MORE LIGHT ON THE GOSPEL

BY THE SAME AUTHOR

Secret of the East

The Oldest Christian People

Key to the Original Gospels

My Neighbor Jesus

The Four Gospels from Aramaic Text

The Gospel Light

The Shepherd of All

The New Testament
  Translated from Aramaic Manuscripts

The New Testament Origin

The Short Koran

The New Testament Commentary

The Holy Bible
  Translated from Aramaic Manuscripts

The Old Testament Light

The Kingdom on Earth

Gems of Wisdom

And the Scroll Opened . . .

The Hidden Years of Jesus

✳ MORE LIGHT ✳
ON THE GOSPEL

Over 400 New Testament Passages Explained

George M. Lamsa

Noohra Foundation
(Formerly Aramaic Bible Center)
BOX 17903   SAN ANTONIO, TEXAS 78217

LIBRARY OF CONGRESS CATALOG CARD NUMBER 68–27125
COPYRIGHT © 1968 BY GEORGE M. LAMSA
ALL RIGHTS RESERVED
PRINTED IN THE UNITED STATES OF AMERICA

This volume is dedicated to Elizabeth J. Moran and William J. Moran, Jr., of Norristown, Pennsylvania, as a token of my deepest and sincerest appreciation for their kind interest and generous help in my work.

CONTENTS

Introduction, *page xxi*

THE GOSPEL ACCORDING TO ST. MATTHEW

1. Baptism of Fire 3:11, *page 1*
2. High Mountain 4:8, *page 2*
3. Angels Ministered 4:11, *page 3*
4. The Land of Naphtali and Zebulun 4:15–16, *page 4*
5. Pure in Heart 5:8, *page 4*
6. Light of the World 5:14, *page 5*
7. Cut Off Your Hands 5:29–30, *page 6*
8. Giving Alms in Secret 6:3, *page 7*
9. Evil 7:11, *page 8*
10. The Golden Rule 7:12, *page 9*
11. God Is Aware of Everything 10:29–31, *page 10*
12. Confess 10:32–33, *page 11*
13. Prophets Revered 10:41, *page 11*
14. A Messenger 11:10, *page 12*
15. Wisdom and Works 11:19, *page 13*
16. Demons Cast Out 12:27, *page 14*
17. Binding the Strong Man 12:29, *page 15*
18. Good Things Out of Good Treasure 12:35, *page 16*
19. Men of Nineveh 12:41, *page 17*
20. The Queen of Sheba 12:42, *page 18*
21. Mustard Seed 13:31, *page 19*
22. Desert Place 14:13, *page 20*
23. Untrue Doctrines Uprooted 15:13–14, *page 21*
24. Pharisees 16:1, *page 21*

25. Sadducees 16:1, *page 22*
26. Calling Peter "Satan" 16:23, *page 23*
27. Take Your Cross 16:24, *page 24*
28. Holy Angels 16:27, *page 25*
29. Taxes 17:25–26, *page 26*
30. Children's Angels 18:10, *page 27*
31. Divorce of Eunuch 19:11–12, *page 28*
32. The Vineyard—God's Religion 20:9–10, *page 29*
33. The Cup of Death 20:22, *page 31*
34. My Cup You Shall Drink 20:23, *page 32*
35. Son of David 20:30, *page 33*
36. Man with Two Sons 21:28–30, *page 34*
37. The Rejected Stone 21:43–44, *page 35*
38. No Marriage in Heaven 22:30, *page 36*
39. God of the Living 22:32, *page 37*
40. God's Name Is Holy 22:44–45, *page 38*
41. Deceptive Men 23:33, *page 39*
42. Zechariah, Son of Barachiah 23:35, *page 39*
43. In the Name of the Lord 23:39, *page 40*
44. Not One Stone upon Another 24:2, *page 41*
45. Iniquity Shall Abound 24:12–14, *page 42*
46. The Sudden Coming of Jesus 24:27, *page 42*
47. Vultures and Carcasses 24:28, *page 43*
48. Universe Shares in Calamity 24:29, *page 44*
49. A Sign in Heaven 24:30–31, *page 45*
50. The Jewish Race 24:34, *page 46*
51. Jesus' Sudden Coming 24:37–39, *page 47*
52. No Wine in Heaven 26:29, *page 47*
53. Shepherd Smitten 26:31, *page 48*
54. Awake and Pray 26:41, *page 49*
55. Perish by the Sword 26:52, *page 50*
56. Jesus Confident 26:53–54, *page 51*
57. Entrusted with Power 26:64, *page 52*
58. Thirty Pieces of Silver 27:9, *page 53*
59. Scarlet Robe 27:28, *page 53*
60. Wine and Gall 27:34, *page 54*
61. Mary of Magdala 28:1, *page 55*

62. Mount of Ascension 28:16, *page 56*
63. To Guard the Teaching 28:20, *page 57*

THE GOSPEL ACCORDING TO ST. MARK

1. Unclean Spirit 1:23–25, *page 58*
2. Jesus Admonished the Leper 1:40–43, *page 59*
3. Your Sins Are Forgiven 2:9, *page 60*
4. The Insane Confess Jesus 3:11, *page 61*
5. Jesus Denounced by Relatives 3:21–22, *page 61*
6. Jesus' Relatives 3:31, *page 62*
7. Touching His Garment 5:30, *page 63*
8. Jesus Sought No Publicity 5:43, *page 64*
9. Great Signs Wanted 6:52, *page 65*
10. Receiving a Child 9:37, *page 66*
11. Jesus Shared His Teaching 9:39, *page 67*
12. Love of Money 10:25–27, *page 68*
13. The Figs Were Picked 11:13, *page 70*
14. Jewish Sects 12:13, *page 71*
15. Like Angels 12:25, *page 72*
16. The Temple Overthrown 13:2, *page 72*
17. A Great Calamity 13:24–25, *page 73*
18. Fruit of the Vine 14:25, *page 74*
19. Meeting in Galilee 14:28, *page 75*
20. Rabbi 14:45, *page 76*
21. A Young Man 14:51–52, *page 77*
22. Pilate Marveled at Jesus 15:5, *page 78*
23. Wine Mixed with Myrrh 15:23, *page 79*
24. Hour of Crucifixion 15:25, *page 79*
25. Jesus' Death Foretold 15:34, *page 80*
26. In a Sponge 15:36, *page 85*
27. An Angel at the Tomb 16:5, *page 86*
28. Speak with New Tongues 16:17, *page 87*
29. Handling Serpents 16:18, *page 88*

THE GOSPEL ACCORDING TO ST. LUKE

1. He Will Be Called 1:32, *page 90*
2. Christ Is Our Hope 2:14, *page 91*

3. Insane, Lunatics 9:1, *page 92*
4. Written in Heaven 10:20, *page 93*
5. Key of Knowledge 11:52, *page 94*
6. Secret Councils 12:3, *page 95*
7. Enemies of the Soul 12:15, *page 95*
8. God's Divine Care 12:6–7, *page 96*
9. Jesus Refused to Meddle 12:13–15, *page 97*
10. Jesus Mindful of His Death 12:50, *page 98*
11. Some Will Not Enter 13:25–26, *page 98*
12. First Will Be Last 13:30, *page 99*
13. Spiritual Food 14:15, *page 100*
14. Dangers of Being a Christian 14:28–30, *page 101*
15. The Old Order and the New 16:16, *page 102*
16. Faith Increased 17:5–6, *page 103*
17. Eagles 17:37, *page 104*
18. Faith Might Be Lost 18:8, *page 105*
19. Jesus Crucified by Romans 18:31–33, *page 105*
20. One Sows, Another Reaps 19:21, *page 106*
21. To Him Who Has Shall Be Given 19:26–27, *page 107*
22. Jewish People Back Jesus 19:47–48, *page 108*
23. The Time of the Gentiles 21:24, *page 109*
24. Coming in a Cloud 21:27–28, *page 110*
25. Sign of the Kingdom 22:29–31, *page 111*
26. Golgotha a Cemetery 24:5, *page 112*
27. Christ's Suffering Foretold 24:26–27, *page 113*

THE GOSPEL ACCORDING TO ST. JOHN

1. God Cannot Be Seen 1:18, *page 114*
2. The Prophet from Nazareth 1:45–46, *page 115*
3. Heaven Opened 1:51, *page 116*
4. The Way of the Wind 3:8, *page 117*
5. Did God Pay a Ransom? 3:16, *page 117*
6. The Only Son 3:16, *page 120*
7. A Samaritan Woman 4:9, *page 121*
8. Jesus Questions the Sick Man 5:6–7, *page 122*
9. Strict Sabbath Observance 5:17–18, *page 123*
10. The Pious Not Judged 5:24, *page 124*

x

11. The Dead Will Hear Jesus 5:25–26, *page 124*
12. Sealed 6:27, *page 125*
13. True Religion Is Simple 6:44–45, *page 126*
14. Some Jews Knew Jesus 7:27, *page 126*
15. Time Too Short 7:34–35, *page 127*
16. Thirsty for Truth 7:37, *page 128*
17. True Judgment 8:16–17, *page 129*
18. Servants Are Not Heirs 8:35–36, *page 129*
19. The Devil Is a Liar 8:44, *page 130*
20. Enlightenment 9:4, *page 131*
21. Jesus' Great Power 10:16–18, *page 132*
22. Jesus Knows His Own 10:28–29, *page 133*
23. A Disciple's Love 11:16, *page 134*
24. Jesus the Resurrection John 11:25–26, *page 135*
25. Jesus Destined to Die 12:27, *page 135*
26. Prince of This World 12:31, *page 136*
27. Jesus Aware of Cross 12:32–34, *page 137*
28. Jesus Spoke for God 12:49, *page 138*
29. Jesus' Method 14:13–14, *page 139*
30. The Comforter 14:26, *page 140*
31. Jesus' Peace 14:27, *page 141*
32. Political and Religious Power 14:30, *page 142*
33. Life Eternal 17:3, *page 142*
34. Jesus Promises a Place 17:24, *page 143*
35. Born to Die on the Cross 18:37, *page 144*
36. Pilate Had No Power 19:11, *page 145*
37. The Hour of the Crucifixion 19:14, *page 146*
38. Friday Not Preparation Day 19:14, *page 147*
39. Sins Forgiven 20:23, *page 147*
40. Peter's Loyalty 21:15, *page 148*
41. Others Will Tie Your Girdle 21:18, *page 149*
42. John Lived a Longer Life 21:22, *page 150*

THE ACTS OF THE APOSTLES

1. Jesus' Second Coming 1:11, *page 151*
2. Universe Mourns 2:19–20, *page 152*
3. God Raised Jesus 2:24, *page 153*

4. According to the Flesh 2:29–30, *page 154*
5. Faith in His Name 3:16, *page 155*
6. Repentance 3:19–20, *page 156*
7. Angel Opened the Door 5:19, *page 156*
8. Hellenistic Jews 6:1, *page 157*
9. Stephen Was a Jew 6:8–9, *page 158*
10. A Greater Prophet 7:37, *page 159*
11. The Tabernacle of Malcom 7:43, *page 160*
12. Jesus of Nazareth 9:5, *page 161*
13. Worshiping Peter 10:25–26, *page 162*
14. Judge of the Living and the Dead 10:42, *page 163*
15. Simon the Carpenter 13:1, *page 163*
16. Paul's Name Changed 13:9, *page 164*
17. By Him 17:28, *page 165*
18. Breaking of Bread 20:7, *page 166*
19. Nazarenes 24:5, *page 167*
20. Bribes Were Common 24:26, *page 168*
21. Paul Exhorts the Passengers 27:21–22, *page 169*
22. Angel Communed with Paul 27:23–24, *page 170*
23. Paul at Appii Forum 28:14–15, *page 171*
24. Paul a House Prisoner in Rome 28:30, *page 171*

THE EPISTLE OF PAUL THE APOSTLE TO THE ROMANS

1. Church in Rome 1:11, *page 173*
2. Judging One's Neighbors 2:1–2, *page 174*
3. Hypocritical Teachers 2:20, *page 175*
4. No Advantage in Circumcision 3:1, *page 176*
5. The Righteousness of God 3:4–5, *page 176*
6. Open Sepulchers 3:13, *page 177*
7. Reconciliations 5:10, *page 178*
8. The Gift of God 5:16–17, *page 179*
9. Sin Has No Power 6:14, *page 180*
10. Speaking Plainly 6:19–20, *page 181*
11. Freed from the Law 7:4, *page 181*
12. Law of Nature 7:23–25, *page 182*
13. The Spirit Is Life 8:10–11, *page 183*
14. The New Man 8:19, *page 184*

15. First Fruits of the Spirit 8:23, *page 184*
16. The Heirs 9:6, *page 186*
17. Esau Put Aside 9:13, *page 187*
18. God Does Not Harden Hearts 9:17, *page 188*
19. The Righteous Believe 10:6–7, *page 190*
20. Gentiles 11:13, *page 191*
21. Chastity 12:1, *page 192*
22. Time to Awake 13:11–12, *page 192*
23. The Living and the Dead 14:9, *page 193*
24. Confessing 14:11, *page 194*
25. The Christians 15:18, *page 194*
26. Crush Satan 16:20, *page 195*

THE FIRST EPISTLE OF PAUL THE APOSTLE TO THE CORINTHIANS

1. The Invited 1:2, *page 196*
2. Simple Gospel 1:21, *page 197*
3. The Unlearned 1:26–28, *page 198*
4. The Mind of God 2:16, *page 199*
5. Human Teachers 3:21–22, *page 199*
6. Words Without Action 4:20, *page 200*
7. Near in Spirit 5:3, *page 201*
8. Suffering from Evil 5:5, *page 202*
9. Judging Angels 6:3, *page 203*
10. Moderation 6:12–13, *page 204*
11. Husband and Wife 7:10–11, *page 205*
12. Past Example 10:11, *page 205*
13. Trials in This Life 10:13–14, *page 206*
14. Falsehood 10:20, *page 207*
15. Covering of the Head 11:10, *page 208*
16. Pagan Jews 12:2, *page 209*
17. We Know Things in Part 13:9, *page 210*
18. Perfection 13:10, *page 210*
19. Unknown Tongues 14:27, *page 211*
20. Women Keep Silent 14:34, *page 212*
21. Interpreters 14:36–37, *page 213*
22. God's Kingdom 15:24, *page 214*

23. Baptism for the Dead 15:29, *page 215*
24. The First Adam 15:45, *page 216*
25. Jesus' Sudden Return 15:51-53, *page 217*

THE SECOND EPISTLE OF PAUL THE APOSTLE TO THE CORINTHIANS

1. Christians Suffer 1:5, *page 218*
2. Diana of Ephesus 1:8-10, *page 219*
3. Paul's Sincerity 1:17-19, *page 220*
4. Christians at Corinth 2:7-8, *page 221*
5. A Sweet Savor 2:14-16, *page 222*
6. Open Face 3:17-18, *page 223*
7. God of This World 4:4, *page 224*
8. Life of Jesus Manifested 4:10-11, *page 225*
9. Earthly Home 5:1, *page 226*
10. Naked 5:3-4, *page 226*
11. Judgment Before Christ 5:10, *page 227*
12. Jesus Died to Save All 5:15, *page 228*
13. The Death of a Sinner 5:21, *page 228*
14. The Right Time 6:2, *page 229*
15. Sorrow Causes Death 7:10, *page 230*
16. Filthiness of Spirit 7:1, *page 231*
17. Obedience to Jesus Christ 10:6, *page 231*
18. Simple Teaching 11:3-4, *page 232*
19. Warning Against False Teachers 11:4-6, *page 233*
20. Paul's Rank 11:9, *page 234*
21. In a Vision 12:1-2, *page 235*
22. Caught up into Paradise 12:4, *page 236*
23. Satan's Angel 12:7-8, *page 237*
24. Miracles of Paul 12:12, *page 237*
25. Corinthians Admonished 13:10, *page 238*

THE EPISTLE OF PAUL THE APOSTLE TO THE GALATIANS

1. Turned to Another Gospel 1:6-7, *page 239*
2. The True Gospel 1:8, *page 240*
3. A Revelation 1:11-12, *page 241*
4. Titus an Aramaean 2:3, *page 242*

5. Law Cannot Save   2:19, *page 242*
6. Gentiles Declared Righteous   3:8–9, *page 243*
7. Promise Made to Abraham   3:16, *page 244*
8. Transgression   3:19, *page 245*
9. Descendants Through Christ   3:29, *page 245*
10. Hagar and Sarah   4:25, *page 246*

THE EPISTLE OF PAUL THE APOSTLE TO THE EPHESIANS

1. The Gospel Will Triumph   1:10, *page 247*
2. Jesus' Name   1:21, *page 248*
3. The Prince of the Air   2:2, *page 248*
4. Resting in Heaven   2:6, *page 249*
5. Saved by Grace   2:11–12, *page 249*
6. Preacher among the Gentiles   3:8, *page 250*
7. God's Wisdom Hidden   3:10, *page 251*
8. Divine Gifts   4:11, *page 252*
9. Struggle Against Evil   6:12, *page 253*
10. The Armor of God   6:13–14, *page 254*
11. Helmet of Salvation   6:16–17, *page 254*

THE EPISTLE OF PAUL THE APOSTLE TO THE PHILIPPIANS

1. Insincere Teachers   1:16, *page 255*
2. Confessing Jesus Christ   2:10–11, *page 256*
3. Partaker of His Suffering   3:10–12, *page 257*
4. Yokefellows   4:3, *page 258*

THE EPISTLE OF PAUL THE APOSTLE TO THE COLOSSIANS

1. With You in Spirit   2:5, *page 259*
2. The Mystery   1:26–27, *page 260*
3. Christ the Main Objective   2:16–17, *page 260*
4. Christ Is the Head   2:19, *page 261*
5. Loyalty to Christ   3:17, *page 262*

THE FIRST EPISTLE OF PAUL THE APOSTLE TO THE THESSALONIANS

1. Dead to Meet Christ 4:15, *page 263*
2. Caught in the Clouds 4:16–17, *page 264*

THE SECOND EPISTLE OF PAUL THE APOSTLE TO THE THESSALONIANS

1. Christ Stands by You 1:12, *page 265*
2. Man of Sin 2:2–3, *page 266*
3. Human Deities 2:4, *page 267*
4. Evil Forces at Work 2:6–7, *page 268*
5. The Anti-Christ 2:8–9, *page 269*
6. Delusion 2:11, *page 269*

THE FIRST EPISTLE OF PAUL THE APOSTLE TO TIMOTHY

1. Paul's Trials and Suffering 1:16, *page 270*
2. Transgression of Moral Law 2:15, *page 271*
3. A Minister's Conduct 3:3, *page 272*
4. Minister to Be above Reproach 4:12, *page 273*
5. Young Widows 5:11, *page 273*
6. Widows' Behavior 5:15, *page 274*
7. True Christian Doctrine 6:3, *page 275*
8. The Christian Challenge 6:12, *page 275*

THE SECOND EPISTLE OF PAUL THE APOSTLE TO TIMOTHY

1. Christians Must Remain Faithful 1:12–13, *page 276*
2. Suffering for the Gospel 2:12–13, *page 277*
3. Snare of the Devil 2:26, *page 278*
4. Scriptures Inspired 3:16, *page 278*
5. Admonishing and Reproving 4:2, *page 279*

THE EPISTLE OF PAUL THE APOSTLE TO THE HEBREWS

1. Jesus an Express Image of God 1:3, *page 280*
2. Fire 1:7, *page 281*

3. Men Brought to Glory 2:10, *page 281*
4. Declaring Jesus' Name 2:12, *page 282*
5. Jesus Entrusted with Power 3:6, *page 283*
6. Jesus Was Obedient 5:8–9, *page 283*
7. One Foundation 6:1–2, *page 284*
8. Only One True Baptism 6:4–6, *page 285*
9. Gospel Will Triumph 8:11, *page 286*
10. Time Is Not Relevant 10:37, *page 287*
11. Promise Made Effective Through Christ 11:39–40, *page 288*
12. Moses Chose to Suffer 11:24–26, *page 289*
13. Putting Aside Negative Thought 12:1, *page 290*
14. Souls Made Perfect Through Christ 12:23, *page 291*
15. Sprinkling of Blood 12:24, *page 291*

THE GENERAL EPISTLE OF JAMES

1. The Engrafted Word 1:21, *page 292*
2. The Devils Also Believe 2:19, *page 293*
3. Shun False Teachings 3:1–2, *page 294*
4. Evil Can Be Defeated 4:7, *page 294*

THE FIRST EPISTLE GENERAL OF PETER

1. Freed Through Christ 1:3, *page 295*
2. Mystery Hidden from Angels 1:12, *page 296*
3. The Term "Holy" 1:16, *page 296*
4. Born Again 1:23, *page 297*
5. Jesus' Destiny 1:19–20, *page 297*
6. Jesus' Preaching in Sheol 3:18–20, *page 298*
7. The Dead Become Partakers 4:6, *page 299*
8. Love Is Supreme 4:8, *page 300*
9. Christians Will Be Judged 4:17–18, *page 300*
10. As a Roaring Lion 5:8, *page 301*

THE SECOND EPISTLE GENERAL OF PETER

1. Christians Must Excel 1:11, *page 302*
2. Eyewitness to the Truth 1:16, *page 303*
3. Backsliders 2:11, *page 303*

4. Eating Their Vomit 2:20–22, *page 304*
5. Scoffers at the Gospel 3:3, *page 305*
6. Slow Changes 3:4, *page 306*
7. Intense Heat 3:10–12, *page 307*

THE FIRST EPISTLE GENERAL OF JOHN

1. The Anointing 2:27, *page 308*
2. The Sons of God 3:2, *page 309*
3. Born of God 3:9, *page 310*
4. "Spirit" Means "Person" 4:1, *page 311*
5. Christ among You 4:4, *page 312*
6. Baptism of Spirit, Water, and Blood 5:6–8, *page 313*

THE GENERAL EPISTLE OF JUDE

1. Repenters Receive Mercy 1:23, *page 314*

THE REVELATION OF ST. JOHN THE DIVINE

1. Readers Are Blessed 1:3, *page 314*
2. Faithful Witness 1:5, *page 315*
3. Kings and Priests 1:6, *page 316*
4. He Cometh with Clouds 1:7, *page 317*
5. First Love 2:4, *page 318*
6 The Tree of Life 2:7, *page 318*
7. Synagogue of Satan 2:9–10, *page 319*
8. Satan's Seat 2:13, *page 320*
9. Sword of the Mouth 2:16, *page 321*
10. Jezebel 2:20, *page 322*
11. Sickbed 2:22–23, *page 323*
12. The Rod of Iron 2:26–28, *page 324*
13. Loyal Members 3:4, *page 324*
14. Pillar in the Temple 3:12, *page 325*
15. To Sit with Jesus 3:21, *page 326*
16. The Slain Lamb 5:6, *page 327*
17. Hiding in Caves 6:15, *page 328*
18. Washed Their Robes 7:14–15, *page 329*
19. Golden Censers 8:3–5, *page 330*

20. Hail and Fire 8:7, *page 331*
21. Third Part of Life Destroyed 8:8–9, *page 331*
22. Star Falling 8:10–11, *page 332*
23. Nature Shares Human Tragedy 8:12, *page 333*
24. Bottomless Pit 9:1–4, *page 334*
25. Desiring to Die 9:6, *page 335*
26. Army of Locusts 9:7–10, *page 336*
27. Abaddon 9:11, *page 337*
28. The River Euphrates 9:14, *page 337*
29. Third of Men Killed 9:16–20, *page 339*
30. Clothed in a Cloud 10:1–3, *page 340*
31. Swearing by God 10:6–7, *page 341*
32. The Witnesses 11:3, *page 342*
33. Two Olive Trees 11:4–6, *page 343*
34. Jerusalem Called Sodom 11:8–9, *page 344*
35. Witnesses Slain for Testimony 11:11–12, *page 345*
36. The Kingdom of Our Lord 11:15, *page 346*
37. The Temple Of God 11:19, *page 347*
38. Great Red Dragon 12:3–4, *page 348*
39. Michael and His Angels 12:7–9, *page 349*
40. Accusers Cast Down 12:10–12, *page 350*
41. Dragon Defeated 12:15–17, *page 351*
42. Beast Rising Out of the Sea 13:1–2, *page 352*
43. Patience of the Faithful 13:10, *page 353*
44. Beast with Two Horns 13:11–16, *page 354*
45. One Hundred and Forty-four Thousand 14:1, *page 355*
46. Died Believing in the Lord 14:13–14, *page 356*
47. The Vials 16:2–4, *page 357*
48. Blasphemed the Name of God 16:8–11, *page 358*
49. Unclean Frogs 16:13–14, *page 359*
50. Covering the Shame 16:15, *page 360*
51. The Beast That Was Is Not 17:8–11, *page 361*
52. Truth Triumphs Over Imperial Powers 18:21, *page 362*
53. Resurrection and Judgment 20:13:14, *page 363*
54. A New Heaven, a New Earth 21:1, *page 364*
55. Aleph and Tau 21:6–7, *page 364*
56. Jesus' Teaching the Light of the World 21:22–23, *page 365*

57. They Shall See His Face   22:4–6, *page 366*
58. The Tree of Life   22:14, *page 367*
59. The Morning Star   22:16–17, *page 368*
Subject Index   *page 369*

INTRODUCTION

The term *Torah,* the Bible, in Semitic languages means "light," the light of God. The light which shines even in darkness. The Psalmist says, "Thy word is a lamp to my feet and a light to my path." (Ps. 119:105)

Light is the most precious and abundant thing in the world, but the light of God is still more powerful and clearer. This is why through His light we see the light, whether there is sunlight or darkness. Many times we read in the Bible, "God is the light of the world." Jesus said, "I am the light of the world."

The Gospel of Jesus Christ is distilled from the teachings of the law and prophets. It is like the clear droplets of dew which fall upon the grass in the early morning. Jesus, through his divine power, and knowledge of God and man, simplified the revelations and visions of the prophets of Israel. His teaching is clear, like water issuing forth from a spring. But the meandering water flows slowly, and gradually it becomes less clear and less palatable to drink. Indeed, what Jesus said, in its original context, even little children can understand. This is why he said, ". . . I thank thee, O my Father, Lord of heaven and earth, because thou hast hidden these things from the wise and the men of understanding, and hast revealed them to children." Jesus is the light of the world. He came to lighten the hearts of man, and to elucidate and make clear what looks hard and harsh and to recover what was lost in the Old Testament.

Unfortunately, mistranslations, misunderstandings of the idioms, misconceptions of Eastern customs and mannerisms of speech have obscured the simple and clear words which fell from the lips of the great master and orator. This happens today when a speech or sermon is translated from one language to another.

It must be understood that the Gospels are as vast as an ocean. They can be surveyed only in part. For many years men have been surveying the ocean and they have only begun to survey it. It will take many more centuries before the Gospels are understood.

For many centuries Christian scholars throughout the world have tried to understand and explain what Jesus preached 2000 years ago to his simple and illiterate disciples. And yet, even today, the quest continues. This is because, from the very inception of the gospel, people throughout the world have been eager to understand it and apply it in their lives and translate it from one tongue to another.

The teaching of Jesus is simple, plain and direct, but it is deep in its meaning and hard in its application and practice. This is because Jesus analyzed the Scriptures and gave the law a new synthesis, and religion a new meaning. For example, it is difficult for men who for centuries have hated their enemies to love them and pray for them. In other words, it is the simplicity and sincerity of the Gospels which make it hard for the scholars and the learned to understand. They are accustomed to live contrary to the teachings of Jesus and they have been used to indirect and obscure terms of speech. In the old days the more obscure and difficult the work of a writer, the more it was admired, and the more the author was esteemed as a learned man. Today, in the East, when we compliment a man on his speech we say, "Your speech was marvelous; we did not understand a word you said!" Which really means, Your speech was so philosophical and deep it was beyond our comprehension. To say we liked and understood your speech would imply that we are equal to you in our learning. This is one reason why many writers chose to write and speak in abstruse and difficult terms.

Jesus disregarded this ancient practice and tried to use simple words, short sentences, and avoided qualifying clauses which often obscure the meaning of what is said. Thus, Jesus' discourses before the masses by the lake, in the market place, and on the mountain created a new norm of speaking and writing which was contrary and alien to that used by the Pharisees, the scribes and all the writers of his day. And the people were amazed at his clarity and his authority. Even his enemies admired the way he spoke, and the direct words he used. Because of the simplicity of his message, many people flocked to him. They came to hear him expound the law and the prophets, because they did not understand what the Pharisees, the scribes and the other Jewish authorities were telling them. Neither did these religious men care whether the people understood. The more they kept them in darkness, the more they were able to exploit them.

For example, if they had told the people God is a loving Father who forgives freely, the people might have stopped bringing sacrifices and offerings. And so the Pharisees and the scribes were angry when Jesus told the sick, "Go your way, your sins are forgiven," and did not demand any remuneration for doing so.

The books of the law and the prophets are clearer than the writings of the elders and the scribes who came centuries after them. When God said to Moses, "Write," He told him to ". . . write and make it plain." (Ex. 17:14) And when He spoke to Habakkuk in a vision He said, ". . . write the vision, and make it plain upon the tablets, that he who reads it may understand it clearly." (Hab. 2:2, Lamsa Bible)

Indeed, the Gospels were written in the simplest language the world has ever known. The language in which God conversed with the patriarchs, prophets, and later with the apostles —the Aramaic language—is the oldest language mentioned in the Bible. It is the language that Abraham, Isaac and Jacob spoke.

One must consider that ancient languages have a limited vocabulary. In those early days people had fewer things, and fewer words to describe them. Sometimes words have many meanings, and only a native-born Aramaean (or Assyrian) would understand their real significance. And at times even a native is deceived by the position of the dots which are placed over or under the letters to determine their meaning. This is so particularly when the manuscript is exposed to flies, and more dots are placed upon it. This is not all. Manuscripts often suffer through humidity and careless handling, and therefore, become harder to read.

On the other hand, translations of the Bible were made by men who really knew only one language—their own. They translated from a text which they could read, but they never spoke the language in which it was written. This is why they were unable to translate an Aramaic idiom into Greek, or a Greek idiom into Latin or English. They took these idioms literally. For example, to say "the banks are on the rocks" in English would mean "the banks are insolvent." In Aramaic it would mean, "they are solvent," like the house built upon a rock that withstood the most violent storms. Moreover, when they came to a word which had several meanings, they used only the meaning they knew. For instance, the word for "camel" also means "rope." Matthew 19:24 should read ". . . It is easier for a rope to go through the eye of a needle . . ." instead of ". . . It is easier for a camel to go through the eye of a needle . . ." Even today in the East we say, "It is like a rope and a needle eye," which means it is a difficult problem. When the man said to Jesus, "I must go and bury my father," the Western translators took it for granted that the man's father was dead, and Jesus was not interested in having him buried. They did not know that "I must bury my father" means "I must take care of my father until he dies." Had this man's father been dead, he would not have come to listen to Jesus' teachings, but would have been busy making preparations for the burial and Jesus would have been one of the mourners. On the other hand, Jesus would not have said, "Let the dead bury your father." No one in the East would have talked to a man who has just lost his father in such a harsh manner.

Many Aramaic words with many meanings were translated literally. For example, the word "spirit" also means "wind," "rheumatism," and "pride." In Luke 13:11 Jesus spoke about a woman who was suffering from rheumatism, but the translators, not knowing the meaning of the word, translated it "suffering from the spirit." And in the first verse in the Sermon on the

Mount we read, "Blessed are the poor in spirit." It should read, "Blessed are the poor in pride," that is, "humble."

One of the worst translations ever made by the translators is found in Luke 14:26. It reads, "If any man come to me, and hate not his father, and mother, and wife, and children, and brethren, and sisters, yea, and his own life also, he cannot be my disciple." It should read, "He who comes to me and does not put aside his father and his mother and his brothers and his sisters and his wife and his children and even his own life cannot be a disciple to me." The word "hate" was mistranslated. Jesus would never have used such a phrase. He was a teacher of love, not of hatred. The wrong rendering of this verse has puzzled many sincere readers of his gospel. More than that, in Near Eastern countries Bibles are burned because of this verse. No Eastern Christian, Moslem or Jew, would ever permit his children to read a gospel with this verse in it. The people in those lands loved their fathers and mothers and children. And because of this mistranslation, communistic and atheistic writers have called Jesus the preacher of hatred. The Aramaic word for "hate" and "to put aside" is written almost identically, as the word "fair" in English ("fair" in color and "fair" in judgment) or the word "light" (well illuminated or light in weight).

In the East even the children know that Jesus was not a preacher of hatred, and therefore would not admonish people to hate their fathers and mothers. What he meant here is, "to put aside" everything, including father, mother, children, and his wife, for the sake of his gospel. In other words, his gospel is to come first. This is why on other occasions he told his disciples and followers that those who love their relatives, fields, houses, and other worldly possessions more than him are not worthy of him. And those who would relinquish them for his sake would receive a hundredfold or more and life eternal. On another occasion he said, "Seek ye first the kingdom of heaven, and other things will be given to you." Jesus was always consistent in his teaching. When one puts God first, all other things will function harmoniously.

As we have said, Jesus chose to use a simple and direct language because the great majority of the people and his disciples were simple folk and slow in understanding. These country peasants and fishermen were accustomed to the usage of idioms, metaphors and maxims in order to understand the abstract terms of speech, and the spiritual truths which were hidden from their eyes. Indeed, the style of the Gospels in their original form have never been surpassed for their simplicity, clarity and directness. It is even richer and clearer than that of the prophets.

Jesus used parables, idioms and metaphors because they were used daily by the provincial people and because they understood figures of speech much better. For instance, Jesus said, "If your hand offend thee, cut it off." This means, "If you are in the habit of stealing, cut it out because it is better than losing other members of your body." In the East, even today, the hands of thieves are amputated, and the lips and noses of shoplifters are cut off. "If your foot offends you" means, "If you are in the habit of trespassing on another man's vineyard or orchard, cut out the trespass." These idioms are well understood by Aramaic-speaking people. This is why in Aramaic- and Arab-speaking countries no one has ever cut off his hand, plucked out his eyes, or amputated his foot. But in other countries countless thousands committed injuries to their bodies because they took these words literally. Likewise, it is also true that many of the American idioms, when taken literally by foreigners, are grossly misunderstood. For instance, "He died on third base," "He was in a pickle for a year," "He was born with a silver spoon is his mouth," "The ladies gave her a shower," "He blew his top," "What he said came out of the horse's mouth," and many other such American idioms should of course never be taken literally.

One of the most difficult Eastern idioms to the American public is, ". . . Unless you eat the body of the Son of man and drink his blood, you have no life in yourselves." (John 6:53) Even some of the Jews from the south who followed him and did not understand the Galilean dialect of Aramaic were puzzled by this statement and left him. They said, "How could this man give us his body to eat and his blood to drink?" But what Jesus meant was this, to eat of his teaching, to make it a part of their lives and to suffer as he was going to suffer on the cross for their sakes. We still say in Aramaic, "He has eaten the book." The prophet Ezekiel was told to "eat the book," which means, "to remember it by heart." Then, again, when people work hard or suffer, they say, "I have eaten my body and drunk my blood," "I have eaten my father and mother," "I have eaten my dead people." These sayings are so common in Aramaic speech that they are often heard in conversation. Jesus likened himself to the lamb which the Jews were going to eat on the passover day and the blood of the lamb which spared the lives of their forefathers in Egypt. It was symbolical of his body and blood, which were to be spiritually eaten and drunk by his followers to the end of time. He did not literally mean that we should eat his body and drink his blood. The Jewish law prohibited anyone from even touching the blood of a dead person. How could Jesus have meant for us to literally eat his body and drink his blood?"

Biblical customs and manners present other difficulties in transmitting thought from one language into another. For example, in America everyone knows the hour when the bride and bridegroom will come to the wedding feast. Readers of the Gospels wonder why Jesus said, "Just as no one knows when the bridegroom comes forth, so no one knows the hour of his return." He used an illustration familiar and understable to everyone in the East. First, Easterners are never punctual. Time means nothing to them. Being late four or five hours is common. Second, the bridegroom and the bride are bathed before the wedding feast, and no one knows when they will be ready because often there is a scarcity of water and it is hard to procure. Therefore, no one but God knows when the bride and bridegroom will be ready to go the wedding house.

Jesus told the people that no one stores new wine in old skins. Even today, in many parts of the East, wine and oil are carried in goatskins. And when the wine is new the vent will cause the skins to burst. What he meant here was this: His teaching was the new wine, and Judaism was the old skins. They could not blend together. On another occasion he told his disciples to go to a town and they would find a donkey with a foal tied to a door. Some Western readers wonder how he could know this, but one does not have to be a prophet to know the answer. A few decades ago one could see many donkeys tied up at the doors of their owners. This would be like seeing many taxis in front of a taxi stand in this country. Donkeys were hired and loaned like taxicabs.

The Pauline Epistles were written in the old Jewish style, which was used by the learned scribes, Pharisees and commentators. This is why they are hard to understand by the reader and need to be explained.

The Epistles of Peter, James and John are simple and clear. Their authors were simple and uneducated men; therefore, they spoke and wrote in a simple language. Moreover, they had sat at the feet of Jesus.

The Book of Revelation came in a vision, and most of the visions are revealed in a symbolic language. Therefore, the reader must understand the meaning of the symbols, figurative speech and metaphors.

See the Introduction to the Book of Revelation, *New Testament Commentary*, A. J. Holman Company.

The author of this book was born and reared in a unique civilization which had remained static from the time of Noah to the dawn of the twentieth century—in a region where customs and manners remained unchanged and unaltered, and where the people conversed in Aramaic the way the patriarchs and Jesus and his disciples did. Moreover, they used the same idioms and mannerisms of speech that were used in the Holy Bible. They wore the same garments and ate the same food, and used the same implements for plowing and threshing as did King David. The area wherein they lived was like a little island in a great ocean. They were surrounded by millions of non-Christians and people who spoke alien languages. Nothing new was introduced into this region until World War I. Only three years ago the Turkish Government opened the door of this land which in the old days, because of its abundant water, fruit trees and vegetables, was called the Garden of Eden.

Moreover, the author was educated under the care of learned

priests of the Church of the East who knew no other language but Aramaic, and highly educated Englishmen, graduates of Oxford, Cambridge and other famous English schools. The author, through God's grace, is the only one with the knowledge of Aramaic, the Bible customs and idioms, and the knowledge of the English language who has ever translated the Holy Bible from the original Aramaic texts into English and written commentaries on it, and his translation is now in pleasingly wide use.

The purpose of this book, like other works I have written, is to throw more light on the obscure passages of Jesus and to elucidate what seems hard and harsh to Western readers and to clarify and strengthen the meaning of the Scriptures. I am a firm believer in the Word of God and the miracles and wonders which were performed by the Hebrew prophets and Jesus. I also believe that the salvation of the world lies in the teaching and the practice of the Holy Word.

All verses on which the following comments are based are taken from the King James version. All other verses and quotations are from Lamsa's translation from the Eastern Aramaic text, published by A. J. Holman Company. No other versions are used or quoted in this commentary. Moreover, many familiar verses are quoted in the comments without giving the reference.

In referring to the Eastern text, I have used various terms such as the Peshitta, which means, "the simple, the straight, the pure," that is, the original. I have also referred to it as the Eastern Aramaic text to differentiate it from other Aramaic texts used by Monophysites in Syria, and as the Bible of the Church of the East. At times I use the term "Lamsa." This is because this translation of the Holy Bible from the ancient Eastern Aramaic manuscripts has now come to be known as "Lamsa's Bible." Bookstores and periodicals refer to it as such. This text is accepted by all Christians in the Near East and India and is revered by the Moslems.

The author wishes to express his deepest and sincerest gratitude to the Reverend Frank Stribling and the Reverend Rocky Errico of Calvary Missionary Church, San Antonio, Texas, for urging and encouraging him to write this commentary, and for selecting most of the passages on which I have commented in this volume, and also to Judge Ralph Keahn for his interest in this work. May the Lord God bless the readers and hearers of this book.

GEORGE M. LAMSA

1. BAPTISM OF FIRE

I indeed baptize you with water unto repentance: but
he that cometh after me is mightier than I, whose shoes
I am not worthy to bear: he shall baptize you with the
Holy Ghost, and with fire.

Matt. 3:11

"Baptism of fire" is an Aramaic saying which means "free
from sin." This is because fire purifies metals and burns the
dross, making the metal shine. In the olden days, when the
crucible was unknown, silver, gold, brass and other metals were
purified by fire, rather than by chemical solutions as they are
today.

Baptism by fire would remove all sins; baptism by water is
symbolic of inner cleansing; and baptism by the Holy Spirit
symbolizes sanctification and salvation.

Jesus had the power to baptize and to forgive sins. The power
of John the Baptist, however, was limited to baptism by water;
the people who came to him confessed their sins but received
no forgiveness.

In the olden days, pagans passed their children through the
fire, burning them alive as an offering to their gods. When the
Jews turned away from their God, they also did the same.

2. HIGH MOUNTAIN

Again, the devil taketh him up into an exceeding high mountain, and sheweth him all the kingdoms of the world, and the glory of them.

Matt. 4:8

The term "high mountain" is used figuratively. It means the high point in human physical aspiration. This temptation was a far greater one than the previous two. This is because the devil, deception, negative thought—anything contrary to the truth—offered Jesus the greatest rewards known to man in order to beguile him, and thus divert him from his great mission. Satan here offered everything which human imagination can comprehend and embrace. It offered the kingdoms of the world and all their glory and splendor.

Satan took Jesus on a high mountain. This means he took him to the summit of his highest human imagination, and he made all these offers to him, if Jesus would but fall down and worship him.

It is interesting to know that the Mount of Temptation is in a wasteland hundreds of feet below sea level. There are no kingdoms or large cities nearby, but small hamlets, sheepfolds and Arab camps. The only town close to it is the humble little town of Jericho.

Jesus, in this temptation, saw himself working with the high priests or learned men of his religion, but he immediately realized that if he should start to work with them, he would be asked to pledge his allegiance to them. In words, he could not have worked with the church authorities without bowing down to them and accepting their teaching, which was so far removed from the truth which God had revealed to Abraham and the prophets. In other words, the new wine could not be contained in the old goatskins, but must be put in the new. Jesus' teaching was so contrary to the doctrines of the elders and to the political and materialistic concepts of the Jewish high priests that they could not be blended.

2

3. ANGELS MINISTERED

Then the devil leaveth him, and, behold, angels came and
ministered unto him.

Matt. 4:11

"Angels ministered to him" is an Eastern idiom meaning
that God, or God's counsel, took care of him. Angels can only
minister to man's soul and guide and strengthen him during
temptation. Angels have no physical body to minister to a person
as a servant does.

Jesus during his temptations was helped by God's counsel
and by the Holy Scripture, which he quoted in order to counter-
act the false thoughts which crept into his mind. In other
words, God's counsel prevailed and Satan, or falsehood, was defeated. God's angels, or counsel, are always ready to assist
those who trust in Him. Angels are constantly ministering to
man.

Jacob said to Esau, "I have seen you as an angel in my
dream." (Gen. 33) Jacob was afraid of Esau, thinking the latter
would avenge the wrongs which Jacob had done him, but when
he met him he found Esau as innocent and harmless as an
angel of God. Angels of God also gave counsel to Joseph and the
Virgin Mary.

In the East we believe that every person has an angel resting
on his right shoulder to guide him. Then again at times we
say that one's angel has gone before him, in other words guiding
and directing him. Children have angel guardians.

Angels, or the counsel of God, were constantly with Jesus
throughout his life. His mission was so fraught with difficulties
he had to rely on God's counsel. In reforming Judaism he was
making of religion a new synthesis, and giving to the law a
new meaning.

4. THE LAND OF NAPHTALI AND ZEBULUN

The people which sat in darkness saw great light; and to them which sat in the region and shadow of death light is sprung up.

Matt. 4:15–16

The reference here is to the Gentiles who dwelt in Galilee. Some of the ancestors of these people had been settled by the Assyrian kings in the lands of Zebulun and Naphtali, the way of the sea, in 721 B.C., when the tribes of Israel were carried captive to Assyria.

The light of the gospel of Jesus Christ shone first upon the Jews, Galileans and Gentiles, and then upon the other people of the world.

5. PURE IN HEART

Blessed are the pure in heart: for they shall see God.

Matt. 5:8

"Pure in heart" in Aramaic means "pure in mind." The ancients believed that the heart was the thinking faculty of man—that is to say, that man thought through his heart. Then again, the heart is the organ through which all of the blood passes, and blood was regarded by the Jews as the secret of life. This is why the Jews refrained from eating and drinking blood and ate only kosher, or bloodless, meat.

The mind must be pure from all impurities such as doubt,

4

greed, and worldly aspirations in order to reflect God. God is the eternal spirit, light, life and truth. Therefore, God cannot be reflected in a mirror smeared with dirt. A telescopic mirror must be clear in order to reflect stars, planets, and galaxies.

The pure in heart are the pious and innocent men and women who never think of harming other people. They feel the presence of God constantly, and they know that God is a good God, and that good cannot be reflected in evil, nor evil reflected in good, just as light cannot mix with darkness, nor fire with water. (Ps. 15:2)

6. LIGHT OF THE WORLD

Ye are the light of the world. A city that is set on an hill cannot be hid.

Matt. 5:14

Righteous men and women are the light of the world. They do not stumble because the light of God directs their steps. Their path is a shining light (Prov. 4:18), but the path of the wicked is dark and the way of the wicked is like darkness. They know not "at what they stumble." (Prov. 4:19)

Light is symbolic of God and enlightenment and is the fastest and most abundant element of the universe. Just as light fills the universe, so God's presence fills the whole space. God is called the Light of the World, and Jesus said, "I am the light of the world." Christians must manifest the light of God in order to be known as the children of God. This light can be manifested by means of faith in God and good works. The author of Proverbs tells us, "But the path of the righteous is like the shining light that shines more and more the perfect day." (Prov. 4:18, Lamsa)

5

7. CUT OFF YOUR HANDS

And if thy right eye offend thee, pluck it out, and cast it from thee: for it is profitable for thee that one of thy members should perish, and not that thy whole body should be cast into hell.

And if thy right hand offend thee, cut it off, and cast it from thee: for it is profitable for thee that one of thy members should perish, and not that thy whole body should be cast into hell.

Matt. 5:29–30

"Cut off your hand and pluck out your eye" is an Eastern idiom meaning "stop stealing, stop envying." "Cut off your foot" means, "Do not trespass in another man's field or vineyard." Such sayings are very common, not only in Aramaic, but in other Eastern languages. Then again, in the East when a man steals, his hands are cut off; when he trespasses, his feet. This was a form of punishment in the days of Jesus which still prevails today in some countries in the Near East.

Mosaic law requires an eye for an eye, a tooth for a tooth, a limb for a limb. And since this punishment was prescribed by Mosaic law, it was universally accepted by Semitic people.

What Jesus meant here was the destruction of the habit of stealing, envying and trespassing, rather than the destruction of members of the body, for members of the body are the agents of the mind. The evil done through these acts is far more serious than the loss of a hand or an eye. In other words, Jesus here hints that it is better for a man to lose a member of his body and to lack the things he covets than to break one of God's laws and receive eternal punishment.

Such bad acts in the East are deplored not only by the government and society, but also by one's own family for many generations. So a man would say, "I wish I might be put to death, rather than bring disgrace to the honor and the name of my forefathers."

6

"Hell" metaphorically means "mental suffering, agony, and regret." The term "hell" is understood in the East, but in the West it is taken literally. Some teachers believe literally that God would burn human bodies as a sort of punishment. Indeed, burning by fire was a form of Babylonian capital punishment, and in the East, when a child cries too much, his mother may say, "Stop it, or I'll put you in the oven." Moreover, in the East, people often say, "He burned me. I have been in fire for a long time," which means, "I have suffered mental agony."

These words should not be taken literally. Mental suffering goes on forever and ever. It is far worse than fire. On the other hand, no human body could withstand being burned forever and ever. A body can be turned to ashes in four hours, but mental suffering never ends and is truly hell. (See Matt. 18:9.)

8. GIVING ALMS IN SECRET

But when thou doest alms, let not thy left hand know what thy right hand doeth.

Matt. 6:3

"Let not your left hand know what your right hand is doing" is an Aramaic idiom meaning, "Let no one know, not even your wife and your brother, what you are doing when you give alms." This is because God knows and sees a good deed even when it is done in secret, and therefore there is no need to publish it.

It often happens that the recipient of alms is embarrassed in the community because of the publicity given by the giver. The name of the almsgiver is sometimes announced in the synagogue and discussed in the market places.

In Jesus' day, many rich men gave alms to the poor to attract public recognition of their piety. This was also done by pagans and by many religious sects. Even today, some religious organizations publish a donor's name in the newspaper and install a plaque in the church in his memory. Some would not give unless they were assured of publicity.

Jesus said, "When you give alms, don't blow the trumpet before you, that is, don't go out announcing and talking about your giving. Your Father, who sees in secret, will reward you for giving. But those who blow their trumpets have already received their reward, from the people who praise their names in the synagogues, street corners, and market places."

9. EVIL

If ye then, being evil, know how to give good gifts unto your children, how much more shall your Father which is in heaven give good things to them that ask him?

Matt. 7:11

The Aramaic term *bisha* has many meanings, including "error," "evil," "bad," "rotten," "cruel," "unreal," "imperfect," "immature"—for example "evil counsel," "evil figs," and "evil tree"; and then again, "misfortune" or "envy."

Bad habits of life are called evil because they are contrary to the good. Aramaic-speaking people know how the word *bisha* is used by the context. They understand that it has nothing to do with the Evil One, or the Devil.

In this instance the term *bisha* means "imperfect," "immature." Jesus did not use the word collectively, in the sense that all who were listening to him were evil, but that they were imperfect. Moreover, when he spoke of an "evil tree" he did not mean that the tree had broken a law. Anything which deviates from the truth is classified as evil or unreal.

8

10. THE GOLDEN RULE

Therefore all things whatsoever ye would that men should
do to you, do ye even so to them: for this is the law
and the prophets.

Matt. 7:12

This important portion of the Scripture is rightly called
"the Golden Rule." It is the core of the law and of the teaching
of the prophets. When men learn to practice this law there will
be no need for other laws or for churches, for evil will cease.
Envy, covetousness, murder, adultery, and the many other things
which cause the downfall of man will come to an end when this
law is practiced.

If a person would only place himself in the position of the
man whom he oppresses, cheats, or mistreats, he would not
wish to be so treated, and would cease doing it to others. Moreover, he would respect the rights of other people just as he ex-
pects others to respect his rights. This is because the law of
compensation is an immutable law. Evil acts, not being of divine
origin, redound on the person who committed them. He who
takes the sword perishes by the sword, and he who oppresses is
oppressed.

All the great imperial powers who violated this law were
measured with the same measure when they were conquered
and oppressed by others. It was done to them as they had done
unjustly to others. (Luke 6:31, Isa. 33:28, Lamsa)

11. GOD IS AWARE OF EVERYTHING

Are not two sparrows sold for a farthing? and one of them shall not fall on the ground without your Father.
But the very hairs of your head are all numbered.
Fear ye not therefore, ye are of more value than many sparrows.

Matt. 10:29–31

Jesus was the first and the greatest teacher of the Word of God—the Holy Bible. He was the first whom we can call a metaphysician. According to his teaching, everything is controlled and sustained by God, from a hair, which seems so small and unimportant, to a little sparrow. There is no other power besides God.

The student of the Bible must distinguish between Jesus' teaching about God and that which we call pantheism. According to Jesus' teaching, there is only one God who reigns over all the universe, but He is manifested in all His creations.

There is only one kind of life and intelligence, and that is God, just as there is only one kind of fire and light in the world. This is because even though life is manifested in many forms, such as animals and flowers, the essence of life is one and the same. And life was created by the only Creator—God, Who cares for it.

Jesus here reveals man's importance in comparison with a little sparrow, or a seemingly useless hair. God is more mindful of man, who is His image and likeness, than of the other creations which He has placed under man's dominion.

12. CONFESS

Whosoever therefore shall confess me before men, him will
I confess also before my Father which is in heaven.
But whosoever shall deny me before men, him will I also
deny before my Father which is in heaven.

Matt. 10:32–33

The Aramaic word *nawdey* means "to give thanks," but
it also means "to confess," that is, to confess the blessings which
the people had received from the Lord.

In this instance, Jesus tells us that those who confess him—
that is, who testify about his teaching and confirm that he is the
Messiah, the Savior of the world—he will also confess (recom-
mend) them before God, his Father.

The term acknowledge him means to acknowledge Jesus'
religion, his way of life.

13. PROPHETS REVERED

He that receiveth a prophet in the name of a prophet
shall receive a prophet's reward; and he that receiveth a
righteous man in the name of a righteous man shall receive a righteous man's reward.

Matt. 10:41

When the prophecy of a prophet was fulfilled, the prophet
was praised, honored and emulated. And then again, a true
prophet lives on through his prophecy. This is why Jesus on
one occasion said, "There are some who are standing here who
shall never taste death." (Matt. 16:28)

When a man sincerely receives another as a prophet, he will receive the reward or the blessing of a prophet. That is to say, he will be rewarded for his good deed because he received the man as a prophet or a good man, even though the other may have been evil. In other words, he did his act of charity faithfully, not knowing whether the one he helped was worthy or not. And one who receives another as a righteous man will receive the reward or the blessing which only a righteous man can bestow.

Those who opened their doors to Jesus' disciples would open their doors to Jesus himself; and those who received Jesus would receive God, Who sent him.

When a person helps a poor man, he will be rewarded for his act whether the one he helped was worthy or not. All those who were to receive Jesus' disciples were to be rewarded for their pious acts regardless of the character of those whom they helped. They did not know these men, but they did what God had commanded them to do. It is the act that counts. God sends his rain upon the good and bad, the just and the unjust.

14. A MESSENGER

For this is he, of whom it is written, Behold, I send my messenger before thy face, which shall prepare thy way before thee.

Matt. 11:10

The Jews expected the return of Moses and Elijah or one of the great prophets before the coming of the Messiah, Christ. These prophets were to come to prepare the way for the Messiah. Nevertheless, centuries had elapsed and none of these prophets had returned.

In the sixteenth century B.C., Moses had promised the people that a greater prophet than himself would come. He said, "The Lord your God will raise up to you a prophet like me from the midst of you, of your brethren; to him you shall hearken." (Deut. 18:15)

Some of the Jews thought that this prophecy referred to Joshua or one of the great leaders who were to defeat the enemies of Israel. Years later they expected a strong and mighty leader different from those of the past, or a prophet greater even than Moses. (John 6:14)

When Jesus was told that Elijah must return before the coming of the Messiah, he answered that Elijah was John, who had already come, but the people did not know him. That is to say, the spirit of Elijah was embedded in John the Baptist, who denounced King Herod Antipas and his wife Herodia, just as Elijah had denounced Ahab, the King of Israel, and his wife Jezebel.

John called Jesus "the Lamb of God" because the lamb is symbolic of meekness and purity. A lamb does not resist those who slaughter it. (Matt. 17:11–12)

15. WISDOM AND WORKS

The Son of man came eating and drinking, and they say, Behold a man gluttonous, and a winebibber, a friend of publicans and sinners. But wisdom is justified of her children.

Matt. 11:19

The Eastern text reads, "yet wisdom is justified by its works." This means that wisdom is verified by the fruits thereof. Just as gold and silver are purified by fire, wisdom is proved or justified by the results of actions caused by it.

Many times wisdom fails, or seems to sound like folly, for not

everything we call wisdom is wise. We must put it into opera-
tion and see its results before we can tell whether it is wisdom
or folly. Foolishness is wisdom to fools, but it is folly to the wise.

16. DEMONS CAST OUT

And if I by Beelzebub cast out devils, by whom do your
children cast them out? therefore they shall be your judges.

Matt. 12:27

The term "your children" in this instance means "your
people." The Jews had many men and women who acted as
healers and who cast out devils—that is, restored the insane to
sanity.

The Hebrew prophets healed the sick, cleansed the lepers,
and even raised the dead, centuries before Jesus. They all performed these miracles in the name of their God, and not in the
name of Beelzebub, the lord of the flies, the prince of the
devils. Jesus contradicted the charge of the Pharisees and
silenced them when he told them that if one devil should
cause a man to be sick and another should heal him, the kingdom of the devil would be divided against itself.

In other words, the forces of evil cannot do good, nor the
forces of good do evil. Jesus' healings were done by the power
of God, who had sent him to preach the gospel, heal the sick
and open the eyes of the blind. God would not grant this power
to evil men. (See Luke 11:20.)

17. BINDING THE STRONG MAN

Or else how can one enter into a strong man's house,
and spoil his goods, except he first bind the strong man?
and then he will spoil his house.

Matt. 12:29

In the East, men who have treasures and other valuables
are constantly armed. At times, they even sleep with their
weapons upon their bodies, so that no one can enter their houses
and plunder their goods without first binding or killing the
owners. This is done also in America, as bandits often bind un-
armed people before they steal their goods.

Jesus told his adversaries, the Pharisees, that if he cast out
devils, that is, restored the insane, by the power of the Devil,
it would imply that the Devil was working against himself. In
the olden days, it was assumed that disease was caused by
devils, while today we say they are caused by germs. The
Easterners had no idea of germs.

If one devil should cause a man to suffer insanity and another
devil should heal him, then the Devil's kingdom is divided
against itself. And when a kingdom is divided against itself, it is
bound to fall. In other words, the Devil's business was to cause
sickness, and then to cause more of it.

No devil could have given power to Jesus or possessed him
without first disarming him. In this case, the strong man is
symbolic of Jesus, who was armed with the truth of God, the
author of good. And as we have said, the Devil, or Beelzebub,
would have had to disarm him before giving him power. But
this was not the case, for Jesus' healing was done by the power
of God. He cast out devils, restored the insane, by the spirit
of God, the healing power of God. Therefore, his enemies
blasphemed when they said, "He does these things by the
power of Satan." It was a blasphemy against the spirit of God,
the Holy Spirit which does the healing. Satan could not have
taken possession of this spiritual power without first winning
victory over God. (See Matt. 12:31, Luke 11:20.)

18. GOOD THINGS OUT OF GOOD TREASURE

A good man out of the good treasure of the heart bringeth forth good things: and an evil man out of the evil treasure bringeth forth evil things.

Matt. 12:35

Treasure, in this instance, is symbolic of the heart, or mind. A wise man brings forth words of wisdom from the treasures of his mind, but a foolish man brings forth folly.

In the East, many good and noble men who are generally admired for their piety and good works possess rich treasures. During banquets, it is their custom to bring out priceless articles from their treasures to show to their guests. On the other hand, evil rich men often bring forth from their treasures imitation articles and display them as though they were costly and precious.

In the East, a good man is known by his good words and deeds, while a bad man is known by his bad words and deeds. On another occasion Jesus said, "By their fruits you shall know them," or in other words, "You shall not judge them by their words or the religion to which they claim to belong."

A good tree is known by the good fruit thereof, and not by its branches and leaves. Many trees in the East look alike but their fruits differ—one is sweet and the other is bitter. No good man can produce evil works, and no evil man will produce good works. Each will bring forth that which he has in the treasures of his heart and mind.

19. MEN OF NINEVEH

The men of Nineveh shall rise in judgement with this generation, and shall condemn it: because they repented at the preaching of Jonas; and behold, a greater than Jonas is here.

Matt. 12:41

Jesus upbraided the Jews because of their disbelief in him as the Messiah. He had performed many miracles and wonders, but still they rejected him. Jesus related Jonah's experience—how the King and the people of Nineveh received him, how they repented from their sins, and how Nineveh was spared from disaster by God. But Jerusalem, being obstinate, was doomed. In the year A.D. 70 the historic and holy city and its colossal temple were destroyed by Titus, the Roman general.

It is interesting to know that the people of Nineveh, the capital of Assyria, were converted to Christianity while Jesus was in Galilee. Jesus sent seventy of his disciples to preach the gospel to the lost tribes of the house of Israel. (Matt. 10:6) These tribes had been carried away captive by the Assyrian kings in 722 B.C., and had settled in Assyria, Syria, Iran and other places. They received the gospel before the people of other races.

Many pagan people revered and feared the God of Abraham, the living God. It is interesting to know that some of the Assyrian kings feared the God of Israel. When they were subjugating Judah, they claimed that they came with the consent of Yahweh. Isaiah called Assyria "the rod of God's anger," that is, His agent. (Isa. 10:5)

Jonah had prophesied that Nineveh would be destroyed, but it was not. In his vision, Jonah argued with God, and wondered why God did not carry out His threats. At last, he was told in his vision that God had spared the people of Nineveh because they repented. (See the article on Jonah in the *Gospel Light*, a commentary on the Gospels published by A. J. Holman Co.

17

20. THE QUEEN OF SHEBA

The queen of the south shall rise up in the judgment with this generation, and shall condemn it: for she came from the uttermost parts of the earth to hear the wisdom of Solomon; and, behold, a greater than Solomon is here.

Matt. 12:42

The "queen of the south" refers to the Queen of Sheba. The term "south" is used because some of the territory of the Queen of Sheba was east of the Red Sea and in southern Arabia, which is south of Judea.

The Queen of Sheba came to see King Solomon, having heard of his wisdom and understanding. She brought him costly presents so that she might sit at his feet and drink of his wisdom.

A greater one than King Solomon there was, even Jesus Christ, but no one paid attention to him or respected his teaching. On Judgment Day, they would be asked by God why they shunned and refused to honor Jesus Christ. But the Queen of Sheba would be commended for her pious act in making such a long journey to see a teacher who was less great than Jesus. She would condemn the Pharisees, Sadducees and scribes, who belittled Jesus and did not recognize him as the Messiah.

Indeed, a prophet or a great man is often more honored by alien peoples than by the people of his own country. It was hard for the Pharisees, Sadducees and scribes to recognize a poor Galilean peasant as the great Messiah, the Savior of Israel.

21. MUSTARD SEED

Another parable put he forth unto them, saying, The kingdom of heaven is like to a grain of mustard seed, which
a man took, and sowed in his field.

Matt. 13:31

This parable was constructed by Jesus to reveal the power
of the Word of God, that is, the power of the gospel of truth
which Jesus had begun to preach to a few people. Jesus
realized that just as the seed grows slowly and multiplies itself,
so a word spoken in truth will ultimately multiply itself and
fill the whole world.

The seed, like the word, is one of the most powerful things
in the world. In the course of time it multiplies itself rapidly,
and the power within it is infinite. The gospel which was proclaimed on the shores of the Lake of Galilee would in due time
be carried on wings of the spirit over seas and oceans.

The mustard seed, though smaller than other seeds, springs up
fast and grows more rapidly than other seeds. As a mustard
seed is small but potent, so the gospel of Jesus Christ is small
when compared with Judaism, paganism, and other religions,
but it is full of the power of God. It has something in it that
no other has. It is the gospel of love and meekness, the two
most powerful weapons in the world—the weapons of the Spirit.

Then again, as grains of mustard seed are rounded and even,
so the truth of the gospel has only one side, not two. The mustard seed cannot be divided in two like some other seeds. So
the gospel, or the teaching, must be based on the truth alone,
and not be divided. Moreover, the mustard seed is hotter than
others, and wherever it grows, other seeds die. Because of its
great power, Christianity was to supplant all other religions. It
could not grow side by side with paganism and other materialistic and sensual religions and philosophies. (Mark 4:30, Luke
13:18)

22. DESERT PLACE

When Jesus heard of it, he departed thence by ship into
a desert place apart: and when the people had heard
thereof, they followed him on foot out of the cities.

Matt. 14:13

The Aramaic word *khorba* means "uninhabited place."
The Aramaic word for "the wilderness" is *madbra,* which means
"a wasteland," or "a land without water or vegetation." Jesus
went to an uninhabited place close to Tiberius.

Until a few decades ago many places around the Lake of
Galilee and around Jordan were uninhabited, and a few still
are. These are the places to which Jesus and his followers
retreated, seeking solitude and rest from the crowds of men
and women who followed him out of curiosity, expecting to
see great wonders.

All great religions were born in desert lands. Moses spent
forty years in the desert, Elijah forty days in Sinai; Paul spent
three years in the desert, and Mohammed, all his life. One
must be in solitude to commune with God. Jesus, as a man,
was often disturbed by the opposition, which was considerable
in the cities, and at times he was tired. He was not in a mood to
meet people at this particular time. Therefore, he went to a
place where no one would disturb him and his followers.

Even today, kings, princes, and religious men seek refuge in
isolated places in order to rest and to make important decisions.

23. UNTRUE DOCTRINES UPROOTED

But he answered and said, Every plant, which my heavenly Father hath planted, shall be rooted up.
Let them alone: they be blind leaders of the blind. And if the blind lead the blind, both shall fall into the ditch.

Matt. 15:13–14

The "plant" in this instance refers to doctrine, that is, the true doctrine which God had revealed to Moses and the prophets, the foundation of the Jewish religion. The Pharisees and scribes had supplanted some of the true teachings of Judaism with their own false doctrines and interpretations.

All of the teachings and doctrines which had not come in a revelation from God were soon to be uprooted and supplanted by the new and true teaching. The truth of the gospel must be preached regardless of the opposition of the Pharisees and the scribes—the blind teachers who were leading the blind.

Jesus' teaching was based on the teaching of the holy prophets of Israel, who in their days had acted as spokesmen for God. Jesus had come to fulfill the law and the prophets, that is, to put them into practice.

Truth always replaces error. It may take time for truth to be understood, but sooner or later it destroys error.

24. PHARISEES

The Pharisees also with the Sadducees came, and tempting desired him that he would shew them a sign from heaven.

Matt. 16:1

The term "Pharisee" is derived from the Aramaic *parash*, "to separate," "to set aside," "to select." Pharisees were the selected ones. They were a group which drew themselves apart from other people. They were the devout nationalists, the Jewish leaders who wanted to restore the political Israel. The party of the Pharisees came into existence after the exile, especially when Judea was occupied by the Romans. There is no mention of the Pharisees in the Old Testament. The scribes are often mentioned in the books of Moses. However, the term *saprey,* or "scribes," has been erroneously translated "officers" in the King James version.

The scribes and Pharisees worked closely together, and both believed in the resurrection of the body and life hereafter. They also believed in helping their enemies if they should meet them in distress on the highways. They knew that enmity and anger blind one's eyes, but love opens them. They revered the prophets of Israel and were looking for the coming of the Messiah, the Blessed One.

Paul was a strict Pharisee who was moved by Jesus' teachings of simplicity, meekness and love.

25. SADDUCEES

The Pharisees also with the Sadducees came, and tempting desired him that he would shew them a sign from heaven.

Matt. 16:1

The term "Sadducee" is derived from the Aramaic *sadak,* to become righteous: *Sadokaye,* Sadducees, that is, "the righteous ones." Such terms as "Sadducees" and "Pharisees" were unknown before the exile in 586 B.C. Neither word is found in the Old Testament.

The Sadducees were members of a Jewish party known as "the righteous ones." In other words, they had declared themselves to be righteous. The Sadducees were not nationalists, nor did they believe in resurrection. As far as they were concerned, one life was enough. Therefore, they did everything they could to enjoy this life.

The Sadducees were satisfied with the Roman Government and the Herodian dynasty, which had been imposed upon the Jews by Roman authorities and their cohorts. Therefore, many Sadducees were employed in the service of the local and imperial governments.

Jesus in his discourses reprimanded the scribes and the Pharisees, often calling them hypocrites and blind guides, but he seldom had any encounter with the Sadducees, for they did not care whether the Jewish religion was reformed or not. Nor did they expect the coming of the Messiah, the great Jewish leader. They were satisfied with things as they were.

26. CALLING PETER "SATAN"

But he turned, and said unto Peter, Get thee behind me, Satan: thou art an offence unto me: for thou savourest not the things that be of God, but those that be of men.
Matt. 16:23

The term "Satan" is derived from the Aramaic *sata*, which means "to mislead," "to miss the mark," "to cause to go astray," "to deviate from one's course."

Peter was trying hard to persuade his master that he was not going to die on the cross. Peter and all the other disciples of Jesus were brought up in Judaism and were told that the Messiah would reign and live forever.

Jesus rebuked Peter because he had told him again and again that the prophecies must be fulfilled, and that the Son of man must die on the cross in order to enter into his glory and establish a new reign, the reign of love, righteousness, and meekness. Peter did not realize that his master's new teaching would be rejected by the high priests, the Pharisees and the scribes, and that he would be condemned to death and crucified by the Romans. Peter had been close to his master and wanted to comfort him, and was not aware that he was offending Jesus by contradicting him.

"Satan" here means "one who misleads." Jesus was angry at Peter; that is why he used such a sharp rebuke. This phrase is very common in Aramaic and Arabic speech. At times a father may call his own son Satan without any malicious intent. Moreover, an ingenious man is also called "Satan" (Arabic: *shitan*).

27. TAKE YOUR CROSS

Then said Jesus unto his disciples, If any man will come after me, let him deny himself, and take up his cross, and follow me.

Matt. 16:24

"Take your cross" in Aramaic is another way of saying, "Risk your life." In Aramaic, we also say, "Take your blood in your hand," which means, "You may be exposed to great dangers, and may die at any time."

It was the custom in Jesus' day for victims to carry their own crosses, signifying that they bore their own guilt. The cross was so dreaded that some people thought they would be defiled if they so much as touched it by accident. This is because its victims were condemned criminals who had committed crimes or unforgivable sins, or had blasphemed against God. Only the worst criminals met this kind of death.

The victims bore their crosses as a sign that they were bearing their own guilt and paying the supreme penalty. While they walked, bent under their heavy crosses, they were mindful of the hour when they would be nailed on the cross. Moreover, the people watched them carrying their crosses, and it was a lesson to those who had evil inclinations, rebellious men and those who dared to resist the imperial government.

Christians were admonished to be ready to die for the teaching of their Lord. Jesus knew his teaching was a contradiction of the old way of life and of the government authorities. Therefore, he knew his followers must be constantly aware of the dangers which would confront them, and that many of them might die on the cross. (Rom. 8:17)

28. HOLY ANGELS

For the Son of man shall come in the glory of his Father with his angels; and then he shall reward every man according to his works.

Matt. 16:27

The Aramaic word for "angel" is *malakha,* which means "a counselor," "a representative of God," "a messenger." Angels are spirits and are God's counsel. God, being the Eternal Spirit, is everywhere, and his counsel also is everywhere. Another meaning of *malakha,* or *malokha,* is "king."

In biblical days, angels were pictured with wings to signify that God's counsel is everywhere. Wings symbolize the omnipresence of God and his spirit. No matter where one seeks God's counsel, it is there in an instant.

Jesus was rejected, repudiated and crucified with malefactors. As far as the world was concerned, he died a defeated man. But he here implies that his death on the cross was not the end of his mission but the beginning thereof. The day will come when his kingdom will be established on earth, and he will come accompanied by holy angels.

The Aramaic term for "kingdom" is *malkotha,* which means "counsel." That is to say, God's counsel will triumph at the end. Moreover, in the East, when a man suffers defeat or loses his political or economic power, we say he is dead. But when he succeeds, we say he has come back again.

How Jesus will return I do not know, but one thing I do know: that his kingdom will be established on earth as it is in heaven, and the ideals for which he died will be accepted by all humanity. Jesus Christ will come in glory in the hearts of all believers. He went up in a spiritual body; he will return in a spiritual body. He has never left his followers; he has always been with them. Whenever two of them are together, he is in their midst. (See Dan. 7:10, other articles on angels in *Gospel Light,* and *Old Testament Light* by the same author.)

29. TAXES

He saith, Yes. And when he was come into the house, Jesus prevented him, saying, What thinkest thou, Simon? of whom do the kings of the earth take custom or tribute? of their own children, or of strangers?
Peter saith unto him, Of strangers. Jesus saith unto him, Then are the children free.

Matt. 17:25–26

In Eastern countries, taxes are collected from workers, strangers in the land, and the poor. Kings, princes, and the noble and rich are exempt from taxes. This exemption also applies to their sons and peers. It would be an embarrassing situation for a tax collector to call upon a rich man and ask him to pay taxes. This is because for centuries these men have been looked upon as the nobles and princes of the realm, and therefore not subject to the ordinances and laws of the land. Some of these men are even allowed to collect taxes from the people for themselves, and to conscript workers for their fields, without pay. This practice is still continued in many countries even today, and is the cause of the people's revolt against the rich.

Jesus knew the customs and manners of the land, and therefore was willing to comply with them in order not to offend the officials.

30. CHILDREN'S ANGELS

Take heed that ye despise not one of these little ones; for I say unto you, That in heaven their angels do always behold the face of my Father which is in heaven.

Matt. 18:10

Easterners for many centuries have believed, and still do believe, in guardian angels. It is said that every man, woman and child has his own guardian angel, God's counsel, who warns him when he is inclined to do evil. It is said that the guardian angel sits on one's right shoulder, and the devil on the left. The term "angel" means "God's counsel."

On the Mountain of Temptation Jesus was ministered to by angels. In the Old Testament we read that angels of God appeared to Gideon, to Samson's parents, to Jacob; and the New Testament tells us that they appeared to Mary, to Joseph, and to the apostles. God's counsel is always with those who seek to do His will and carry out His orders.

In the East, children are not treated as tenderly as they are in America. When they draw near to the presence of a holy man or a high government official they are rebuked, chased away, and at times scolded or even beaten.

Jesus loved children and wanted to have them seated close to him, listening to his words, because the children are pure in mind. One must be like a child, innocent and harmless, in order to enter into the kingdom of God. Moreover, most prominent Eastern men would have shunned children, but Jesus took them in his arms as examples of the true children of God.

31. DIVORCE OF EUNUCH

But he said unto them, All men cannot receive this saying, save they to whom it is given.
For there are some eunuchs, which were so born from their mother's womb: and there are some eunuchs, which were made eunuchs of men: and there be eunuchs, which have made themselves eunuchs for the kingdom of heaven's sake. He that is able to receive it, let him receive it.
Matt. 19:11-12

Jesus was not opposed to legal divorce, but he was against those who deserted their wives without any cause. He was also against lax enforcement of the laws on divorce, which were seldom upheld by the religious authorities.

Jesus upbraided the Jews who deserted their wives and did not give them divorce papers according to the law of Moses. The Jews, like other Eastern people, took their marriage covenants very lightly. And when they were angry with their wives or did not love them, they deserted them without even bothering to give them divorce papers. According to Jesus, adultery was ground for divorce. As the result of the lax enforcement of this law, many innocent women suffered unjustly and were forced to commit adultery when they married other men, for they were still married to their former husbands, not having been given legal divorce papers.

The disciples thought that Jesus' admonition relative to divorce was too harsh, and therefore hard to comply with. They had been brought up in the Jewish religion, where women were regarded as inferior. This custom was universal at that time, and still prevails in many lands.

Jesus' saying does not apply to every man, because some are eunuchs, who are not fit to be married. In Matt. 19:7, he points out that there are cases where a woman can divorce her husband on the grounds of incapability, because, as we have said, there are some men who are born eunuchs, some who have made themselves eunuchs, and others who were made eunuchs by force.

The Church of the East grants divorces on such grounds. The author of this article was appointed to examine such cases and report to Church authorities.

There are also women who are not sexually normal to be married. In such cases both men and women can apply for divorce. (See *Gospel Light*, Matt. 5.)

32. THE VINEYARD—GOD'S RELIGION

And when they came that were hired about the eleventh hour, they received every man a penny.
But when the first came, they supposed that they should have received more; and they likewise received every man a penny.

Matt. 20:9–10

The man in the parable, the owner of the vineyard, symbolizes God; the laborers are the people who have started to work in God's religion at various times. The vineyard is God's religion, Judaism. Early morning suggests the beginning of the gospel, while agreement over the wages symbolizes the period in which the laborers worked.

The Jews were the first people to work in God's vineyard. The Gentiles and the pagans came later, and at the end all of them received the same wages. In the realm of the spirit there is no time. It is willingness and loyalty that count.

All these laborers are the preachers of the gospel who began their work after Jesus' ascension and those who will labor later at the end of time, who will receive the same wages. Some of these men who came too late to work in the vineyard could not have come first, because they were not yet born. Those who had started early had suffered persecutions, but those who came later did not. The gospel had already triumphed over the world. The word "evening" refers to the late hours. The workers whom no one had hired and never heard of the gospel.

The beginning and the end are in God's hands. No one can be blamed for being too late to accept the gospel. No one but God has authority over the wages, that is, the rewards which God will offer for those who have worked in His religion. The Jews came first and the Gentiles later, but the wages will be according to the service rendered and not the length of time. (Mark 10:31, Matt. 22:14, Luke 14:24)

33. THE CUP OF DEATH

But Jesus answered and said, Ye know not what ye ask.
Are ye able to drink of the cup that I shall drink of,
and to be baptized with the baptism that I am baptized
with? They say unto him, We are able.

Matt. 20:22

The cup and the baptism in this instance are symbolic
of the arrest, the suffering and death of Jesus. This is because,
in the East, the cup was poisoned and handed over to the
guests whom the host had marked for death.

The sons of Zebedee, James and John, were to suffer and
die for the gospel of their Lord. Nevertheless, in order to sit
on his right hand and his left, they had to do the will of God.

Jesus could not promise them seats in his kingdom. They
must earn them by drinking from the cup which he was going
to drink, and by being baptized with the same baptism with
which he was going to be baptized—that is, the baptism on
the cross, when his body would be covered with his blood.
In other words, such high places in the kingdom of God could
not be given to anyone just because they asked for them, or
as gifts or favors. Christians must earn such places by complete dedication to the cause of the gospel, and by hard work
and suffering.

These high places were to be given to those who deserved
them. God has granted them to the apostles and the martyrs
who have followed in the footsteps of Jesus Christ and given
their lives for the sake of the gospel. (See Cup in *Gospel
Light*.)

34. MY CUP YOU SHALL DRINK

And he saith unto them, Ye shall drink indeed of my cup,
and be baptized with the baptism that I am baptized with:
but to sit on my right hand, and on my left, is not mine
to give, but it shall be given to them for whom it is prepared of my Father.

Matt. 20:23

"My cup you shall drink" means, "The death I die, you
shall also die." That is to say, you will be hated, condemned
and put to death because of my teaching and your loyalty to
me.

In the East, when a host wants to do away with his enemy,
he gives a banquet in his honor, and then he poisons the cup.
Kings and princes and noblemen usually employ cup and food
tasters. Our English word "assassin" comes from the Persian word
hashashin, which is derived from *hash-hash.* (See article on
Cup, Matt. 20:22.)

Nearly all of Jesus' disciples met with violent deaths. Some
were crucified, some were beheaded, and others died by the
sword.

Just as Jesus' body was washed with his own blood, so his
disciples were also to be baptized with the baptism of blood;
that is to say, were to give their earthly lives for the sake of
the life hereafter.

35. SON OF DAVID

And, behold, two blind men sitting by the wayside, when they heard that Jesus passed by, cried out, saying, Have mercy on us, O Lord, thou son of David.

Matt. 20:30

The term "Son of David" was often used as a token of admiration and respect, not necessarily because the person was an actual son. It really means David-like, but could also mean a descendant of David, depending upon how the term is used. In the East, gallant men are often called sons of kings and great men who have died centuries before them. Jesus called a woman whom he had healed "daughter of Abraham," though she was born two thousand years after Abraham. What he meant was that she was a member of the faith of Abraham, or one of his descendants. Mohammed calls the Virgin Mary a daughter of Aaron.

David lived a thousand years before Jesus. The Jews expected the Messiah to be of David's line or to be David-like, or even greater than David, so that he might deliver them from their enemies and establish a universal and lasting kingdom.

Jesus did not claim to be a descendant of any king or prince. The Pharisees and scribes rejected him on the grounds that he was not a descendant of David. (See John 7:11–42, Matt. 22:41–46.) They said, "When Christ comes, we will know who he is, and he will be born in Bethlehem, the City of David." Apparently, the Pharisees and scribes and other Jewish authorities knew nothing about Jesus' birth in Bethlehem, nor did Jesus defend his birth. On the contrary, he quoted Psalms 110:1: "The Lord said unto my Lord, Sit thou at my right hand, until I make thine enemies thy footstool." Jesus was looked upon as a Galilean, and, according to the Jews, was not entitled to be called "Messiah."

David was the true founder of the Hebrew monarchy. He

33

was a great leader, a conqueror, and a true servant of God. Jesus called himself the son of man and the son of God. In his humanity he was a man like us, and in his divinity, God.

36. MAN WITH TWO SONS

But what think ye? A certain man had two sons; and he came to the first, and said, Son, go work today in my vineyard.

He answered and said, I will not: but afterward he repented, and went.

And he came to the second, and said likewise. And he answered and said, I go, sir: and went not.

Matt. 21:28–30

Jesus recited this parable to teach his disciples and followers that there are many men and women who pretend that they are ready to do any good errand or deed, but when the time comes to do it, they refuse. On the other hand, there are those who say they cannot do it, but after thinking the matter over, they do it.

There are many people who brag about what they believe, and some would die for the beliefs of their denomination, but when it comes to doing something about their faith (religion), they do nothing. Moreover, there are those who do not boast about what they believe, or can do, but when the time comes to act, they go ahead and do what needs to be done.

Jesus places emphasis on action, or work, rather than on empty or pleasing words, which are like hot winds. On one occasion he said, "It is not the one who says, 'My Lord, My Lord,' but the one who hears my word and does it."

The Pharisees and scribes boasted of the things they were going to do, but they never tried to do them. Christianity is not like pagan creeds; rather, it is a life full of good actions. Christians must work hard in order to hasten the kingdom of God.

The term "man" is used figuratively, to represent God. The two sons represent the people—the Jews and the Gentiles. The vineyard is the Gentiles who at the beginning did not obey God's prophets, but at last accepted the gospel of Jesus Christ from his apostles.

The younger son is symbolic of the Jews, for they received the law from Moses, but at the end they trampled upon it and despised it.

It is not the word that counts; action and faithfulness are more important.

A remnant of the Jews did accept the gospel, and many of Jesus' followers were recruited from the common people or the lower classes, who were looked upon as sinners. Because of their acceptance of the gospel, they became first in the kingdom.

37. THE REJECTED STONE

Therefore say I unto you, The kingdom of God shall be taken from you, and given to a nation bringing forth the fruits thereof.
And whosoever shall fall on this stone shall be broken: but on whomsoever it shall fall, it will grind him to powder.

Matt. 21:43–44

The "stone" in this instance is Jesus Christ. The rejection of the stone by the builder indicated that the teaching of Jesus would be opposed by the adherents of other religions, and his followers persecuted and put to death. (See Matt. 24:9–14.) But ultimately Jesus' teaching was to destroy false pagan doctrines.

Then again, kings and princes of this world who would try

to destroy Christianity would be destroyed by the stone, the truth, which is not cut by human hands. (See Dan. 2:34–35.)

In other words, all who would oppose the truth of Christ only harm themselves, and merely cause it to spread more rapidly, for persecution is the very life of a new movement.

The kingdom, Christ's religion, was taken from the Jews and given to the Gentiles who accepted the gospel. Nevertheless, many Jews did become converts to the gospel. Most of the first Christians were Jews.

38. NO MARRIAGE IN HEAVEN

For in the resurrection they neither marry, nor are given in marriage, but are as the angels of God in heaven.

Matt. 22:30

"Like the angel of God" is an Eastern phrase which means "Godlike," "innocent." God is the Eternal Spirit, and spiritual man was created in His image and likeness—good, eternal, and indestructible.

Marriage was ordained by God to replenish the face of the earth. In heaven there will be no multiplication; therefore, sex will cease, and men and women will be spiritual, like angels of God, or God Himself.

Some teachers of religion believe that life in heaven will be similar to life on earth, but much easier and full of joy. They also maintain that people will enjoy everything without laboring for it. In other words, they maintain that heaven is a place for idlers and loafers.

The Babylonians and Egyptians believed in another life on this earth. This is why the wives and servants of kings and other great men were buried with them.

Angels are God's counsel and His messengers. No one has seen an angel except in a vision. They have spiritual bodies which can only be seen with spiritual eyes. When angels appear to men, they appear as humans, but only in visions.

39. GOD OF THE LIVING

I am the God of Abraham, and the God of Isaac, and the God of Jacob? God is not the God of the dead, but of the living.

Matt. 22:32

The God of Israel was the God of the living, because the Hebrews believed in immortality. The gods of other nations were human beings, who were forgotten after their deaths. But Abraham, Isaac, and Jacob, though they were departed from this life, were living somewhere else. So the Hebrews' God was the God of the living. (Ex. 3:6) The Hebrew concept of death was different than that of the Gentiles and pagans. Moses and Elijah were expected to return and to prepare the way for the coming of the Messiah.

On the other hand, the God of the Jews was the living God, the God of all generations, the creator of the heavens and the earth.

Jesus did not believe in the power of death; he did not believe that death was an end, a finality. A living and indestructible God would not have created a destructible man. This is why Jesus knew that death had no power over him, and that the same God Who is the Lord of life is also the Lord of death. (Mark 12:26, Luke 20:35)

40. GOD'S NAME IS HOLY

The LORD said unto my Lord, Sit thou on my right hand,
till I make thine enemies thy footstool?
If David then call him Lord, how is he his son?

Matt. 22:44–45

In the New Testament, both Jesus and the Lord God are referred to as "the Lord." In Aramaic, capital letters were unknown. The word Lord was written the same, whether it be the Lord God, Jesus, or a human lord. The Jews, however, later made the name of the Lord God distinct.

David calls the Messiah "my Lord," and he calls God "the Lord." This is why in this passage he says, "The LORD said unto my Lord."

The names of *Mariah*, "Lord," and of *Mari*, "my Lord," were written in a distinct manner. In Hebrew it is called *Shem, Prash,* that is, "the separate name," "the Holy One," "the Most High." The name *Yahweh* was also used. This name was given by Moses, and it was written differently and was not supposed to be uttered with the mouth because of reverence for God. It is abbreviated and written *Yah* (Jah). (See *Gospel Light,* Matt. 22:41–42.)

41. DECEPTIVE MEN

Ye serpents, ye generation of vipers, how can ye escape
the damnation of hell?

Matt. 23:33

"Serpents and the offspring of scorpions" is an Aramaic
phrase which means "deceptive" or "subtle," and "without guidance from God." (See comment on scorpions, *Gospel Light*,
Matt. 3:7.)

42. ZECHARIAH, SON OF BARACHIAH

That upon you may come all the righteous blood shed
upon the earth, from the blood of righteous Abel unto the
blood of Zacharias son of Barachias whom ye slew between the temple and the altar.

Matt. 23:35

Zechariah is the son of Jehoiadah the priest who was later
called Barachiah. (II Chron. 22:11) Brakhiah is his spiritual
name, which was given to him when he put the queen Athaliah
to death, and placed Joash, the son of Ahaziah, King of Judah,
upon the throne of his father. Jehoiadah, the priest, had married
Jehoshabeath, the daughter of King Jehoram, and Jehoshabeath hid Joash from Athaliah, who had slain all the princes of
Judah. He also cleansed the temple of God and restored the
true religion.

After the death of Jehoiadah, the princes of Judah conspired
against God's religion, and returned to Baal worship. Then
Zechariah, the son of Jehoiadah, warned the people, saying that

just as they had forsaken the Lord their God, so would he also forsake them. Because of his warnings and admonitions, Zechariah was stoned, by command of the king, in the court of the house of the Lord. (II Chron. 24:20–23) His brothers also were slain, because they too opposed Baal worship.

Some Bible authorities were led to believe that Zechariah, the son of Barachiah, was the father of John the Baptist, who lived about six centuries later.

43. IN THE NAME OF THE LORD

For I say unto you, Ye shall not see me henceforth, till ye shall say, Blessed is he that cometh in the name of the Lord.

Matt. 23:39

"Coming in the name of the Lord" is an Aramaic saying meaning "coming as an ambassador of the Lord," that is, "appointed and sent by the Lord to deliver a message to the people." An ambassador is a representative of the king who sends him.

The Messiah was an ambassador of God, representing God and His religion. What he said and did was approved by God, or was done in God's name, according to His laws and religion.

In biblical days, many false prophets and messengers came in their own name, for the Lord God had not sent them, and this is why their predictions did not come true.

Jesus Christ was sent by God to reveal the true way, the true religion, which was revealed to Abraham, Moses, and the prophets. He preached that which the Lord had spoken through His holy prophets. He had come to fulfill the law and the prophets.

44. NOT ONE STONE UPON ANOTHER

And Jesus said unto them, See ye not all these things?
verily I say unto you, There shall not be left here one stone
upon another, that shall not be thrown down.

Matt. 24:2

The temple of Solomon, rebuilt by Herod, was destroyed by Titus in the year A.D. 70. The ruins of the beautiful and colossal temple and those of the city remained there in Jerusalem. Thousands of the Jews were slaughtered; some were carried away captive; and some were sold in the slave markets. Such was the fate of the once great city Jerusalem and the holy temple which King Solomon had built to the God of Israel, the universal God.

Jesus' prophecy was fulfilled when Emperor Hadrian uprooted Jerusalem from its foundations and built a new city, calling it Elia Heliopolis.

Today all of the stones of the temple are at Baalbek, Lebanon, about 160 miles north of Jerusalem. Not one stone was left on another. This happened because the once holy temple had been defiled by pagan practices—Baal worship—and during the time of Jesus had become a den of thieves and was used as a business institution. (Jer. 26:13)

45. INIQUITY SHALL ABOUND

And because iniquity shall abound, the love of many shall
wax cold.
But he that shall endure unto the end, the same shall be
saved.
And this gospel of the kingdom shall be preached in all
the world for a witness unto all nations; and then shall the
end come.

Matt. 24:12–14

The reference here is to the false prophets and false
teachers of religion who were to cause men and women to go
astray from the true religion, and who were to introduce
materialistic philosophies and teachings contrary to the gospel
of Jesus Christ.

Those who accepted the challenge and endured persecution
and suffering would ultimately triumph over the material world
and man-made doctrines. God always keeps a remnant, and a
remnant, no matter how small, is a majority with God.

46. THE SUDDEN COMING OF JESUS

For as the lightning cometh out of the east, and shineth
even unto the west; so shall also the coming of the Son of
man be.

Matt. 24:27

In the East, lightning is supposed to be the fastest thing
in the world, but science tells us that light is the fastest, and that
it travels 186,300 miles per second. Nevertheless, lightning is

the fastest thing our eyes can see in motion, for we cannot see the motion of light.

Jesus states that his coming will be as fast as lightning. Just as lightning is seen in both the East and the West in the same second, he will be seen likewise by all eyes everywhere. Moreover, the events that will precede his coming will take place in rapid succession.

No one will be able to foretell the day and the hour of his coming, just as no one knows when a thief will come at night. Therefore, Christians are admonished to be alert and not to be misled by false prophets, who for their own worldly gain would predict his coming and thus deceive the faithful. Moreover, his followers are admonished to be constantly watchful and ready to greet him when he comes. In other words, no one should say, "I have plenty of time to repent, to be ready to greet him." Christians are warned to keep their candles burning, and provide plenty of oil for their lamps (good works) in order to be able to greet him at any time he should come, and to enter into his kingdom. (See the parable of the virgins, Matt. 25:1-13.)

47. VULTURES AND CARCASSES

For wheresoever the carcass is, there will the eagles be gathered together.

Matt. 24:28

The term "eagles" may be wrong. Jesus might have said "vultures." Even though the eagle is a bird of prey, akin to the hawks, and it does kill, it is not a scavenger.

On the other hand, vultures hover over highways and deserts to find dead bodies. They usually eat spoiled meat which other birds and wild beasts shun. They are true scavengers.

"Carcass" in this instance is symbolic of the Jewish race. The

43

Jews had lost their freedom and the precious teaching of their prophets. And now, they were like a carcass ready to be devoured by the vultures, or the birds of prey—the pagan nations—which were their enemies round about them. They had already been devoured by the Assyrians, the Chaldeans, the Syrians, and now they were to be the victims of the Romans, whose flags bore the image of the eagle, which means omnipresence. The Romans had conquered and occupied all the lands around the Mediterranean. Now they were slowly but gradually annexing Judea.

In the year A.D. 70, the Roman legions under General Titus took Jerusalem and destroyed the temple, taking thousands of Jews captive. Thus Jesus' prophecy was fulfilled.

48. UNIVERSE SHARES IN CALAMITY

Immediately after the tribulation of those days shall the sun be darkened, and the moon shall not give her light, and the stars shall fall from heaven, and the powers of the heavens shall be shaken.

Matt. 24:29

When the events which will precede the coming of Jesus Christ shall take place, the whole universe will share in this human tragedy. Such sayings are generally used figuratively.

Jesus in this instance indicates that the stars will fall, and all the powers of the universe will be shaken up. The term "stars" also means "great men, emperors, and princes who control the world." The Scriptures hint that there will be an end to the universe. Such statements were also made by the Hebrew prophets centuries before Jesus. (Isa. 13:10, Ezek. 32:7) On the other hand, the Scriptures also state that the universe is from everlasting to everlasting, indestructible.

Some of the stars and planets in our universe may collide and explode. It will be a great calamity—greater than any other catastrophe known in the history of man. (See Dan. 7:13.)

49. A SIGN IN HEAVEN

And then shall appear the sign of the Son of man in heaven: and then shall all the tribes of the earth mourn, and they shall see the Son of man coming in the clouds of heaven with power and great glory.
And he shall send his angels with a great sound of a trumpet, and they shall gather together his elect from the four winds, from one end of heaven to the other.

Matt. 24:30–31

Jesus' followers will be informed of his coming through a revelation: The sign of his coming will appear in heaven. Moreover, he will send his angels, which means he will send his messengers to announce his coming and prepare the way so that his followers may be ready to go out to greet him.

The "four winds" signify the four corners of the earth; the trumpet is symbolic of the important announcement of his coming. Jesus' followers will gather from all parts of the earth to greet him.

The term "heaven," in this instance, means "universe." The Aramaic or Hebrew word *Shamaya* means "heavens," "universe," or "sky." The Scripture implies that the chosen ones will come from everywhere. No one has ascended to heaven except Jesus Christ, who came down from heaven.

It must be remembered that this is a revelation, and should not be taken literally. The term "trumpet" is used figuratively; heavenly messengers need no trumpet to announce them. They come in the stillness of the day and the silence of the night.

Jesus' coming will be spiritual; that is to say, he will come in a spiritual body, free of space and time. When he comes, space and distance will disappear and every eye will see him. (Dan. 7:13, Mark 13:4)

50. THE JEWISH RACE

Verily I say unto you, This generation shall not pass, till all these things be fulfilled.

Matt. 24:34

The Aramaic word *sharbta* means "a family," "a tribe," "a nation," "a generation," or "genealogy." But in this instance it means "a race," that is, the Hebrew race or the Jewish people. (The Jews at this time were known by their religion. Israel as a state or a political entity had come to an end in 586 B.C.)

Jesus wanted his disciples to know that they had a great work ahead of them, and that it would take many centuries before Jews were converted to Christianity.

Two thousand years have elapsed and only a few Jews have been converted to the true teachings of Jesus which he taught in Galilee and Judea.

The Jews will remain as Jews, as a witness to the Jewish race; but the day will come when those who call themselves Christians will truly accept the true and simple teachings of Jesus. At that time the Jews will embrace Christianity, for true Christianity is true Judaism—the truth which God had revealed to Abraham, Moses and the prophets.

Throughout centuries the Jews have played an important part in religion; they have preserved the sacred writings and the entity of God.

51. JESUS' SUDDEN COMING

But as the days of Noe were so shall also the coming of
the Son of man be.
For as in the days that were before the flood they were
eating and drinking, marrying and giving in marriage, until
the day that Noe entered into the ark,
And knew not until the flood came, and took them all
away; so shall also the coming of the Son of man be.

Matt. 24:37–39

When Noah in his day warned the people of the impending disaster, the great deluge, they laughed at him. They
were so confident in their materialistic way of life and the pros-
pects of a happy future that instead of repenting or preparing
to protect themselves from the flood, they were planting vineyards, marrying and giving in marriage, not realizing that the
end was nigh. (Gen. 7:1)

When the end comes, those who trust in the material world
and their own wisdom will again be caught unawares, because
they will not accept guidance or listen to warnings from those
who believe and are in communion with God.

52. NO WINE IN HEAVEN

But I say unto you, I will not drink henceforth of this
fruit of the vine, until that day when I drink it new with
you in my Father's kingdom.

Matt. 26:29

The Aramaic term *khamra*, "wine," has many other meanings, including "teaching," "joy," and "inspiration." These terms

are common in Semitic speech and are still in use in both classical and vernacular tongues, and are well understood. The word for "wine" is written exactly like the word *khamara*, which means "donkey," but it is pronounced with a slight difference.

What Jesus meant by drinking wine in heaven was this: "I shall not have this joy until I see you in heaven." Heaven does not contain wine, but it does contain the eternal joy of everlasting life and the presence of God.

The term "wine" also means "teaching" or "inspiration." Jesus said, "No one puts new wine in old skins." The "new wine" is his teaching, and the "old skins," Judaism. (See Mark 14:25; *Gospel Light*, John II.)

53. SHEPHERD SMITTEN

Then saith Jesus unto them, All ye shall be offended because of me this night: for it is written, I will smite the shepherd, and the sheep of the flock shall be scattered abroad.

Matt. 26:31

When the shepherd is slain by robbers, the sheep scatter. This is because they have no one to lead them, and they know they are in danger, so they all run in different directions. Moreover, when sheep smell blood, they become agitated. When the flock is at peace, the shepherd stands with his staff in his hand where all the sheep can see him. His presence comforts the sheep. They know they are safe from wild animals and thieves. Jesus quoted this saying from the prophet Zechariah. (Zech. 13:7, I Kings 22:17)

Sheep are very timid. At times, they are frightened even by the presence of strangers. They know the voice of the shepherd, but the voice of a stranger terrifies them.

The prophet Ezekiel says, "And my sheep were scattered, because there is no shepherd; and they became food for all the wild beasts of the field." (Ezek. 34:5)

Jesus was the Good Shepherd of Israel, who had come to gather the scattered sheep, to seek those who were lost, to bind those who had been injured, and even to give his life for their sake.

When Jesus was arrested, his disciples saw the danger of being implicated, arrested, and probably put to death. So they fled in the dark hours in Gethsemane, even as the sheep flee when the shepherd is slain.

54. AWAKE AND PRAY

Watch and pray, that ye enter not into temptation: the spirit indeed is willing, but the flesh is weak.

Matt. 26:41

Jesus admonished his disciples to pray that they might not enter into temptation; he did not ask them to pray that God would not tempt them. In Matthew 6:13, when he taught his disciples how to pray, he said, "Do not let us enter into temptation."

In the East, one often hears a wife saying to her husband, "Do not let us be in want." No husband would think of causing his family to be in want. God strengthens those who seek his help to overcome temptation. The disciples needed help during this dark hour.

The disciples were in need of prayer so that they might not enter into temptation, like Judas, who had sold Jesus for thirty pieces of silver. Moreover, their faith in Jesus as the Messiah was weak. They did not believe that the Messiah had to die on the cross in order to win a victory over evil forces. Then again,

Jesus' concept of the Messiah was too alien to their simple minds.

The disciples could easily have turned against Jesus and denounced him as a great deceiver who had lured them away from the Jewish religion, just as Peter did when he swore and cursed, saying he did not know Jesus at all. To many people, their life is more precious than their religion. (Mark 14:38, Luke 22:40)

55. PERISH BY THE SWORD

Then said Jesus unto him, Put up again thy sword into his place: for all they that take the sword shall perish with the sword.

Matt. 26:52

Jesus knew the Old Testament by heart. He had spent the early years of his youth studying the Scriptures. He knew that those who had taken the sword had perished by the sword. For example, Absalom, who slew Amnon, the firstborn of David, was slain by Joab; and Joab, who slew Abner and Amsa with the sword, was slain by Benaniah with the sword.

This was also true of great empires which had taken the sword; all of them had perished by the sword. Force, like a two-edged sword, works both ways. This is because force is generally met by a greater force. (See Matt. 10:34.)

56. JESUS CONFIDENT

Thinkest thou that I cannot now pray to my Father, and
he shall presently give me more than twelve legions of
angels?
But how then shall the Scriptures be fulfilled, that thus
it must be?

Matt. 26:53–54

Jesus was so confident in God and in the ultimate victory.
He knew that God would send legions of angels to deliver
him if he should ask for help. Nevertheless, he knew that
death on the cross was his destiny, and that the Scriptures
must be fulfilled. (Isa. 53:7) Jesus had again and again tried
to impress on the dull minds of his disciples that he must die
on the cross, and that his death was inevitable. He knew that
the authorities of his religion would reject him, and that his
departure from the old concept of religion as advocated by the
religious authorities, would cause his death.

Jesus had to die the death of a malefactor on the cross.
The Scriptures had predicted his rejection and death. During
his trial, he told the Roman Governor Pilate, "For this cause
came I, to bear witness to the truth." (John 18:37) "To bear
witness to" in Aramaic means "to die for." Jesus was not afraid
of death, because he was confident of ultimate victory over
death and the grave, for he knew that death was not a finality,
and that there was life beyond the grave.

Jesus also knew that since God is indestructible and eternal,
so spiritual man is indestructible and eternal. In other words,
God could not have created man in His own image and likeness,
only to make him destructible.

Jesus had surrendered his human will to the divine will.
The flesh was weak but the spirit was willing. Jesus never
doubted God; he trusted in Him to the last moment.

57. ENTRUSTED WITH POWER

Jesus saith unto him, Thou hast said: nevertheless I say
unto you, Hereafter shall ye see the Son of man sitting on
the right hand of power, and coming in the clouds of
heaven.

Matt. 26:64

"Sitting at the right hand of power" here means that God
will entrust him with all things. In the East, the queen is
accorded the seat at the right hand of the king, and when
the queen is absent, the place of honor is generally occupied
by princes and nobles of the realm or relatives of the king.
(Ps. 110:1)

Clouds are symbolic of glory, honor, and the highest success.
(Dan. 7:13) Figuratively speaking, God was supposed to dwell
in the clouds and to ride upon them. He made the clouds
His chariots.

In a few generations, Christianity surpassed Judaism in numbers and became a worldwide religion with tremendous power
which shook the world, and frightened kings and emperors.
The priests construed a statement such as the above as blasphemy, simply because they thought that God is too holy and
man too sinful even to come close to His presence.

The priests could see this hidden power growing; therefore
they were alarmed, for their positions were at stake.

58. THIRTY PIECES OF SILVER

Then was fulfilled that which was spoken by Jeremy the prophet, saying, And they took the thirty pieces of silver, the price of him that was valued, whom they of the children of Israel did value.

Matt. 27:9

The Eastern text reads, "Then what was spoken by the prophet was fulfilled, namely, I took the thirty pieces of silver, the costly price which was bargained with the children of Israel." Jeremy, or Jeremiah, is wrong; it was Zechariah, and not Jeremiah. (See Zech. 11:12–13.) Evidently the error was caused by the author or the copyist.

The price of a man was settled at thirty pieces of silver; the price of a woman was much less. In those early days, men were sold in the market place to the highest bidder. Joseph was sold in the market place in Egypt for thirty pieces of silver. (See Gen. 37:28, Ex. 21:32.)

Judas sold Jesus for the same price as Joseph. The prophecy of Zechariah was fulfilled.

59. SCARLET ROBE

And they stripped him, and put on him a scarlet robe.

Matt. 27:28

This kind of royal robe in Aramaic is called *klamis dazkho-rita*, which means "scarlet" (a color of cloth made in Lebanon from seashells). Only kings wore this kind of costly garment. One legend has it that the scarlet robe belonged to one of the

Maccabean kings and was kept in the temple, and that the high priest had it put upon Jesus to show that they had no other king but Caesar. Be that as it may, I prefer to believe that the scarlet robe was one of Herod's old royal garments, and it was used to mock Jesus and to repudiate his Messianic claims. Easterners would take great delight in dressing a man who had claimed to be a ruler in king's clothing before he was put to death. An Arab caliph did the same thing. Jesus was wrongly accused as a political disturber who claimed to be a king. (Luke 23:11, Isa. 53:3)

60. WINE AND GALL

They gave him vinegar to drink mingled with gall: and when he had tasted thereof, he would not drink.

Matt. 27:34

Vinegar mixed with gall was given to prisoners in order to lessen their suffering on the cross. Jesus tasted it, but refused to drink it. Jesus was thirsty for water. Apparently he had had no water to drink since his arrest. And then again, loss of blood intensifies thirst.

61. MARY OF MAGDALA

In the end of the sabbath, as it began to dawn toward the first day of the week, came Mary Magdalene and the other Mary to see the sepulcher.

Matt. 28:1

This Mary is not Mary the sister of Lazarus (Aramaic *Lazer*), but one Mary of Magdala, a town in Galilee far from the town in which Lazarus and his sister had lived. (Luke 23:55–56) Some commentators have confused this Mary with the sister of Lazarus. They think that she was called Magdala because she had built a *magdla*, "tower," with the money she had earned by her whoredom. But this is a gross falsehood. In the East, harlots never build memorials, nor are they wealthy.

Moreover, in the East, men and women are often known by the name of the town from which they come; for example, Jesus of Nazareth, and Joseph of Ramtha (wrongly called Joseph of Aramathea).

Mary, sister of Lazarus, was a pious woman, not a harlot. The name *Miriam*, Mary, is very common in Eastern countries. There were so many Marys that no one can know for sure just which one is being referred to. The term Magdalene is used to distinguish this Mary from the others. (Mark 16:1, Luke 23:56)

62. MOUNT OF ASCENSION

Then the eleven disciples went away into Galilee, into a
mountain where Jesus had appointed them.

Matt. 28:16

Matthew says that Jesus ascended from a mountain in
Galilee. In Matthew 26:32, we read that Jesus, before his
arrest and crucifixion, told his disciples that he would be in
Galilee before them. (Mark 16:7) And John tells us that he
appeared to them while they were fishing on the Lake of
Galilee. (John 21:1) Evidently, all of the disciples had gone
back to their homelands and now were back at their old
business, fishing, in order to make a living. Some American
preachers seem to think they went fishing because they had
been overtired in Jerusalem during the tragic week preceding.
But this is not the case. The disciples were not fishing for
recreation; they fished to support themselves.

In the Gospels of Matthew and Mark we read that the
ascension took place from a high mountain in Galilee. But
Luke claims the ascension took place on the top of a small
mountain near Jerusalem called the Mount of Olives. (Acts 1:12)
We might note that the Book of Acts was written by Luke,
a disciple of Paul, many years after Jesus' ascension. Mark is
a copy of an earlier text of Matthew. John is more authoritative
than Luke because he was constantly with Jesus. Matthew and
John were of the twelve; Luke was not yet born. Luke's Gospel
is a compilation from the Gospel of Matthew and the stories
he obtained from eyewitnesses who were still living in his day.

Be that as it may, the most important thing is not the place
from which Jesus ascended, but the ascension itself.

63. TO GUARD THE TEACHING

Teaching them to observe all things whatsoever I have commanded you: and, lo, I am with you alway, even unto the end of the world. Amen.

Matt. 28:20

"Teach them to keep or to guard everything which I have taught you" is a divine command. Jesus in his last hours with his disciples warned them to guard his teachings against false teachers who were sooner or later to come to teach falsehood in his name. On other occasions he said to them, "If you love me, keep my commandments." Jesus always laid emphasis on doing the things he had taught them, not on merely confessing his name, his greatness, and the miracles and wonders he had performed.

For many years, Jesus' disciples and their followers adhered to what their Lord had taught them, and the good news of the pure gospel spread over all the known world.

But when the Christians began to depart from Jesus' teaching and to rely on man-made doctrines, the Church split asunder. The true teaching for which Jesus Christ gave his life was supplanted with man-made doctrines and the rapid spread of the gospel was checked. The progress of the true gospel is still being hampered today, for glory, honor, and worldly rewards are valued higher than the teachings for which Jesus died on the cross.

The Gospel According to St. Mark

1. UNCLEAN SPIRIT

And there was in their synagogue a man with an unclean
spirit; and he cried out,
Saying, Let us alone; what have we to do with thee, thou
Jesus of Nazareth? art thou come to destroy us? I know
thee who thou art, the Holy One of God.
And Jesus rebuked him, saying, Hold thy peace, and come
out of him.

Mark 1:23–25

The Aramaic words *rokha tamtha* mean "the unclean
spirit," a person who is unruly, insane, or has an evil inclination.
In the East, any wrong inclination is considered unclean,
whether it be a person, food, speech, or teaching.

Medical terms were unknown in biblical days. The people
who suffered mentally were considered possessed by an evil
inclination, or mentally disturbed. The term "spirit" in Aramaic
also means "inclination," "rheumatism," "temper," "pride," or
"a person."

When this insane man saw Jesus in the synagogue he could
not control his anger toward him. He had heard people dis-
cussing Jesus, and many attacking him, considering him a dangerous man, an enemy of the Jewish religion. This was because
in his discourses on religion, he ridiculed the scribes, Pharisees,
and the Jewish rabbinical authorities.

The mentally disturbed man spoke out. "I know who you
are, Holy One of God," was said sarcastically. Such remarks
can only be determined by the facial expression and the gestures
of the hands. In the East, an insane man can even rebuke a
prince or a king without offending him, and not be punished
for his bad conduct.

There were others in the synagogue who disagreed with Jesus' teachings and looked upon him as an alien teacher and a prophet from Galilee, but they did not dare to speak.

A remark such as Jesus made, "You can destroy this temple, and I shall build it in three days," was offensive, and considered blasphemous. Jesus rebuked the insanity and the man was restored. (Luke 4:33–35)

2. JESUS ADMONISHED THE LEPER

And there came a leper to him, beseeching him, and kneeling down to him, and saying unto him, If thou wilt, thou canst make me clean.

And Jesus, moved with compassion, put forth his hand, and touched him, and saith unto him, I will; be thou clean.

And, as soon as he had spoken, immediately the leprosy departed from him and he was cleansed.

And he straitly charged him, and forthwith sent him away.

Mark 1:40–43

Evidently, the leper sought healing from Jesus while Jesus was preaching in the synagogue, healing the sick and restoring the insane. (Mark 1:39) When the leper was healed, he was so overwhelmed that he forgot to do his duty according to the Mosaic ordinance concerning leprosy. Instead of rushing to see the priest who had the sole authority to declare him clean, he kept talking and boasting about his healing. Jesus knew that without the order of the priest the leper could not come to him, "Why do you talk about it? Go and show yourself to the priest, who will give you a bill of clearance." (Lev. 14:2–3)

Here we see that Jesus had no intention of weakening the

Mosaic law and ordinances, but sought to strengthen them. This confirms what he had previously taught: "I have not come to weaken the law and the prophets, but to strengthen them, and put them into practice." Indeed, Jesus did not wish any conflict with the Jewish authorities. (Matt. 8:2–4, Luke 5:12–14)

3. YOUR SINS ARE FORGIVEN

Whether is it easier to say to the sick of the palsy, Thy sins be forgiven thee; or to say, Arise, and take up thy bed, and walk?

Mark 2:9

To say to a man suffering from palsy, "Take your bed quilt and walk," is far more miraculous than to say, "Your sins are forgiven." This is because palsy is a difficult disease to heal. Many teachers of religion can easily say, "Your sins are forgiven." Judges can forgive people their trespasses; kings and governors can commute death sentences. But to say to a man suffering from palsy, one of the most dreaded diseases, "Take your bed quilt and walk," is a more difficult situation. Most healers would shun such a case.

The Pharisees were told that no one can forgive sins but God, and the high priest was the only one who could make an offering on behalf of the people to absolve them from their sins. But Jesus, being sent by God, had the power to forgive sins, and to heal any kind of disease. Indeed, any teacher of religion endowed with such tremendous power could forgive sins, and heal people. (Matt. 9:5)

4. THE INSANE CONFESS JESUS

And unclean spirits, when they saw him, fell down before
him, and cried, saying, Thou art the Son of God.

Mark 3:11

The term "unclean spirits" means "insane," "unruly," and
"evil inclinations." When insane men came to Jesus they
felt his divine presence, so they fell down and worshiped
him as an act of reverence.

In the East, even violent, insane men honor and bow down
to priests and holy men; they know them by their priestly
garments. Many insane men are constant attendants at prayer
meetings. Evidently, these insane men had seen Jesus as he
preached, and had heard of his healing power. They called
him the Son of God, the highest title given to a holy man;
that is, Godlike. It was the insane men who cried out and not
the devils. (See Luke 4:41.) Had it been the devils, they would
never have confessed Jesus as the Son of God.

5. JESUS DENOUNCED BY RELATIVES

And when his friends heard of it, they went out to lay hold
on him: for they said, He is beside himself.
And the scribes which came down from Jerusalem said,
He hath Beelzebub, and by the prince of the devils
casteth he out devils.

Mark 3:21–22

The Aramaic word *khyanaw* means "relatives," and the
word for "friends" is *kariwan*.

It was his relatives who came to seize Jesus, not his friends, because the relatives thought he had lost his mind. We are also told of other occasions when his brother did not believe in him. (John 7:5) Others also said, "He has a devil," that is, "He is crazy." (John 10:20)

The relatives of Jesus were embarrassed by his actions and his claims to Messiahship. They were afraid of the religious authorities, who might expel them from the synagogue. That is why Jesus said, "No prophet is without honor except in his own town and among his own relatives." Probably this is one reason he did not go out to meet his mother and his brothers when they called on him. (Mark 3:31–35)

6. JESUS' RELATIVES

There came then his brethren and his mother, and, standing without, sent unto him, calling him.

Mark 3:31

Evidently Jesus' relatives did not follow him because of fear of being expelled from the synagogue. When he pronounced himself as the Messiah, the Savior of the world, at the synagogue in Nazareth (Luke 4:18–23), the people took him out to throw him from the brow of the mountain and kill him (Luke 4:29), but he escaped and fled to Galilee.

At the outset, Jesus' relatives did not want to have any part in his Messianic claims because of their fear of the Jewish authorities. A Jew would choose to die rather than be excommunicated and disowned by his people.

When Jesus became popular and began to gain friends in the cities around the Lake of Galilee, his relatives came to see him, but he did not go out to greet them because they had branded him as insane and he did not want to interrupt his discourse. (Mark 3:21) He pointed to his disciples and told the crowd that these men, his disciples, were his relatives because they had left everything and followed him.

This is true today. An American missionary is highly honored in a foreign land, but not in his own city and among his own people where everybody knows who he is. Jesus' relatives, his friends, and the inhabitants of Nazareth knew him as a child, as a youth, and as a mature man. They did not believe that he could be the Messiah.

7. TOUCHING HIS GARMENT

And Jesus, immediately knowing in himself that virtue had gone out of him, turned him about in the press, and said, Who touched my clothes?

Mark 5:30

When this woman tried to see Jesus, she found it difficult. (See Mark 5:27–28.) In the first place, the crowd which followed Jesus was large, and in the second place, women are shy in the presence of holy men. In some parts of the East, they are so shy they cover their faces when in the presence of a holy man. And then again, women are discouraged from approaching a prince, a nobleman, or a holy man.

This woman's faith in Jesus was so strong she believed that if she only could touch his garment, it would be sufficient to heal her of her infirmity. Her faith was enhanced by the fact that she knew she would not have an opportunity to see Jesus and discuss her problem with him.

The Aramaic phrase "touch his garment" does not mean that she simply touched the cloth. She held the hem in her hand and tugged, which means, "I urgently want to see you." Jesus knew the meaning of the touch, so he immediately realized that there was a person behind him who was eager to talk to him, but because of the crowd he could not.

The term "virtue" means "strength," or "feeling," or "vibration." When one person touches another he transmits the feeling, which we might call vibrations. The woman's touch was like a beggar knocking at the door. The people inside the house know the difference between a guest's or a relative's knocking, and that of a beggar. The beggar knocks softly and the tones of the knocking indicate that he is in need. The woman's sincere touch for help indicated that she needed him badly. Therefore, Jesus responded. (See Mark 5:34, Luke 6:19, 8:46.)

8. JESUS SOUGHT NO PUBLICITY

And he charged them straitly that no man should know it; and commanded that something should be given her to eat.

Mark 5:43

The meaning of such a command cannot easily be ascertained without seeing the speaker's face. In the East, speakers often warn, "Don't tell this to anyone," but the listener knows the intended meaning by the motions of the hands and the facial expression of the speaker.

Of course, some people, wishing to publicize something, make a secret of it, telling people not to repeat it, thus making sure it will be told. But in this case Jesus was being cautious because of the reaction from religious authorities. On the other hand, on another occasion he told his disciples and followers, "What I tell you secretly, preach in the market places and from the housetops."

There was nothing secretive about healing this little girl; such a miracle could hardly be hidden from the people. There were

64

times when Jesus' popularity and his miraculous healings were opposed by the religious authorities, who thought that these miracles were exaggerated, and that Jesus was deceiving the public, and therefore sought to arrest him. At times it is wise to keep one's mouth shut. God and the one who was healed know what has taken place, and this is more important than publicity.

When Jesus raised Lazarus from death, the religious leaders were alarmed, took cognizance of his work, and decided to have him arrested. In the East, it is not a wise thing to boast about healings and miracles, for the healer is sure to incur the wrath of the religious authorities unless he has been authorized. On the other hand, true healers shun publicity and do their work quietly. They do not receive any reward for their healings; they do it gratis. Freely they have received and freely they give.

9. GREAT SIGNS WANTED

For they considered not the miracle of the loaves: for the heart was hardened.

Mark 6:52

The Eastern text reads: "Neither did they understand the miracle of the loaves of bread, because their hearts were confused." When Jesus appeared to the people, they were mystified and alarmed because they did not expect to see him. Some Eastern writers maintain that on such occasions Christ, rather than the man Jesus, appeared to them. Evidently, some of the disciples and followers either did not think about the miracle of the bread, or else discounted the miracle. Hebrew prophets also multiplied bread. In the East, when people go to see religious men, they always take food with them as a gift. (See

I Kings 14:1.) The people wanted Jesus to perform a greater miracle than feed a crowd.

Other men who had witnessed the miracle of the feeding of the 5000 wanted to know where Jesus had been when they met him at Capernaum. Jesus said to them, "You seek me not because you saw the miracle, but because you did eat of the loaves." (John 6:25–26) And later they said to him, "What miracles do you perform, that we may see and believe in you?" (John 6:29) In other words, even those who had seen the miracle of bread did not take it seriously. The people in Palestine were looking for greater and more spectacular signs —something which had never been done before. They expected the Messiah to perform miracles, wonders and signs to surpass anything in history. But Jesus refused to do anything spectacular. He did what the Hebrew prophets had done, and even greater healings than they. Moreover, he told his disciples that they should do greater things than he had done. The Christian gospel is not proved by miracles, but by the changing of the human heart. (Matt. 16:9–11)

10. RECEIVING A CHILD

Whosoever shall receive one of such children in my name, receiveth me: and whosoever shall receive me, receiveth not me, but him that sent me.

Mark 9:37

"Receive a child in my name" is an Eastern saying which means, "Receive the child the way I would receive him." In the East, children are chased away when they appear in the presence of holy men, high government officials or other dignitaries. The servants of the official or the host generally rebuke them and tell them to keep away, sometimes even cursing them. It is an embarrassing situation for a host to see children playing in the house, talking or watching his guests as they recline at the meal. Neither women nor children sit down to eat with important guests or holy men.

When children came around Jesus, as they usually did when they saw a prominent man walking or entering the town, Jesus' disciples rebuked them and chased them away. Jesus was indignant. So he took one of the children in his arms and said, "One must be like a child in order to enter into the kingdom of God." Then he told them that anyone who did a favor to a child, even to the extent of troubling himself to give the child a cup of water, would receive his reward.

This may be difficult for the Western world to understand. But Easterners know why Jesus placed such importance on a cup of water, for it is very scarce in Palestine. An honorable guest or a high government official may have plenty of water on the table, but children often go thirsty. This is why water and thirst are so often mentioned in the Bible. To give a cup of water to a thirsty child in the East is a great favor.

According to Jesus the little children were pure and free from the evils of this world. They were Godlike. (Matt. 10:42, Luke 9:48)

11. JESUS SHARED HIS TEACHING

But Jesus said, Forbid him not: for there is no man which shall do a miracle in my name, that can lightly speak evil of me.

Mark 9:39

Trades and professions, in the East, are generally handed down secretly from father to son. Many silversmiths, carpenters and other tradesmen never disclose the secrets of their trades to strangers. On the other hand, artisans who find the secrets are favored by the artist; they glory in them, especially when the secrets come from a well-known and skillful man.

Jesus knew that the men who wrought miracles in his name or by his method could hardly speak against him, because this would weaken their own position. The disciples who reported this to him were unaware of these facts, for they were fishermen and illiterates. All those who were performing miracles in the name of Jesus were helping to spread his gospel and his fame.

From this we learn that we should welcome and encourage those who do what we do and who say what we say, whether they give us credit or not, for as Jesus says, "Whoever is not against us is for us."

12. LOVE OF MONEY

It is easier for a camel to go through the eye of a needle, than for a rich man to enter into the kingdom of heaven. And they were astonished out of measure, saying among themselves, Who then can be saved?
And Jesus looking upon them saith, With men it is impossible, but not with God: for with God all things are possible.

Mark 10:25–27

Jesus in this instance upbraided the rich men who had made wealth their God, and who went tax-free and oppressed the poor. Jesus was not against riches, but against the love thereof.

In this case Jesus referred to the rope and the needle. The term "camel" is wrong. This error was caused by translators, simply because the same word is used for "camel" and for "rope." Needles in the early days were large and made of oak. Women could thread a cord through the eye of a wooden needle.

On the other hand, in Aramaic literature we read that when a man strikes an easy friendship with another, he says, "Our friendship is like thread and needle"; but when it takes a long time to understand one another and become friends, one says, "Our friendship was difficult, like a rope passing through the eye of a [wooden] needle."

When a thick cord is passed through a needle, a part of it comes off. A rich man must likewise give up some of his luxuries and his love for money in order to enter into the kingdom of God.

The disciples thought this was a harsh saying. If the acquisition of money or wealth was evil, nobody would be saved. They felt it would be difficult for people to become Christians if they must give away their fortunes.

The disciples again and again misunderstood their wonderful teacher. God can cause men to give up their bad habits and their love for wealth. Matthew did it. St. Francis of Assisi renounced all his father's wealth and went barefoot, preaching the Christian gospel. What is impossible with man is possible with God, Who is the creator of the Universe. (See Jer. 32:17; see article in *Gospel Light*, Matt. 19:24.)

Jesus was against the greedy rich people of his day who did not pay the wages of their laborers nor their taxes. He was not against the pious rich whom God had blessed. These men were God's agents, entrusted with His wealth, to be distributed to the poor.

13. THE FIGS WERE PICKED

And seeing a fig tree afar off having leaves, he came, if haply he might find any thing thereon: and when he came to it, he found nothing but leaves; for the time of figs was not yet.

Mark 11:13

The phrase "the time of figs was not yet" is a marginal note originally written by a scribe or a learned man who thought the reason figs were not on the tree must be that it was not yet fig season. Years later, this marginal note, like many others, was copied and made an integral part of the gospel. We know that this is a marginal note. There are many such notes in the Bible. Moreover, we know that Jesus, as the Messiah, and with his knowledge of the country and its agricultural and pastoral life, would not have gone to a fig tree searching for figs out of season. Not even an ignorant desert dweller would do such a thing.

The tree had no figs on it simply because other hungry travelers who had walked the same road had already picked them. In the East, poor people, and especially hungry travelers, do not wait until the fruits are fully ripe. They eat them before they are ripe, for if they do not, someone else will pick them.

These fig trees, a few decades ago, were still there on the road between Jerusalem and Bethany. And the fruit of these trees is still picked by travelers as of yore. Moreover, in the East a tree by the highway or a branch thereof is the property of the wayfarer and the poor.

Jesus, being a man, was disappointed when he failed to find fruit, and therefore he was seemingly disappointed. He cursed the tree. Easterners do this when they fail to find water in a well or fruit on a tree.

The tree served as a great lesson to the disciples. Jesus told them if they had faith, they could not only cause a tree to wither, but could also remove a mountain, a seemingly insurmountable problem. (Matt. 21:21)

14. JEWISH SECTS

And they send unto him certain of the Pharisees and of
the Herodians to catch him in his words.

Mark 12:13

There were three important parties in Judaism: namely,
the Pharisees, the Sadducees, and the Herodians, not counting
the scribes, who were employed by all of these, and other small
and peculiar sects.

The term "Herodians" means those Jews who supported
Herod's royal dynasty. Herod himself was an Edomite, who
became a usurper and took the kingdom from the Hashmonians
(Maccabees). Herod was hated by the Jews and looked upon as
a foreigner. He was a very cruel man, who even put his own
sons to death. But many Jews who were employed in the state
government under Herod and in the service of the imperial
government of Rome, manifestly were supporters of the house
of Herod, in order to keep their government positions; but in
their hearts they were enemies, as were the other Jews.

Jesus' teachings were so revolutionary that they undermined
all these parties. When the party leaders saw that many of the
Jews were flocking to Jesus, they became alarmed. Fearing they
would lose their positions, they forgot their differences for a
while and became united against Jesus. They took counsel to
see how they could stop him from attacking their way of life
and their ideologies. (Matt. 22:15, Luke 20:20–21; see also articles on Pharisees and Sadducees.)

15. LIKE ANGELS

For when they shall rise from the dead, they neither
marry, nor are given in marriage; but are as the angels
which are in heaven.

Mark 12:25

The term "as the angels" in this instance means "spiritual"
—that is, without physical bodies. "Angel" means "God's counsel." The Hebrew prophets in their discourse with simple people
tried to transform a spiritual idea into a physical one in order
that the unlearned people might understand it. The Bible tells
us that the angels are spirits: "He made His angels spirits." The
term "spirit" in Aramaic means "omnipresent," "all-embracing,"
"everywhere."

In heaven there is no marriage, because there are no physical
bodies. In the new life hereafter, men and women will be like
angels, freed from their physical bodies, physical limitations,
and worldly desires.

16. THE TEMPLE OVERTHROWN

And Jesus answering said unto him, Seest thou these great
buildings? there shall not be left one stone upon another,
that shall not be thrown down.

Mark 13:2

This prophecy was fulfilled when General Titus captured
Jerusalem and destroyed the temple in the year A.D. 70. All
of the great stones and pillars of the first temple, which was
built by King Solomon and later rebuilt by Zerubbabel and

72

Herod the Great, were removed to a town in Lebanon called Baalbek, about 160 miles north of Jerusalem.

It seems that the Romans tried to build a temple to Zeus or Jupiter, but something happened, probably a war with Persia, and the construction of the temple was abandoned. Or possibly the temple was built and then later destroyed.

The town of Baalbek was invaded by many conquerors, who coveted the most beautiful mountain in the known world, Mount Lebanon. Jesus' prophecy was fulfilled: Not one stone was left upon another. (Luke 19:44)

17. A GREAT CALAMITY

But in those days, after that tribulation, the sun shall be darkened, and the moon shall not give her light,
And the stars of heaven shall fall, and the powers that are in heaven shall be shaken.

Mark 13:24–25

"The sun will be darkened and the moon will not give light" is an Aramaic saying symbolic of a great universal disaster. When people in the East lament the death of a great ruler or some other tragedy, they say, "The sun became dark and the moon refused to give light; the stars did not appear." This means the calamity was so great that the universe shared in it. Such statements are frequently found in the Bible as well as in other Eastern literature. (Isa. 13:10)

According to Jesus' teachings, when the end comes there will be a universal upheaval, everything will collapse. There will be a new world and a new heaven. God's own light will surpass the light of the sun, moon, and stars. The prophet Zephaniah says, "That day is a day of wrath, a day of trouble and distress, a day of confusion and desolation, a day of darkness and gloominess, a day of clouds and thick darkness." (Zeph. 1:15, Eastern text) And Luke says: "And there will be signs in sun and moon and stars. . . ." (Luke 21:25, Matt. 26)

18. FRUIT OF THE VINE

Verily I say unto you, I will drink no more of the fruit of the vine, until that day that I drink it new in the kingdom of God.

Mark 14:25

The Aramaic word *khamra,* or "wine," has many other meanings. Metaphorically it means "joy," "inspiration," and "teaching." It is written exactly like the word for "donkey" but is pronounced with a slight difference.

This verse has been a stumbling block to many theologians and readers of the Bible. Some students of the Bible use it to support their belief in a physical life hereafter. They believe there will be wine in heaven "because Jesus said so," and since there will be wine, why not other physical things?

The term "fruit of the vine" means "the product of the vine," that is, "wine." What Jesus meant is: "I shall never have joy with you until we meet again in heaven." The Scripture tells us wine makes the heart merry. Jesus was to be crucified very soon; this was the last time he would taste the product of the vine, that is, the joy he was experiencing with his beloved disciples.

On other occasions Jesus used the term "wine" when he meant "teaching." He said, "no one puts new wine in old skins." (Matt. 9:17) "New wine" in this instance means "Jesus' teachings," while "old skins" means "Judaism."

Moreover, it is often said in the East, "This is the wine of the Church of the East," or of the Baptist Church, etc., meaning their teachings. The people know the meaning of such figurative speech. However, such metaphors are not used in Western languages, and the term "wine" is therefore taken literally and misunderstood.

19. MEETING IN GALILEE

But after that I am risen, I will go before you into Galilee.
Mark 14:28

Jesus was so sure about his triumph over death and the grave and his resurrection that he wanted to make a date with his disciples to meet them in Galilee before they returned to their own villages. Note: all the disciples of Jesus, with the exception of Judas, were Galileans; after the feast of the Passover they would return home with others to Galilee.

Jesus' disciples, however, took this saying lightly, or perhaps misunderstood it, for in the first place, they did not believe that he would die on the cross. Secondly, they were not sure of his resurrection. This is why, when the rumors of his resurrection spread, they were reluctant to believe them.

The term "Galilee" was used to make his resurrection definite, as one person says to another, "Don't worry . . . I'll see you in your own homeland." The young man, the angel at the sepulcher, told the women to tell Jesus' disciples that Jesus would meet them in Galilee: "Tell his disciples and Peter that he will be before you in Galilee; there you will see him, just as he has told you." (Mark 16:7, Eastern text)

20. RABBI

And as soon as he was come, he goeth straightway to him,
and saith, Master, master; and kissed him.

Mark 14:45

The term *Rabbi* is Aramaic. Jews acquired it during the
captivity in Babylon. *Rabbi* is equivalent to the English word
"doctor" or "professor." It is derived from the word *rab*, "great."
Thus to call one "Rabbi" means, "my great Professor," (or Doctor
or Teacher). This title is given only to learned men. The term
malpana is also used to mean "professor" or "teacher."

Jesus was an educated man. He had studied at the synagogue and could read and write. The Evangelist tells us that
Jesus read the Scriptures in the synagogue, and that he also explained them so that the simple people might understand their
message. Had he been uneducated, he could not have taught
the people. Even his enemies called him "Rabbi." (Luke 4:16–
22)

Jesus .spent all eighteen years of his early life, studying the
Scriptures. Nearly all of his teaching is quoted from the Mosaic
law and the prophets, which he knew by heart.

Evidently Jesus, while studying the Scriptures, made notes
just as we do today. He always spoke with authority, because he quoted the Scriptures. Matthew might have had access
to these notes when he wrote his Gospel. This is why his Gospel
is the first record of Jesus' teachings. Matthew was a chief tax
collector. One must read and write to be appointed to such an
important position.

Judas addressed Jesus just as he had addressed him on all
other occasions; students always called their teacher "Rabbi."

21. A YOUNG MAN

And there followed him a certain young man, having a
linen cloth cast about his naked body: and the young
men laid hold on him:
And he left the linen cloth, and fled from them naked.

Mark 14:51–52

The young man might have been one of the followers of
Jesus who had accompanied him and his disciples to the
Garden of Gethsemane. Or he might have been a young man
who just happened to be there at that time. There is no indica-
tion that he was one of Jesus' disciples.

Gethsemane is a public park. Many wayfarers and strangers
who cannot find lodging in the city on feast days spend the
night there, sleeping under the olive trees. When Jesus was
arrested, his disciples fled, so the young man fled too, fearing
he might be implicated.

Many poor people in Palestine, especially in those early
days, had only one garment, or a large piece of cloth, which
covered their bodies. Such poor people are still found in many
villages of India, North Africa, and Palestine. Undoubtedly, this
man was poor; that is why he was spending the night in Gethsemane.

Some commentators think this man was Mark. Mark was
not yet born; he was a disciple of Paul and Peter, and as a
young man he traveled with them, sharing their itinerary. Be
that as it may, the Gospel does not tell us who this young
man was, simply because he was not a disciple or a relative
of Jesus, or even a relative of one of the disciples. They really
did not know who he was. He might even have been an alien
who had come to the feast of the Passover.

22. PILATE MARVELED AT JESUS

But Jesus yet answered nothing; so that Pilate marvelled.

Mark 15:5

Jesus gave no answer simply because he knew that his time had come, and he had to die on the cross. All the accusations against him were false. Both the accusers and the governor, Pilate, knew that Jesus had done no evil. An answer would have done no good; it might even have implicated him more. The prophet Isaiah had predicted that he would not open his mouth or protest. (Isa. 53:7)

In the East, a person who is accused is judged by his words. People believe that the less the accused talks, the better. Jesus said, "By your words, they shall judge you."

When a false charge is brought against an innocent man in the East, he feels that the charges are not worthy even to be answered. The governor was already aware of the fact that Jesus had never said that he was a political king. Pilate could see that the haggard and poorly dressed man from Galilee who stood before him was far from being a political leader or a revolutionary. Therefore, he needed no answer; the case spoke for itself. The innocence of a person is sometimes evidenced by the fact that he does not try to defend himself. Self-defense throws some doubt on one's innocence. Moreover, Jesus also knew that the Roman governor was helpless, and that his political position meant more to him than justice. (John 19:9)

23. WINE MIXED WITH MYRRH

And they gave him to drink wine mingled with myrrh:
but he received it not.

Mark 15:23

Before victims were crucified, they were given wine mixed
with myrrh to lessen their suffering. This drink is similar to a
novocaine shot given by a dentist or a medical doctor.

Jesus was thirsty. He had not drunk water since his arrest on
Thursday evening. Prisoners in the East, especially those
charged with political crimes, are seldom fed or given water.
They are not treated like prisoners in America.

Moreover, the loss of blood made Jesus even more thirsty.
He asked for water, but there was no water on Golgotha. Who
would go down to the town to bring a pitcher of water? Therefore, the soldiers gave him some of the wine mixed with myrrh
which was at hand. But Jesus refused to drink it. He was thirsty
for water. And he did not want to drink anything that might
lessen his suffering on the cross. (See Ps. 69:21.)

24. HOUR OF CRUCIFIXION

And it was the third hour, and they crucified him.

Mark 15:25

According to the Gospel of Mark, Jesus was crucified on
the third hour, that is, nine o'clock in the morning. This method
of keeping time is still used in some Eastern and European
countries.

Matthew says "from the sixth hour," twelve noon, darkness

covered the earth, and Luke agrees. It was about the sixth hour, that is, twelve noon, and the darkness covered the earth until three P.M. (Matt. 27:45)

John mentions the hour when Pilate told the Jews, "Behold your king." In other words, John mentions the time when the sentence of death was pronounced upon Jesus. (John 19:14) We must remember that John was the only disciple who was at the scene when Jesus was crucified. Luke and Mark were not yet born.

The authors of the Gospels, like any other Easterners, were not interested in giving the reader the exact hour and minute of the events which transpired on Friday. In the East, time is not relevant. The disciples were not at the governor's palace; nearly all, with the exception of John, had fled. Therefore, to the bereaved disciples, time was not important. What the authors wanted to say was that it was on Friday, the sixth day of the week, when the crucifixion took place.

In the East, a man who has waited for a friend for two hours might say, "I have been waiting for you all day." (Matt. 27:45, Luke 22:44)

25. JESUS' DEATH FORETOLD

And at the ninth hour Jesus cried with a loud voice, saying, Eloi, Eloi, lama sabachthani? which is, being interpreted, My God, my God, why hast thou forsaken me?

Mark 15:34

Mark translates the words on the cross from Palestinian Aramaic into the Chaldean, or southern, Aramaic. Mark was with Peter; Eastern scholars believe that both Peter and Mark were in Babylon. For some time, Jesus had admonished his disciples to go first to the sheep which were lost from the tribes of Israel. These were the ten tribes who were carried to Assyria in 722 B.C., and the Jews of the second captivity, who had been in Babylon since 586 B.C. Most of the well-to-do and prosperous Jews had remained in Babylon after the restoration, rather than returning to Judea. Indeed, there was a large Jewish colony in Babylon; the Babylonian Talmud was written there; and the city was a center of learning for the Jews for many years.

Matthew uses Palestinian Aramaic and does not explain the words on the cross, because the people and the Jewish authorities who stood near the cross understood the meaning of the words. In Mark, the words are interpreted.

We must not forget that when Jesus made this outcry, his lips were parched with thirst, and he had lost much blood. His words were not too clear. This is why the thousands of spectators who stood by the cross said, "He is calling on Elijah." The word for *God* and the word for *Elijah* are written almost alike, but in the Chaldean or Babylonian Aramaic the word for God is *Alaha*, while in Palestinian Aramaic it is *Eli*. The final letter *i* shows the possessive case, "my God."

The difference between Matthew and Mark is this: Matthew uses *Eli*, "my God," but Mark uses the Chaldean term, *Alahi*, "my God." The Term *El* is a Semitic name for God. Jacob changed the name of a town, Luz, "Almonds," to *Bethel*, "the House of God." Later, when the holy name of God, *Yahweh*, was considered so holy it was not pronounced, the term *El* was used, as *El Shaddi*, "the great God," or "the God Almighty."

We know that Matthew, being a Palestinian Jew, wrote for the people of Palestine, in their vernacular, and that his Gospel was the first gospel. Mark was not even born when Jesus died on the cross. Mark, at the outset, was a disciple of Paul, and later joined Peter. But even Paul had never seen Jesus. He was converted to Christianity many years after Jesus' death.

As we have said, Mark translated the words of Jesus on the cross into the language of the people where he and Peter were preaching, to the Jews in Babylon who had been expecting the promised Messiah. There is no mention in the New Testament of Peter and Mark visiting Rome. If they had, it must have been after the Gospel of Mark was written. A tradition says that Peter died in Rome. Assuredly, the Gospel of Mark was written prior to the apostles' visit to Rome.

The Gospel of Mark was transcribed from early scrolls written by Matthew. This is why Mark's Gospel does not contain the account of Jesus' birth and his genealogy. Undoubtedly, the genealogy was written later, after Christianity had spread, and people wanted to know more of the background and life of its founder. All biographies and genealogies of great men are written after they become famous or have died. Had Mark written his Gospel in Rome, he would not have translated the words on the cross into the Chaldean Aramaic, for the Jews who were in Rome were Palestinians who had been dispersed by the Romans.

The ancient writers of the Church of the East state that God was in Jesus when he was in the womb, He was with him when he was on the cross, and He was with him in the grave. God never forsook Jesus. Jesus suffered and died and was buried as a man. His divinity, or the God within him, never suffered or died on the cross, nor was it buried in the grave. Jesus the man, and Christ—God in him—were inseparable, but distinct.

Jesus had often told his disciples that he would be rejected, condemned to death, and crucified, and that the Scriptures concerning his death must be fulfilled. Isaiah, the great Hebrew prophet, had foretold Jesus' rejection and death. (Isa. 53:1–5) Jesus had also assured his disciples that he would meet death on the cross, but that he would rise up on the third day.

Moreover, on their last journey to Jerusalem he predicted that his disciples would leave him, and would flee for their lives. He said, "For behold, the hour is coming, and it has now come, when you will be dispersed, every man to his own country, and you will leave me alone; and yet I am never alone, because the Father is with me." (John 16:32)

Then again, while praying in Gethsemane, Jesus had surrendered his human will to His divine will, and was willing to drink the cup of death. He could have asked God for help, and we are told that many legions of angels would have been sent to his aid, but Jesus was not afraid of death. He was willing to prove that sinister death and the fearful grave were not a barrier between man and God. He was going to prove that man is immortal and indestructible, because he is the image and likeness of God, and God is indestructible. Jesus, through his death on the cross, was to triumph over death, and through his resurrection give a new meaning to life.

A famous Eastern writer and commentator known as Eshoo-Dat of Khedata says that these words were uttered on the cross to make known Jesus' immeasurable love toward God. Jesus was obedient to God to the extent that he shed his blood on the cross for the sake of humanity. How could God the Father forsake His beloved son, who laid down his life for the sake of His children?

Furthermore, this Eastern writer states that it was not because God had forsaken him that Jesus said this, but that he was willing to suffer continually for our sakes. In his commentary on Matthew 27:46, he tells us that God never forsook Jesus on the cross. He further states that the sun and the moon darkened as a sign of mourning. The whole universe was sharing in this great tragedy.

Jesus was allowed (Aramaic: *shabak*) by God to die on the cross in order to demonstrate that there is resurrection and life hereafter. The death on the cross was to reveal the secrets of life. Jesus could have escaped death as he had done before.

Peter says, "But with the precious blood of the Lamb without blemish and without spot which is Christ, Who verily was fore-ordained for this very purpose before the foundation of the world, and was manifest in these last times for your sakes." (I Pet. 1:19–20)

Then, again, Jesus in the garden said, ". . . O my Father, deliver me from this hour, but for this cause I came to this very hour." (John 12:27) That is to say, "This is my destiny, to die for the sake of the truth." He said almost the same thing as he stood before Pilate, when he said, "For this cause came I into the world, to bear witness concerning the Truth." (John 18:37) The term "bear witness" in Aramaic means "to die for the sake of the truth." Martyrs were viewed by many people who came to bear witness or see their death. Indeed, death on the cross was the fulfillment of Jesus' destiny.

Jesus cried on the cross, "My God, my God, for this I was spared," and the Jewish people who stood near the cross thought he was calling on Elijah. None of them said that God had forsaken him. Even today, Easterners, when they suffer tragedies, say, "I was spared by God to see this tragedy with my own eyes." Such phrases are very common in Eastern speech, and are well understood by the people. The ancient Greek texts also use the term "spared," or "allowed."

Had Jesus said that God had forsaken him, his enemies could then have told the people that Jesus had confessed that he was a sinner. The Scriptures say that God does not forsake the righteous; nor does God forsake those who trust in Him. The Jews near the cross said, "He has trusted in God; let us see if God will deliver him." How is it that the thousands of people who stood around the cross did not say that God had forsaken him? How is it that translators of the New Testament, who lived 1600 years later in England, knew more than the people who stood on the hill of Golgotha and witnessed Jesus' death, and heard his cries, in their own language? Indeed, the testimony of those who stood near the cross is greater than that of all the scholars in the world!

No doubt the difficulty in translating the words on the cross was due to the two Aramaic words: *lamana*, for "this," and *shabak*, "to spare," "to leave," "to desert," "to forgive," "to allow." The translators mistook the word *lama*, "why," for *lamana*. In the vernacular Aramaic, we use the word *lamodi*, or *lamodmindi*, that is, "for what cause," "for this reason or cause." When *lamana* is used to mean "why," it is always preceded by the word *mital*; *mital lamana*, "why," appears throughout a book which was written by a great scholar and physicist named Job, of the Church of the East, in the ninth century A.D.

The word *shabak* is one of the most difficult words to translate, especially for foreigners who read, but cannot converse in, Aramaic. They mistranslated the word *shabak*—which in Matthew 5 means "to desert" or "to leave one's wife"—as meaning "divorce." In the East, innocent and legally divorced men and

84

women can remarry, but it is unlawful for a man to marry a woman who has been deserted but not divorced. Therefore, the words *lamana shabaktani* that appear both in Matthew and Mark mean, "For this cause, or thing, I was spared." That is to say, "This is my destiny." At times, this expression is used as an exclamation, with a shaking of the head—"What an end!"

Jesus, throughout his life, trusted in God and was guided and directed by Him. He never doubted or questioned his Father's wisdom. He was always in accord with Him, and never felt that he was alone or without the presence of God.

After his resurrection, Jesus upbraided some of his disciples and reminded them that he told them many times that the Messiah must die and the Scriptures be fulfilled. From the day on which Jesus embarked on his mission, he was mindful of his death on the cross. He knew that his new teaching—of loving-kindness and meekness—would be rejected by the religious authorities, and that he would meet death for speaking against the doctrines of the elders. But he was also confident of his ultimate victory over death on the cross, and the triumph of his gospel. That is why his last cry was to entrust his spirit into the hands of his Father.

26. IN A SPONGE

And one ran and filled a sponge full of vinegar, and put it on a reed, and gave him to drink, saying, Let alone; let us see whether Elias will come to take him down.

Mark 15:36

The reference here is to Mark 15:23. Wine mixed with myrrh was given to Jesus in a sponge fastened on the end of a reed, rather than in a cup, as the cross was so high. (Matt. 27:48, John 19:29)

Generally, victims were given this drug before they were crucified. This drink was ministered to Jesus after he cried on the cross, "My God, my God, for this I was spared," and the people who stood near the cross thought he was calling on Elijah.

Even today, Easterners, when they suffer tragedies, say, "I was spared by God to see this tragedy with my own eyes," or, "Why didn't I die before this happened?" Such phrases are very common in Eastern speech, and are well understood by the people.

Had Jesus said that God had forsaken him, his enemies would have told the people that Jesus had confessed that he was a sinner. The Scripture says that God does not forsake the righteous; God does not forsake those who trust in Him. The Jews near the cross said, "He has trusted in God; let us see if God will deliver him." How is it that thousands of people who stood around the cross did not say that God had forsaken him? How is it that the translators who lived 1600 years later, knew more than the people who stood on the hill of Golgotha and witnessed Jesus' death?

27. AN ANGEL AT THE TOMB

And entering into the sepulchre, they saw a young man sitting on the right side, clothed in a long white garment; and they were affrighted.

Mark 16:5

Angels appear to pious men and women in a vision or a trance, as human beings. Angels appeared to Mary, to Joseph, to Gideon, and to Hebrew patriarchs and prophets. God always guides and directs those who believe in and walk in His way. He also admonishes and counsels good men and women, and answers their prayers by sending His messengers to them to comfort them. Jesus' followers were bereaved and sad.

White is symbolic of purity. Kings, princes and priests wore white linen garments. No matter how the angel appeared, it appeared unto Jesus' followers. Others who might have been there could not see him, just as Jesus after his resurrection appeared only to those who believed in him and were mourning his death. He was not seen by others. (Luke 24:3)

28. SPEAK WITH NEW TONGUES

And these signs shall follow them that believe; In my name shall they cast out devils; they shall speak with new tongues.

Mark 16:17

"Speak with new tongues" does not mean that the disciples were to speak in strange or unknown tongues, but that they were to speak the languages of other races and peoples who were to receive the Christian gospel. That is to say, when Jesus' disciples were to go as missionaries to other lands far away from Judea, the Holy Spirit would help them to learn to speak the new tongues, which were hitherto unknown to them. Moreover, the Holy Spirit was to facilitate the learning of idioms and new tongues. The disciples were to converse in Arabic, Persian, Greek, Latin, Chinese, and other languages, some of which they had never heard before. Jesus also assured his disciples that the Holy Spirit would continuously guide and teach them.

All the needs of these early Christian missionaries who had dedicated their lives to God and were willing to die for the gospel of Jesus Christ were to be met.

It is interesting to know that at that early time most of the languages spoken today were unknown. Languages such as English, German, French, Italian, Spanish, Russian, and many others did not yet exist.

Then again, in the East, when a gospel of peace and good news is proclaimed, it may often be called "a new tongue," a peaceful and gentle message full of hope. And when a king upbraids his people, we often say, "He is speaking in a strange tongue" or "in an unknown tongue," as, "He is speaking in a harsh tone." Such mannerisms of speech are still found in many Eastern languages.

On the other hand, God, or His spirit, can enable one to speak in an unknown or new tongue. People who happen to be moved by the Holy Spirit would understand, despite the speaker's incomplete knowledge of the language.

Today, American missionaries speak in tongues which, until recently, were unknown to them. (See Acts 2:4, 5:16.)

29. HANDLING SERPENTS

They shall take up serpents; and if they drink any deadly thing, it shall not hurt them; they shall lay hands on the sick, and they shall recover.

Mark 16:18

"Handling serpents" is an Aramaic idiom which is also common in other Eastern languages, and which is still used today. It means "overcoming one's enemies." In the East, an enemy is called a serpent or a snake because he acts slyly. Even today we say, "When you go to a certain city, be careful. There are many snakes [enemies] there."

The apostles had many enemies who were opposed to the teachings of their Lord. But Jesus assured them that the Holy

Spirit would help them to overcome all dangers and oppositions which were ahead of them.

Moses handled a serpent, Pharaoh, by his tail; that is, he triumphed over him. Drinking poison means attacks against one's character. These harmful attacks were not to reflect on the character of the disciples, nor would they hinder the progress of the gospel.

Jesus' disciples understood what he was telling them. Even though these verses are sometimes taken literally in Europe and America, neither Jesus nor his disciples had ever tried to handle a snake or drink deadly poison; had they done so they would have tempted God, which the Scriptures admonish us against doing.

Today some Americans who take these words literally do handle snakes, and are sometimes bitten by them. Some Western scholars have deleted a number of verses from this chapter, stating that Jesus could not have encouraged his followers to handle deadly snakes and to drink poison.

On the other hand, when one picks up a snake by mistake, the snake may not harm him. Paul was bitten by a viper, but the poison of the viper did not harm him. The Eastern text reads, ". . . and bit his hand, but Paul felt no harm." (Acts 28:3–6)

The Gospel According to St. Luke

1. HE WILL BE CALLED

> He shall be great, and shall be called the Son of the Highest: and the Lord God shall give unto him the throne of his father David.
>
> Luke 1:32

Many Bible students wonder why the angel did not say, "He is the Son of the Highest," instead of, "He shall be called the Son of the Highest." The reason for saying "He shall be called" is this: Both the angel and the author of the Gospel knew the customs and the temperament of the Eastern people, especially the Jews. To call a man the son of God implies that the Jewish God was married, as the pagan gods were. Such a statement would be taken as a blasphemy and as a pagan doctrine, but "He shall be called the Son of the Highest" is well understood by all Semitic people. God called Solomon, "My son." (I Chron. 28:6) Jesus called God his Father, and he is known as God's son in a spiritual and not in a physical sense.

Note that Matthew states, ". . . He that is to be born of her is of the Holy Spirit." (Matt. 1:20) That is to say, Jesus was conceived by the power of the Holy Spirit. Such terms of speech are common in Semitic languages and well understood and accepted. (Isa. 9:6-7, Jer. 33:15)

Easterners believe that that which is impossible to man is possible to God and to His Holy Spirit. Nevertheless, the Jews and the Moslems resent any remark that implies that God is married or conceived and born, because God is spirit, life, and truth; and these attributes are not subject to conception and birth. Jesus said to the woman in Samaria, "For God is Spirit; and those who worship Him must worship in spirit and in truth." (John 4:24)

The phrase "son of God" has been a stumbling block to millions of Jews and Moslems as well as some Christians. This is because their concept of God is like that which was expressed by Jesus, that God is spirit. And since He is spirit, He never begets nor is begotten, but is from everlasting to everlasting. The Moslems and Jews in particular resent such statements. This is why the Moslems call the Christians unbelievers and blasphemers.

In Aramaic, to say to a man, "You will be called the Son of God," is like saying to an American, "You will be called the President," meaning that you will be as highly honored and respected as a president, not that you will actually be a president or the son of a president.

In the Roman imperial system, the emperors were worshiped as gods of the realm, and their sons were known as the sons of God. Tiberias, Nero, and other emperors were all looked upon as deities. This is the reason why the Romans persecuted the Christians, who claimed that Jesus of Nazareth was also the son of God, hence a deity.

Persian, Greek, Egyptian, and other pagan emperors were also worshiped as gods. Therefore, it was easy for Western people to say, "God has a son," but difficult for the Semitic people, who were taught that God is the Eternal Spirit.

2. CHRIST IS OUR HOPE

Glory to God in the highest, and on earth peace, good will toward men.

Luke 2:14

The Eastern text reads, "Glory be to God in the highest, and on earth peace and good hope for men."

The term "will" is a mistranslation. The word will has some resemblance to the word "wish," but the Aramaic word *sabra* means "hope," "good tidings," "good news," "the gospel of Jesus Christ." (See also Luke 2:10.) In other words, the angel brought glad tidings of a better hope, a better future—a future wherein the Messianic hope would be fulfilled, Israel freed from her oppressors and the kingdom of heaven established on earth. (Isa. 9:6–7)

For centuries the Hebrew prophets had expected the coming of the Messiah, who would establish a new kingdom and a harmonious order wherein people of all races would dwell in peace, and the great and small powers would respect one another. Indeed, this was the greatest Jewish expectation and hope of salvation. And because this prophecy of an everlasting peace and God's reign has not been fulfilled, the Jews believe that the Messiah, Christ, has not yet come.

Today, the wolf and the lamb are far from dwelling together; the leopard and the kid are not lying down together. Many centuries have elapsed since the angels sang this song of a good future, and yet the powerful nations have constantly oppressed the small nations, and the strong have devoured the weak. Even today, after 2000 years, many small, weak nations are still suffering under the yoke of the stronger ones. This is because Christians have not put the gospel of Jesus Christ into action. This is why the universal reign of righteousness and peace has not been established, and why the nations have not forged their instruments of war into plowshares and sickles.

3. INSANE, LUNATICS

Then he called his twelve disciples together, and gave them power and authority over all devils, and to cure diseases.

Luke 9:1

The Aramaic term *shadey* means "the insane," "lunatics," or "those who suffer from mental disorders." This term is still in common use in Aramaic and Arabic languages. *Shedana* means "one who is crazy or possessed by an evil inclination," which is often called an evil spirit.

Since God is the only spirit, how could there be an evil spirit? The Aramaic word which means spirit can also mean a person, the wind, rheumatism, pride, or an inclination.

"The insane" in Arabic are called *Magnooneen*. In Persian, they are called *dewana*, which means "those who live a wild life, suffering from mental disorders."

In the olden days, medical terms as we know them today were unknown. Insanity and mental disorders had no names in these languages. So the people called them devils and demons. In the Gospel of Matthew they are called unclean spirits. (Matt. 10:1) In the Gospel of Mark we read, "And unclean spirits, when they saw him, fell down before him, and cried, saying, 'Thou art the Son of God.'" (Mark 3:11, King James) The spirit has no body with which to fall down and worship. The insane or lunatics did it, and after they were healed they confessed that Jesus was the son of God. (Luke 10:20)

4. WRITTEN IN HEAVEN

Notwithstanding in this rejoice not, that the spirits are subject unto you; but rather rejoice, because your names are written in heaven.

Luke 10:20

The term "written in heaven" is used metaphorically, meaning, "You are saved," or, "You are the chosen one." In the olden days, the names of men who were to be honored and promoted were written in the Chronicles of Kings.

Such statements should not be taken literally. Heaven has

no bookkeepers and accountants. Nevertheless, every human act is evident, and God sees and knows everything. These terms of speech were used because the names of valiant and faithful men were written in the books of kings as a reward, as in the case of Mordecai. (Esth. 6:2–3)

5. KEY OF KNOWLEDGE

Woe unto you, lawyers! for ye have taken away the key of knowledge; ye entered not in yourselves, and them that were entering in ye hindered.

Luke 11:52

The scribes, who were also known as lawyers, had sole authority over the interpretation of the Scriptures. But they did not go deep in order to understand the spiritual meanings, nor did they let others do the thinking and the interpretation. The scribes were opposed to all those who differed from them. (Matt. 23:13)

The scribes, Pharisees, and other Jewish higher authorities relied on the doctrine of the elders, the traditions and teachings of the great rabbis of the past. Even today, millions of Christians are supposedly guided by the theological teachings of men which differ and are contrary to the teachings of the Scriptures.

6. SECRET COUNCILS

Therefore whatsoever ye have spoken in darkness shall be
heard in the light; and that which ye have spoken in the
ear in closets shall be proclaimed upon the housetops.

Luke 12:3

The phrase "in darkness," in this instance, means "in secret." In the East, some important councils are held in partially
dark places so that the people will not know what is being
said. A group of men can be seen assembled and seated in a
corner of the house whispering to one another.

The inner chamber, or closet, is a small place in the house
wherein people find privacy. Some of the important secret
councils are held in inner chambers. In some houses these
chambers are used for sleeping and prayer, especially in the
homes of the rich. They are small private rooms. (I Kings
22:25, II Kings 9:2)

In the East, when things are spoken secretly, they are generally made known, for the people tell one another. Remarks
are interpreted by facial expressions and gestures of the hands.
(Mark 4:22, Luke 8:17)

7. ENEMIES OF THE SOUL

But I will forewarn you whom ye shall fear: Fear him,
which after he hath killed hath power to cast into hell;
yea, I say unto you, Fear him.

Luke 12:15

Jesus here is speaking of the enemies of the truth, those
who were opposed to the Christian gospel. Many of Jesus'

95

followers were sooner or later to die for the truth they were representing.

Jesus admonished his followers not to fear those who kill the body, because they cannot harm the soul. The body is nothing but a garment in which the soul is clothed or manifested.

Jesus' disciples and followers were warned to be careful of false teaching, sin and evil forces, which can destroy not only the body but also the soul. Some evil teachers caused the faithful to go astray from the way of God and worship pagan gods, thus succeeding in destroying their souls.

The term "hell" means "mental suffering" or "the eternal torment." God, being a good and loving Father, is not the author of hell. Man creates his own difficulties and his own hell, and he overcomes them with the help of God.

8. GOD'S DIVINE CARE

Are not five sparrows sold for two farthings, and not one of them is forgotten before God?
But even the very hairs of your head are all numbered. Fear not therefore: ye are of more value than many sparrows.

Luke 12:6-7

God's divine care is manifested throughout the universe. Jesus here assures his disciples of God's guidance and His continual protection against the evil forces. (See Luke 12:5.) God is constantly mindful of all His creatures; even the little sparrows which look so unimportant to us are clothed and protected by Him. God also knows when they are sold.

Man is more important than sparrows and other creatures. This is because man is created in the image and the likeness of God, and therefore, when even a hair falls from a man's head, God feels it and knows it.

9. JESUS REFUSED TO MEDDLE

And one of the company said unto him, Master, speak to
my brother, that he divide the inheritance with me.
And he said unto him, Man, who made me a judge or a
divider over you?
And he said unto them, Take heed, and beware of covetousness: for a man's life consisteth not in the abundance of
the things which he possesseth.

Luke 12:13–15

In the East, many disagreements are settled by pious
men and friends at the town gate or on the housetops. Most
of the disputants shun the government officials and regular
judges. Probably this man was trying to tempt Jesus.

Jesus refused to meddle between the two brothers. The one
who asked him to speak to his brother about dividing the
inheritance with him was greedy. He wanted Jesus to induce
his brother to give him a larger share of the inheritance, which
he probably did not deserve; he may have been the younger
son, who usually receives a smaller portion of an inheritance.

Then again, Jesus was not a judge or a divider of property.
There were priests and scribes who took care of this.

We should never meddle with the affairs of others, except
when they sincerely seek our help and counsel.

10. JESUS MINDFUL OF HIS DEATH

But I have a baptism to be baptized with; and how am I straitened till it be accomplished!

Luke 12:50

Jesus in this instance spoke of his death. He was to be sprinkled with his own blood. (See Baptism of Spirit, Water, and Blood.) The picture of his death on the cross was continuously mirrored in his mind and oppressed him. (Matt. 20:22)

The prophets had predicted his rejection and his death. They themselves had been put to death for the sake of the truth which they preached.

11. SOME WILL NOT ENTER

When once the master of the house is risen up, and hath shut the door, and ye begin to stand without, and to knock at the door, saying, Lord, Lord, open unto us; and he shall answer and say unto you, I know you not whence ye are:
Then shall ye begin to say, We have eaten and drunk in thy presence, and thou hast taught in our streets.

Luke 13:25–26

Jesus is speaking of the Last Day. The master of the house in this instance is the Lord himself.

The preaching of the gospel is to continue. Many will embrace Jesus' teaching and will enter into his kingdom. At the end the door will be closed; only those who have accepted the gospel and have done good works will enter. The others will not, because they will have failed to practice Jesus' teaching. (See the parable of the ten virgins, Matt. 25:1–13.) In other words, some people preach the gospel, but do not live it.

Many believers in Christ will be disappointed because they cannot enter into his kingdom. Some of these will be religious leaders and high church authorities, who have failed to do good works. (Luke 6:46)

12. FIRST WILL BE LAST

And, behold, there are last which shall be first, and there are first which shall be last.

Luke 13:30

In the preceding verse we are told, ". . . . and they will come from the east and from the west and from the south and from the north, and sit down in the kingdom of God." (Luke 13:29) That is to say, in days to come many races from all over the world will embrace Christianity—nations which during the time of Jesus had not even been heard of, nations and peoples not yet born.

The Jews, who had been called first, will be the last to be converted. They were the first people in the world to whom God had sent prophets and given His law and His commandments. Some Jews were among the first to accept Christ, but others rejected him. Those who rejected him will be the last.

Jesus came first to the Jews because they had been called by God and shepherded by the holy prophets. He also admonished his disciples to preach first to the Jews and then to the Gentiles. In other words, the Jews were given the first opportunity to come to the great banquet and to enter into the Messianic kingdom. But when they refused to come, others, the Galileans and the Aramaeans, were called and therefore became the first. (Matt. 19:30, 20:16, Mark 10:31)

13. SPIRITUAL FOOD

And when one of them that sat at meat with him heard these things, he said unto him, Blessed is he that shall eat bread in the kingdom of God.

Luke 14:15

"Eat bread" (in the kingdom of God) is an Eastern idiom which means "to be well received." In the East, to eat bread with a king or a prince is a great honor. Kings and princes never eat with those who are unwelcome in the palace. One can hear people say, "I dined with the ruler," meaning, "I was well received and favored."

There is no physical food in the kingdom of God. The reference here is to the truth and the eternal joy. The term "bread" also means "truth," that is, "the bread of life."

Jesus also spoke of drinking wine in the kingdom of God, by which he meant "rejoicing when he meets his followers in the kingdom." In Aramaic, "wine" also means "joy," "inspiration," and "teaching." Jesus used these words metaphorically, and the people understood this.

Those who suffer for the sake of the truth will rejoice in the life hereafter. The kingdom of God means peace, eternal joy, harmony, and inner understanding of the spiritual life.

14. DANGERS OF BEING A CHRISTIAN

> For which of you, intending to build a tower, sitteth not down first, and counteth the cost, whether he have sufficient to finish it?
> Lest haply, after he hath laid the foundation, and is not able to finish it, all that behold it begin to mock him, Saying, This man began to build, and was not able to finish.
>
> Luke 14:28–30

The towers were built around a city wall, a sort of fortification. In peacetime they were generally manned by watchmen, who kept watch day and night. All ancient cities had walls, with towers for the watchmen and for the soldiers during times of danger. Towers were built in villages and in vineyards, as well.

What Jesus means here is this: Before he starts building a tower in his town or vineyard, a man first sits down and estimates the cost before he lays the foundations thereof, to see whether he has enough money to finish the job, lest he find after he has laid the foundations that he has no money to complete it, and would therefore be embarrassed.

In Luke 14:26 we read, "He who comes to me and does not put aside his father and his mother and his brothers and his sisters and his wife and his children and even his own life cannot be a disciple to me." (Eastern text) The King James version wrongly translates the words "put aside" as "hate."

Jesus admonished his disciples and followers that before they joined his ranks they must sit down and examine their strength and courage; to become aware that in following him they placed themselves in danger to the extent of being arrested, convicted, and forced to carry their own crosses to the place where they would be crucified. This is a warning to anyone who might think that to be a Christian is easy.

101

Perhaps today it is easy; no one carries his cross. Moreover, Christians are on the whole highly respected, and their leaders are revered and highly paid. (Matt. 16:24, Mark 8:34)

15. THE OLD ORDER AND THE NEW

The law and the prophets were until John: since that time the kingdom of God is preached, and every man presseth into it.

Luke 16:16

The law and the prophets spanned the period from Moses until John the Baptist. They were the heralds of the new law, the new covenant, and the spiritual kingdom which was to come. In other words, John was the last prophet of the old order, the Old Testament, or the old covenant. With Jesus began the New Testament, the new order, or the second covenant.

Until John, the kingdom, that is, the Jewish religion, was dominated by worldly men—princes, kings, and high priests who fought for power and who oppressed the people. And from the time of John until the time of Jesus the kingdom of heaven suffered violence. It was dominated by force, and only those who were powerful ruled over it. (Matt. 11:12–13)

Jesus, through his teaching and his death on the cross, brought to the law and the prophets a new synthesis and gave to religion a new meaning. He came not to weaken the law but to fulfill it, that is, to put it into practice. He came not to be ministered to, but to minister. Now many men and women were pressing to enter into the kingdom of heaven.

16. FAITH INCREASED

And the apostles said unto the Lord, Increase our faith.
And the Lord said, If ye had faith as a grain of mustard seed, ye might say unto this sycamine tree, Be thou plucked up by the root, and be thou planted in the sea; and it should obey you.

Luke 17:5–6

The apostles, not being well trained in religion, thought that faith could be increased like material things, that is to say, by adding to it or acquiring it by the means of knowledge.

Jesus told them that faith could not be increased by material means, nor could it be imparted from one person to another. To acquire faith, one must become like a little child who has faith in his father and mother and believes whatsoever they tell him.

All we need in order to increase our faith is to attain a spark thereof. As Jesus puts it, faith is like a small mustard seed, which bores into rocks, absorbs the sun and grows into a large plant.

Faith is measured by quality, not quantity. A single spark of fire can burn the world. When faith is put into action, it increases. This is because through faith one contacts the universal forces. When one has faith, the whole universe works with him.

Moreover, faith ignites the forces which are within man and gives him the assurance of true success. It was Abraham's faith in God that enabled him to make his long and hazardous journey successfully and become the father of the believers. Abraham trusted in God and used that which he had at hand. The Lord God did the rest. When we work with God our faith in Him increases.

The disciples were afraid to practice healing. They were like one who is learning to drive a car but is afraid to drive alone. After all, Jesus' disciples were students who had been traveling with him in order to learn from him, just as Elisha the prophet traveled with Elijah, his master.

Then again, in the East, students keep silent while their teacher or master is present. They refuse to try to do anything in the presence of their master, fearing that they will be unable to do it well; generally they expect the master to do it for them.

Moreover, the disciples had always relied on Jesus, and they themselves were not taking any responsibility. This is why the apostles did not have enough faith to heal the boy who was epileptic. After Jesus' ascension, they were forced to rely on themselves; they started healing and preaching the gospel, demonstrating what Jesus had taught them.

17. EAGLES

And they answered and said unto him, Where, Lord? And he said unto them, Wheresoever the body is, thither will the eagles be gathered together.

Luke 17:37

The term "eagles" in this passage probably means "vultures." The latter are scavengers and devour dead bodies. The carcass in this instance represents Judaism. The Jews had lost both their political power and their prophets and seers. Now they were oppressed and harassed by the pagans and Gentiles who were round about them. Thus Judaism resembled a corpse, ready for the vultures to alight upon it and devour it.

The Jews had already been conquered—by the Assyrians, by the Chaldeans, by the Greeks, by the Syrians—and soon they were to be trampled by the Romans. In the year A.D. 70, Titus put an end to the Jewish state. He destroyed Jerusalem and its magnificent temple, and dispersed the Jews.

18. FAITH MIGHT BE LOST

I tell you that he will avenge them speedily. Nevertheless
when the Son of man cometh, shall he find faith on the
earth?

Luke 18:8

Jesus knew that a great many of his followers would recant
and return to pagan religions. He also knew that the material
and physical world has many alluring rewards to offer, and
some would esteem this physical and temporal life more than
the eternal life to come.

When Jesus returns, there may be no true Christian on the
face of the earth. Today the trend is toward paganism, materialism, and false philosophies. There are many who claim to be
Christian, but how many of them practice the teachings of
Jesus Christ, and how many of them are carrying crosses?

19. JESUS CRUCIFIED BY ROMANS

Then he took unto him the twelve, and said unto them,
Behold, we go up to Jerusalem, and all things that are
written by the prophets concerning the Son of man shall
be accomplished.
For he shall be delivered unto the Gentiles, and shall be
mocked, and spitefully entreated, and spitted on:
And they shall scourge him, and put him to death: and the
third day he shall rise again.

Luke 18:31–33

Jesus was crucified not by Jews, but by soldiers who were
in the service of the Roman Army. The Jews had no authority

to crucify or even to stone a man from Galilee. The Jewish high priest was an ethnarch, that is, the head of the nation, with spiritual authority and limited political power over his people.

The Jewish punishment for blasphemy was stoning. When Stephen was convicted of blasphemy he was stoned by the Jews. The Roman governor had nothing to do with the case, because Stephen was a Jew from Judea, and therefore was under the jurisdiction of the high priest, who had authority in spiritual matters.

On the other hand, Jesus' case was different. He was considered a Galilean, even though he was a member of the Jewish religion. Jesus was from Galilee, and Galilee was under the jurisdiction of Herod Antipas. This is why Pilate, the governor, sent him to Herod to be judged. And when the governor said to the high priest, "Take him and judge him according to your own law," the high priest answered, "We have no authority." This is because Jesus could not be convicted on religious grounds. Therefore, they had made a political charge against him, stating that he had told the people he was king of the Jews. Thus, Pilate was the only one who could judge him and convict him under such a charge, for to say he was king was treason.

20. ONE SOWS, ANOTHER REAPS

For I feared thee; because thou art an austere man: thou takest up that thou layedst not down, and reapest that thou didst not sow.

Luke 19:21

In the East, it often happens that one sows but another reaps. One plants a vineyard, but another drinks its wine. This is because during wars and persecutions, farmers and owners of vineyards were either slain or fled to another country, and the persecutors reaped their crops and picked their grapes. This condition still prevails in some backward countries, but no longer exists in the Arab lands.

The prophets of Israel had planted the vineyard, the Kingdom of God, and had sown the seed, God's Word, and many of them had died for its sake. But now the apostles were reaping the wheat and picking the grapes.

Even today, it is true that some men labor hard but never taste the fruits of their labor, while others reap and enjoy it. Nevertheless, all those who labor and suffer for the sake of their good work shall live forever. The generations which come after them will praise their names. For example, all the prophets who died for the sake of their true teaching are now living in the holy literature which they left behind as a great heritage; their names are handed down from one generation to another. Their lives are emulated, and their words are published and read in hundreds of languages.

21. TO HIM WHO HAS SHALL BE GIVEN

For I say unto you, That unto every one which hath shall be given; and from him that hath not, even that he hath shall be taken away from him.
But those mine enemies, which would not that I should reign over them, bring hither, and slay them before me.
Luke 19:26–27

Most of the land in the East is owned by princes and rich landlords, who lease it to the farmers, who in turn raise the crops and divide them with the owner. In some cases, the peasants receive a small portion of the produce, which is barely enough to supply them with food until the next harvest.

The good peasants who work hard and raise good crops are granted more land, but as for those who fail, their land is taken away from them and given to those who have done better. Jesus illustrated this point by the parable of the talents. Those who had made good were given more money, but the money was taken from the one who had failed and given to those who had done well.

This is also true in business or trade. Those who succeed are given more money, but the little they have is taken away from those who fail, and given to those who were successful.

Jesus in this instance means that more power and knowledge will be given to those who made good in the preaching of the gospel, but even the little which they have will be taken away from those who fail through negligence. (See Matt. 13:12; also, article on Luke 19:13, *Gospel Light*, p. 289.)

22. JEWISH PEOPLE BACK JESUS

And he taught daily in the temple. But the chief priests and the scribes and the chief of the people sought to destroy him,
And could not find what they might do: for all the people were very attentive to hear him.

Luke 19:47–48

Jesus had a great many followers in Judea. Even though the majority of his converts were Galileans, many Jews in the south, who were tired of the high priest, the corrupt Herodian dynasty, and the imperial government which constantly taxed them and added to their burdens, looked upon Jesus as a savior. This is the reason the Jewish authorities arrested Jesus at night and tried him during the dark hours. They feared the masses of the Jewish people who had sided with him. Moreover, the Jewish authorities were afraid of the people who had been flocking to Jesus and acclaiming him as a reformer, a prophet, and even as the great Messiah.

Every attempt to reform the corrupt government in Judea was crushed by Roman authorities and the supporters of the Herodian dynasty. The Jewish authorities were afraid that resistance against the government might cause the Romans to deprive them of their religious freedom and power.

23. THE TIME OF THE GENTILES

And they shall fall by the edge of the sword, and shall be led away captive into all nations: and Jerusalem shall be trodden down of the Gentiles, until the times of the Gentiles be fulfilled.

Luke 21:24

During the time of Jesus, the Jews were ruled by the iron yoke of the Romans and oppressed by people of other races, who acted as cohorts of the Romans. For example, King Herod the Great was an Edomite by race, but a Jew by religion. He was a vassal in the hands of the Romans and he collected heavy taxes and tribute which he shared with the Roman officials.

The Roman rule lasted until the early part of the seventh century A.D., when it was superseded by the Arab conquest. Nevertheless, other stern Gentile rulers ruled over Palestine, oppressed the Jews, murdered them by the thousands, and carried many of them away captive.

When the Gentile rule comes to an end, and the kingdom of

heaven is established on earth, people of all races, colors and religions will live together peacefully, and love one another. Then a lasting peace will reign. (Dan. 9:27)

24. COMING IN A CLOUD

And then shall they see the Son of man coming in a cloud with power and great glory.
And when these things begin to come to pass, then look up, and lift up your heads; for your redemption draweth nigh.

Luke 21:27–28

The term "cloud" is used metaphorically, meaning "glory," "honor," and "majesty." Jesus used symbolic language in order to explain his coming to simple people who did not understand philosophical and metaphysical terms. Jesus is here right now. He said, "Lo, I shall never leave you." He also assured his disciples and followers that whenever two or three of them are together he is with them. Whenever two people meet in the East, following the greeting they ask one another, "What is your way [religion]?" Then they begin to discuss religious matters. Whenever we are spiritually minded, thinking and talking about God's kingdom, Christ is there. (Rev. 1:7)

Jesus' second coming will be a glorious coming; that is, good will triumph over evil. Hence, every eye will see him coming in glory and every heart will feel his presence. This is because his spiritual kingdom, the reign of God, will be established on earth.

25. SIGN OF THE KINGDOM

And I appoint unto you a kingdom, as my Father hath
appointed unto me;
That ye may eat and drink at my table in my kingdom,
and sit on thrones judging the twelve tribes of Israel.
And the Lord said, Simon, Simon, behold, Satan hath desired to have you, that he may sift you as wheat.

Luke 22:29–31

God, through the Hebrew prophets, promised a universal
kingdom based on justice and righteousness. And the Messiah,
the Prince of Peace, will be the ruler, or the king, over this
spiritual kingdom, which in due time will embrace the whole
world and bring all peoples to the way of God.

The Aramaic term *malcotha*, "kingdom," also means "counsel."
Hence, the kingdom of God means God's counsel, God's way of
ruling the world—God's way of life.

Jesus promised his disciples a reign based on justice and
harmony, where everyone will live in peace, happiness and
tranquility.

These words, or figures of speech, are not to be taken literally.
There will be no eating or drinking in the kingdom of God.
Such terms are symbolic of a righteous reign of truth, harmony
and happiness, which are the eternal bread of life.

26. GOLGOTHA A CEMETERY

And as they were afraid, and bowed down their faces to
the earth, they said unto them, Why seek ye the living
among the dead?

Luke 24:5

"Why seek ye the living among the dead?" means, "Why
do you search for me in a cemetery?," for Golgotha, the skull,
was a cemetery.

Some of the women followers of Jesus who had come with
him from Galilee had followed the men who had put his body
temporarily in an empty tomb. And now, very early on Sunday
morning, they had returned to the sepulcher and brought with
them spices to give Jesus' body a proper and final burial. This
was because Jesus' body had been hastily placed in the tomb on
Friday evening because the Sabbath was drawing near.

Evidently the sepulcher was close to the place where Jesus
and the two malefactors were crucified: Golgotha, "the skull."
At that time the top of this hill was a cemetery for foreigners
who had died in Jerusalem. The Jewish cemetery is on the other
side of the Brook of Kedron, across from the holy city.

The temporary sepulcher, I believe, was one of the caves
across from the Damascus Gate. These three caves look like the
face of a man, two eyes and a mouth, and the top of the hill
resembles a human skull.

Jesus was surprised that they were looking for his body in a
cemetery. He had told them that he would be arrested, condemned, crucified, and buried, but that he would rise again.
Nevertheless, as we see from the Gospels, neither the women nor
the disciples had taken his words seriously. They could not see
how anyone could triumph over death and rise from the grave.

27. CHRIST'S SUFFERING FORETOLD

Ought not Christ to have suffered these things, and to enter into his glory?
And beginning at Moses and all the prophets, he expounded unto them in all the scriptures the things concerning himself.

Luke 24:26–27

Jesus, prior to his crucifixion, had told his disciples and followers that he would be rejected, condemned and crucified. He had wanted to prepare them for what they thought was a tragic end. Nevertheless, his followers could not see or understand how such a great and holy man, who had wrought miracles and wonders, could meet with death on the cross. Nor did they expect him to rise again.

The holy prophets were still lying in their graves, and to the minds of the simple disciples, death was an end, a finality; but to Jesus, death was nothing but triumph over the forces of evil, and the beginning of a new life.

The Gospel According to St. John

1. GOD CANNOT BE SEEN

No man hath seen God at any time; the only begotten Son, which is in the bosom of the Father, he hath declared him.

John 1:18

In the Book of Exodus we read, "And the Lord spoke to Moses face to face, as a man speaks to his friend." (Ex. 33:11) "Face to face," in Semitic languages, means that God conversed with Moses openly, not in metaphors, parables, or figurative speech. To the prophets and seers, he spoke in dreams and visions, using Semitic and figurative speech, but to Moses God spoke openly, that is to say, Moses felt the presence of God and heard His voice intuitively, for Moses had a great understanding of God and spiritual things. Therefore there was no need for figurative speech.

Isaiah tells us that the angels covered their faces when they approached the presence of God. God has no face and no form; God is substance, essence, and the intelligence which governs the universe. Therefore no one has seen God, and no one could describe Him. The Bible tells us that even Elijah could not see God's face.

God reveals Himself in similitudes so that man may understand Him. He often appeared as a man in a vision or trance, but He is not a man.

God can only be seen in spirit and truth, and Jesus is spirit, life, and truth. That is why he said, "Whosoever has seen me has seen God." In other words, he was good as God is good, for only good can reflect good, and evil reflects evil. (John 4:23–24)

2. THE PROPHET FROM NAZARETH

Philip findeth Nathanael, and saith unto him, We have found him, of whom Moses in the law, and the prophets, did write, Jesus of Nazareth, the son of Joseph.

And Nathanael said unto him, Can there any good thing come out of Nazareth? Philip saith unto him, Come and see.

John 1:45–46

Nazareth was a small town in Galilee. The town was despised by some of the Jewish sects, for Nazareth was inhabited by Gentiles who had become Jews by religion.

Centuries before, the King of Assyria had brought men from the other side of the River Euphrates, and settled them in Galilee, after the ten tribes of Israel were taken away captive in 722 B.C. The Jews rejected the Galilean claim to the Jewish religion because these people were of mixed races. That is why they said to Nicodemus, "Examine the scriptures; no prophet shall rise from Galilee."

When the Jews returned from capitivity, the ancestors of the Galileans came to Zerubbabel and to the chiefs of the fathers, and offered to help rebuild the temple. They said that since the captivity they had been worshiping the God of the Jews. But the Jews refused their help. (Ezra 4:1–4) So we see that even centuries before Christ, the Jews rejected the Galileans, who were called the adversaries of Judah and Benjamin.

Jesus and his disciples were known as Galileans, and spoke the Galilean, or northern, dialect of Aramaic.

The prophet Isaiah calls Galilee the land of the Gentiles, the people who dwell in darkness. He predicted that a great light would shine from Galilee. (Isa. 9:1–2) He also told the Jews that the Messiah would become a light unto the Gentiles.

115

3. HEAVEN OPENED

And he saith unto him, Verily, verily, I say unto you,
Hereafter ye shall see heaven open, and the angels of God
ascending and descending upon the Son of man.

John 1:51

The term "angel" means "God's counsel," "messenger," or
"minister." "Ye shall see heaven open, and the angels of God
ascending and descending upon the Son of man [Jesus]" means
that henceforth there will be constant communication between
heaven and the son of man; or, that what had been a mystery
would be revealed through Jesus.

In the East, when a king and his princes and governors are
at peace, emissaries continue to carry messages between them,
but when they are not on good terms such communications
cease.

Jesus died as a repudiated teacher of religion. No religious
authorities would believe that he had anything to do with God.
Jesus lived in an era when religious teachers were telling the
people that God had become disgusted with this world, and
would have nothing to do with it. This period in Jewish history
is called Deism. Morever, during this period no prophets or
seers had appeared. The Jews had been without them for
many years. In other words, God had been silent; but now the
heavens were to open and God's messengers were to come on
earth.

John, the last prophet of the old order, had already come,
and was bearing witness to Jesus. Jesus' teaching was the revelation of God to mankind. This revelation was to come, through
angelic powers and the Holy Spirit, to all men.

4. THE WAY OF THE WIND

The wind bloweth where it listeth, and thou hearest the sound thereof, but canst not tell whence it cometh, and whither it goeth: so is every one that is born of the Spirit.

John 3:8

Even though the wind is made manifest by the elements which are found in the air, no one knows whence it comes and whither it goes, nor where it begins and where it will end.

Now, if we cannot tell whence comes the wind and whither it goes, how then would we understand the ways of the Spirit, which has no elements in it—and which is the essence, the finest thing in nature? (Eccles. 11:5) This is why God is called Spirit. There is nothing finer than Spirit. The Spirit, like electricity, can be felt, but cannot be seen by human eyes or discerned by any other means. We can contact it and understand it only through the Spirit of God which is in us.

The things of the Spirit can only be discerned spiritually. Unfortunately, Nicodemus took everything literally, and therefore did not understand what Jesus had told him.

5. DID GOD PAY A RANSOM?

For God so loved the world, that he gave his only begotten Son, that whosoever believeth in him should not perish, but have everlasting life.

John 3:16

No verse in the Holy Bible is more quoted than this one, and yet none is probably more theologically misunderstood. This is because the Western reader does not understand Eastern customs and mannerisms of speech.

Indeed, many scholars and preachers of the gospel sincerely believe that God sacrificed Jesus of Nazareth to appease the Devil and the evil forces. Some teachers say that God, through Jesus' death on the cross, paid a debt to the Devil in order to free man from sin. Others use the term "redemption," meaning that God paid a ransom or a price in order to redeem mankind from evil forces. Still others say that God reconciled or appeased His own wrath against humanity through the death of His beloved son.

It is interesting to note that nearly all the passages which in the King James version read "redemption," in the ancient Eastern, or Aramaic, text (Lamsa) read *porkana*, "salvation." Redemption is made effective by means of a payment or a ransom, but no price is ever paid when a person is saved from danger.

It is often said that Jesus Christ died for our sins, and that our sins could never have been forgiven without his death. The Aramaic word *mitol* means "because," or, "on account of," or "for," but the preferred meaning is "because." I am inclined to believe that Jesus died because of our sins, because of man's transgression against God's law.

Humanity, in Jesus' day, was just as sinful as it is today. The world has been dominated by sin since Adam and Eve first transgressed the law. If man had not broken the law, Jesus would not have had to die. On the other hand, God, being the loving Father, does not need to be appeased by his children. No human father would try to appease his wrath by putting one of his sons to death.

Now, if we assume that Jesus died to appease the forces of evil, then seemingly evil was stronger than the good—God. On the other hand, it is usually the weaker who pays the stronger, the vanquished who pays tribute to the victor. Therefore, such an act would not only prove that the Devil, or Satan, is an entity, but also a force or power equal to or greater than God.

Moreover, if God delivered His son to sinful men to be crucified to appease His own wrath and thus reconcile Himself with His children, then He could hardly be a God of love, a loving Father. Customarily, only pagans killed their sons in honor of kings and princes. They also offered them as sacrifices in order to appease their wrath, and redeemed captives by payment of ransom. The King of Moab offered his son, the crown prince, who was to reign in his place, to appease the wrath of the kings who fought against him. (II Kings 3:27) Moreover, feudal chieftains, in order to settle blood feuds, sacrifice a member of their tribe to bring reconciliation. Baal worship was founded on this idea of reconciling gods through human sacrifices and other offerings. But the Jews, having been admonished by God, inaugurated the practice of animal rather than human sacrifice.

Some theologians say that Jesus took our sins upon himself and offered them to God; others say that God forsook Jesus on the cross because He could not look on the sins Jesus was bearing. Yet in the Gospel we read that when Jesus forgave sinners, all he said was, "Go and sin no more." He did not say, "Offer something to appease God's wrath." Of course the Jews, like the pagans, often tried to appease God's wrath by means of sacrifice and offerings, at times even offering their children. Moreover, in the Bible we read that God sees every evil thing which man does, and nothing is hidden from His eyes.

Assuredly, the death of Jesus on the cross was predicted by the prophet Isaiah. The latter knew that anyone who would venture to challenge the temple religion and the corrupt systems of this world would meet with death. The prophet did not at any time say that Jesus' death would reconcile God or pay a debt to the forces of evil.

Jesus, in his teachings, condemned hypocrisy, injustice, exploitation and the misuse of religion. All the Hebrew prophets who had spoken out against evil kings and princes and the wicked order of their days had met with the same fate, and for this cause they were all killed or stoned.

Jesus' death was different in that he was willing to die, knowing that he would rise again from death. Therefore, his death was a triumph, and his grave is still the only empty one. In other words, God permitted the death of His beloved son in order to reveal the depth of His love to humanity.

The Scripture says God is love. Indeed, love could not demand human sacrifices, because there is nothing in love to be appeased. Jesus died on the cross not to appease God or the evil forces, but to prove that life is indestructible and everlasting because God is indestructible and everlasting. Moreover, Jesus through his death on the cross inaugurated a new world order, the order of meekness and loving-kindness.

6. THE ONLY SON

For God so loved the world, that he gave his only begotten Son, that whosoever believeth in him should not perish, but have everlasting life.

John 3:16

The Aramaic word *ykhidaya* means "the only, the sole, begotten one." This term is used because Jesus was the only child of the Virgin Mary. Some authorities state that he was the first child. No one can know this for sure. But the reference here is to Jesus' humanity and not to his divinity. For God, being the Eternal Spirit, could not be the firstborn, neither is he subject to birth or death. That the apostle John spoke of Jesus' humanity is very clear. Jesus, in his divinity, was with God from the very beginning—before the earth was created.

Jesus was the second Adam because he was the first to restore man's divinity and to triumph over sin and death, and thus he became the begotten son of God—a new Adam. And through his method we also become the children of the living God.

7. A SAMARITAN WOMAN

Then saith the woman of Samaria unto him, How is it
that thou, being a Jew, askest drink of me, which am a
woman of Samaria? for the Jews have no dealings with
the Samaritans.

John 4:9

The Samaritans, like the Jews, were expecting the coming
of the Messiah. Moses, fifteen hundred years before, had assured the people that the Lord God would send them a
prophet greater than himself, and had admonished the people
to listen to him. (Deut. 18:15)

The Samaritans, however, did not accept the books of the
prophets, nor were they under the authority of the Jewish
scribes and Pharisees. However, the Samaritans did accept the
five books of Moses, and seemingly were ready to accept a
change in the Jewish religion, especially in the temple ordinances, the rituals, and the doctrines of the Jewish elders,
which were not based on the law of Moses or the teaching of
the prophets.

Then again, the Samaritans were not Israelites by race. They
were descendants of those who had been settled in Galilee in
722 B.C. by the King of Assyria. These people had accepted the
law of Moses and some of the teachings of the Jewish religion;
nevertheless, the Jews still looked upon them as aliens. (See
Ezra 4:1–4.)

8. JESUS QUESTIONS THE SICK MAN

When Jesus saw him lie, and knew that he had been now a long time in that case, he saith unto him, Wilt thou be made whole?

The impotent man answered him, Sir, I have no man, when the water is troubled, to put me into the pool: but while I am coming, another steppeth down before me.

John 5:6–7

Jesus knew that this man who had spent so many years in the temple grounds had been helpless to get into the water before the others. But he also knew that the man was making a good living by begging, and was probably better off than many healthy laborers, who were often unemployed. That is why Jesus asked the man if he was willing to be healed. Indeed, some beggars, making a good living at their begging, might have been unwilling to be healed, no matter how helpless they seemed.

Even today, many people might refuse to be healed because they would lose the indemnities they receive from the government and insurance companies. But this sick man wanted to be healed and start a new life, to trust God for his daily bread.

9. STRICT SABBATH OBSERVANCE

But Jesus answered them, My Father worketh hitherto, and
I work.
Therefore the Jews sought the more to kill him, because
he not only had broken the sabbath, but said also that
God was his Father, making himself equal with God.

John 5:17–18

The Jews, during the time of Jesus, had become very
dogmatic. They had written vast commentaries, trying to explain
the law and the ordinances of Moses. They had forgotten the
simple religion of their prophets.

Any act done on the Sabbath day was considered a violation
of the Sabbath, but this was not the case before the Babylonian
captivity, when the Jews were a pastoral people, needing to
take care of their sheep and cattle on the Sabbath day. The
Sabbath was made in order to give man a day of rest.

The Jews were angry at Jesus because he said, "My Father
doeth the work, so I do it too," which implied that God did not
rest on the Sabbath day. Then again, at this particular period,
the people had forgotten that God was their Father, who cared
for them and met their needs on every day of the week. Moreover, God's name was so holy that they hesitated to utter it
with their mouths. In other words, the God Who in olden days
helped and supplied the needs of their forefathers had now
become dependent on their offerings and sacrifices. (See article
on Sabbath, *Gospel Light.*)

10. THE PIOUS NOT JUDGED

Verily, verily, I say unto you, He that heareth my word,
and believeth on him that sent me, hath everlasting life,
and shall not come into condemnation; but is passed from
death unto life.

John 5:24

God, Who had sent Jesus, would not, on the Judgment
Day, try those who harkened to his teaching—the pious ones.
That is to say, on the Day of Judgment the pious will not be
tried like the wicked; but they will pass from this mortal life
into eternal life without any hindrance.

11. THE DEAD WILL HEAR JESUS

Verily, verily, I say unto you, The hour is coming, and
now is, when the dead shall hear the voice of the Son of
God: and they that hear shall live.
For as the Father hath life in himself; so hath he given
to the Son to have life in himself.

John 5:25–26

The hour will come on the Resurrection Day, when even
the dead will hear Jesus' voice. That hour is here and now to
those who are living but have not accepted the light of the
truth. Those who believe in Jesus' teaching will have everlasting life. On that day, the dead who hear his voice and
believe in him will be saved and live forever.

Since God is eternal and indestructible, the spiritual man is
also eternal and indestructible. Man was created in the image

and likeness of God. Moreover, God had placed all power in the hands of Jesus Christ, who therefore had the authority to grant everlasting life to those who would believe in him.

12. SEALED

Labour not for the meat which perisheth, but for that meat which endureth unto everlasting life, which the Son of man shall give unto you: for him hath God the Father sealed.

John 6:27

The Aramaic term *khetam* means to "seal," but also means to "attest," "confirm," and to "determine."

God had determined from the very beginning that Jesus Christ would come into the world to feed people with the bread of life, which is the truth. God knew man would go astray from the way of truth, and follow after his own evil devices, and labor for material things which perish.

However, when people are fed spiritual food, that is, the true understanding of spiritual life, then peace and harmony reign, and material things abound.

13. TRUE RELIGION IS SIMPLE

No man can come to me, except the Father which hath
sent me draw him: and I will raise him up at the last
day.
It is written in the prophets, And they shall be all taught
of God. Every man therefore that hath heard, and hath
learned of the Father, cometh unto me.

John 6:44–45

What Jesus means in this instance is that some men, no
matter how learned they are, will not follow him. Only those
whom God would draw to him would be ready to accept him
and his new teaching. This is because it is difficult for the wise
and the prudent to receive a humble teacher and accept a
simple teaching, giving up that which they had worked for
many years to acquire.

God's truth is too simple, too good to be believed. Only those
who are simple and pure in heart are drawn to it and taught
by the spirit of God. The learned and the wise cannot understand the truth; it is too simple. (Isa. 54:13)

14. SOME JEWS KNEW JESUS

Howbeit we know this man whence he is: but when Christ
cometh, no man knoweth whence he is.

John 7:27

Some Jews knew Jesus and they supposed him to be the
son of Joseph and Mary. They had seen him in the streets, in
the market place, and in the fields, and had heard him preach

in the synagogue. After all, to them he was just another citizen of Nazareth. They did not know that he was the Messiah, the Christ.

The Jewish people were taught that when the Messiah came, no one would know from whence he came or whose son he would be. Jesus, Joseph and Mary were well known to the people of Nazareth and the neighboring towns in Galilee. This was one reason why it was hard for the Jews to accept him as the promised Messiah, the Savior of the World. Evidently they found it difficult to accept such a meek and humble man as the Messiah—the King of Kings. Even today, most people throughout the world look for mighty and wealthy leaders.

No prophet is without honor except in his own town and among his own people.

15. TIME TOO SHORT

Ye shall seek me, and shall not find me: and where I am, thither ye cannot come.
Then said the Jews among themselves, Whither will he go, that we shall not find him? will he go unto the dispersed among the Gentiles, and teach the Gentiles?

John 7:34-35

This saying was aimed at the Pharisees who were never to see Jesus or find him again. Jesus spoke of his death and his departure from this life, but they understood him not. After the resurrection, Jesus appeared to his disciples and followers alone, and when they saw him again they rejoiced in him. But the Pharisees and scribes did not see him.

The unbelievers could neither see him nor go where he was going. That is to say, they could not go to the cross for the sake of God's truth. But his disciples and followers were to see him again, and they were also ready to die the same kind of death for the sake of his teaching.

The reference here is to the lost tribes from the house of Israel, who were now dispersed among the Gentiles. Jesus had sent out seventy of his disciples with instructions to go to no one but the lost sheep from the house of Israel. Most of the descendants of the ten tribes were now in Assyria, Iran and other adjacent lands.

The ten tribes of Israel were carried captive by the Assyrian kings in 722 B.C. (See II Kings 17–18, John 8:21.)

16. THIRSTY FOR TRUTH

In the last day, that great day of the feast, Jesus stood and cried, saying, If any man thirst, let him come unto me, and drink.

John 7:37

"Let him come to me and drink" is an Aramaic idiom which means, "Let him come to me and learn from me." In the East, we often say, "I ate the book," which means, "I committed it to my heart," "I drank the knowledge like water." And when we show our affection to a · child we say, "I eat you." Such expressions as "eat the book" and "drink the water of life and truth" are common in the Bible.

The people were more thirsty for the knowledge of God than for water. (See Isa. 55:1.) Though water was scarce in Palestine, people could get enough to drink from wells and brooks, but the knowledge of God was very precious.

The people in the past had gone astray from the God of their forefathers, and had transgressed against His laws and ordinances. And now the doctrines of the elders had replaced the precious truth, which was taught by the prophets.

17. TRUE JUDGMENT

And yet if I judge, my judgment is true: for I am not
alone, but I and the Father that sent me.
It is also written in your law, that the testimony of two
men is true.

John 8:16–17

By "I am not alone" Jesus meant, "I do not pass judgment
all alone, but God also sits in judgment with me." What he was
saying here was that he does nothing by himself, without consulting God, and that his judgment is according to the judgment of God. This is because he was always in accord with
God his father. (See John 8:26.)

The Mosaic law required two witnesses in order to convict
a man of crime or of blasphemy against God. The judgment
of two or three judges is more acceptable than that of a sole
jurist. (John 14:10)

18. SERVANTS ARE NOT HEIRS

And the servant abideth not in the house for ever: but
the Son abideth ever.
If the Son therefore shall make you free, ye shall be free
indeed.

John 8:35–36

Stewards and servants are not hired permanently. Some of
them change positions quite often. A servant always knows that
he is a hireling, and that his work may be temporary; he may
be dismissed by his lord at any time. But a son is the heir, or
one of the heirs, and stays at the home of his father forever.

The Pharisees and scribes were servants of God, but Jesus Christ was the son and the heir to whom God had entrusted everything.

Jesus spoke of freedom from ignorance, not political freedom. The Jews were subjected by the Gentiles and pagans simply because they had departed from the way of God and gone after pagan gods.

God's promises to David were conditional. David's descendants would sit on his throne provided they walked in the way of God and obeyed His laws as David did. But when they failed to remain loyal to God, the covenant which God had made with David would be canceled and they would be carried away captive.

Both Israel and Judah suffered the same fate and lost their freedom, becoming vassals and paying tribute, now to Assyria, now to Egypt, and now to Syria.

But when they knew the truth, and became aware of their calling and of the divine promises, repenting from their evil-doings, they would regain their freedom. But before the yoke of the oppressor would be removed, they must first repent from their sins and their evil ways.

19. THE DEVIL IS A LIAR

Ye are of your father the devil, and the lusts of your father ye will do. He was a murderer from the beginning, and abode not in the truth, because there is no truth in him. When he speaketh a lie, he speaketh of his own: for he is a liar, and the father of it.

John 8:44

The Aramaic term *Akelkarsa* means "an accuser," "an adversary," "the tempter," or "him whom we call the devil." Figuratively, it was *Akelkarsa,* the adversary, who took Jesus into the wilderness to tempt him. An adversary can be anything which is adverse to the truth. Jesus was tempted as a man; God cannot be tempted with evil, nor does He tempt anyone.

The Pharisees and scribes who debated with Jesus claimed that they were the descendants of Abraham, the father of the believers. But Jesus challenged their claim and told them that their father was *Akelkarsa,* the accuser. This was because they did not believe in him, and, like the adversary, they accused him of blasphemy and wanted to trap him. Jesus told them that if God and Abraham had been their spiritual fathers, they would have recognized and accepted his teachings, because he taught that which God had revealed to the holy prophets.

Now the true religion of Abraham and that of the prophets was almost forgotten. Man-made doctrines and falsehood had replaced it.

The adversary is a liar and the father of lies. God did not create him, and did not give him power or authority over man. When man knows the truth, he becomes free from evil and from deception and lies, which are contrary to the truth.

Any negative thought is a man's adversary. Any idea which deflects him from the true course of his life is his enemy.

We know that God is not the author of evil or opposed to truth, for God is the light and the truth.

20. ENLIGHTENMENT

I must work the works of him that sent me, while it is day:
the night cometh, when no man can work.

John 9:4

Darkness is symbolic of ignorance and superstition; and light, of enlightenment. When God said, "Let there be light,"

He meant, "Let there be enlightenment and understanding." That is to say, Let man know that he is the image and likeness of God, his creator. God is often called the light.

Jesus is the light of the world. As long as he was with his followers, they could see their way and do their work, but when he was gone, no one would be able to work, because they would not have the light or the understanding of God. So the disciples and his followers were to work hard while he was with them, guiding them and preaching to them. (John 12:35)

In the East, when electricity and kerosene were unknown, men and women worked by the light of an oil lamp after six o'clock in the evening. When there was a shortage of oil they could not work. God's light is abundant and inexhaustible, but man-made light is temporary and limited. The light of Jesus Christ continues centuries after his death and resurrection.

21. JESUS' GREAT POWER

And other sheep I have, which are not of this fold: them also I must bring, and they shall hear my voice; and there shall be one fold, and one shepherd.
Therefore doth my Father love me, because I lay down my life, that I might take it again.
No man taketh it from me, but I lay it down of myself. I have power to lay it down, and I have power to take it again. This commandment have I received of my Father.

John 10:16–18

Jesus was willing to die for the sake of his teaching, because he was sure that he would rise again. No one had power over him, but he himself was willing to prove that death was not a finality or an end, but the beginning of a larger life. No one before Jesus had ever dared to demonstrate this. (Acts 2:24) Even the great Hebrew prophets feared death, and when in danger, escaped for their lives. They looked upon death as sinister.

The term "other sheep" means "the Gentiles" and pagans, who were not yet in Jesus' fold, but who were soon to accept him as the savior of mankind and to practice his teaching.

Jesus, like the prophet Isaiah, saw the universality of the Jewish religion. Therefore he advocated that the light of God, the Holy Scriptures, should be shared with the Gentile world as the only means of securing an everlasting peace and creating a new order wherein both Jews and Gentiles would live together peacefully and happily.

Isaiah had predicted that the Messiah, Christ, would become a light to the Gentiles and ruler over the universal state which would embrace all lands, to the outer ends of the world. The prophet had also envisioned the reign of everlasting peace and righteousness. (Isa. 9:1-2)

22. JESUS KNOWS HIS OWN

And I give unto them eternal life; and they shall never perish, neither shall any man pluck them out of my hand. My Father, which gave them me, is greater than all; and no man is able to pluck them out of my Father's hand.
John 10:28-29

"Pluck them out of my hand" means "snatch or seize them." A good shepherd would fight and die before he allowed his sheep to be seized by wild animals or stolen by thieves. "Sheep" in this instance means "people," that is, believers in Jesus Christ.

The term "sheep" is frequently used throughout the Bible.

God is often pictured as a shepherd. The kings, prophets, and men of God are also portrayed as God's shepherds, watching over His people. This is because sheep are very timid, and must be led by good shepherds, just as men are led by prophets and men of God. (John 10:11)

23. A DISCIPLE'S LOVE

Then said Thomas, which is called Didymus, unto his fellow disciples, Let us also go, that we may die with him.

John 11:16

Jesus' disciples were not sure of his resurrection, even though their master had often assured them that he would rise again. They could not understand it. This is because the concept of resurrection was at that time naïve and not well crystalized.

The Pharisees believed in resurrection, but the Sadducees denied it. Moreover, there were other Jews who were satisfied with one life, and had no desire for another.

Some of Jesus' disciples loved him so much that they were willing to die with him. In the East, faithful servants who love their lord offer their lives instead of his, or are willing to die with him, or go to jail. Thomas, who in Aramaic is called *Thoma* or *Thuma*, "the twin," was willing to die with Jesus.

In Aramaic we often say, "I'll die for you," meaning, "I'll die instead of you," or, "I will make myself an offering for you."

24. JESUS THE RESURRECTION

Jesus said unto her, I am the resurrection, and the life:
he that believeth in me, though he were dead, yet shall
he live:
And whosoever liveth and believeth in me shall never die.
Believest thou this?

John 11:25–26

Jesus' gospel gave to mankind a clear and definite hope of
resurrection and eternal life. This is because Jesus in his teaching proved that man is a child of God, made in his image and
likeness, and that the spiritual man is indestructible. This doctrine he proved through his death on the cross and his resurrection from the grave. No prophet or man of God has ever
been able to rise from the grave. Jesus' grave is the only empty
one.

Those who believe in Jesus Christ are assured of life eternal.
They will pass from this earthly life into life everlasting. No
other religion, before Christianity, has ever assured its adherents such a true and sure hope of life hereafter. Without resurrection and life hereafter, life is dark, hopeless, and meaningless.

25. JESUS DESTINED TO DIE

Now is my soul troubled; and what shall I say? Father,
save me from this hour: but for this cause came I unto
this hour.

John 12:27

Jesus was the first teacher of religion who saw victory
after death. No other prophet or man of God had ever taught
that death and the grave were conquerable. Jesus, from the very

beginning of his ministry on earth, foresaw his rejection and his death. The great prophet Isaiah, centuries before him, had foreseen the Messiah's rejection and death, but his prophecy was not understood by the Pharisees and other learned Jews. (Isa. 53) This is because no one believed that meekness would ever triumph over force, and love over hatred; no one could see that force and the sword had failed and that all the nations who had resorted to them had perished by them. In other words, no one had ever before taken the words of the prophet Isaiah seriously. Most people believed that the Messiah was not supposed to die; he was to conquer the world and live forever.

Jesus, like any other man, was disturbed. His body resisted, but his spirit was willing to let his body die so that he might demonstrate that death has no power over those who believe in God, and who are created in His image.

During his trial, Jesus said to Pilate: "For this I was born, and for this very thing I came to the world, that I may bear witness concerning the truth." (John 18:37) Jesus had come to bear witness to the truth, or, in Aramaic, to become a martyr, or die for the sake of the truth.

26. PRINCE OF THIS WORLD

Now is the judgment of this world: now shall the prince of this world be cast out.

John 12:31

The "prince of this world" refers to the Jewish high priest, the Herodians and the Romans who ruled over the people. These worldly authorities were dominated by greed, hatred, pride and worldly aspirations. But now their days were numbered. The temple was to be destroyed in the near future and

Jesus' gospel of good news and hope was to triumph over the Roman Empire; and the kingdom of righteousness envisioned by the Hebrew prophets was to be established on the earth.

Jesus was facing the darkest hour of his life. He was soon to be delivered to the wicked princes and leaders of this sinful world. The sinless one was to be tried and convicted by the sinful; the innocent was to be crucified by the wicked. (Luke 10:18)

27. JESUS AWARE OF CROSS

And I, if I be lifted up from the earth, will draw all men unto me.

This he said, signifying what death he should die.

The people answered him, We have heard out of the law that Christ abideth for ever: and how sayest thou, The Son of man must be lifted up? who is this Son of man?

John 12:32–34

"Lifted up" is another manner of saying in Aramaic, "crucified." This is because the victims were lifted up to their crosses and then crucified. Evidently, the crosses were erected beforehand. Even today, the gallows are prepared in advance. The victims were lifted up so that everyone in the crowd could see them crucified.

John 12:33 might be a footnote which was added later to show that Jesus knew beforehand what manner of death he was going to die, the death on the cross, the severest punishment that could be inflicted.

When Jesus was lifted up, thousands of men and women who had heard of him but had never seen him, saw him dying the death of a malefactor. Many of them believed he was a right-

137

eous man dying the death of a sinner. In the eyes of others he was dying as a malefactor.

From that moment on, Jesus began to draw men and women to him. The cross would stand forever in the hearts of those who would believe in him.

Had Jesus died in Nazareth the world would have been robbed of a wonderful gospel, the gospel of good tidings, meekness, and freedom from evil, which was made possible through his death on the cross. Without the cross he could not have demonstrated that death was conquerable.

28. JESUS SPOKE FOR GOD

For I have not spoken of myself; but the Father which sent me, he gave me a commandment, what I should say, and what I should speak.

John 12:49

Jesus gave all glory and honor to God, his Father. He said nothing of his own accord, but only that which God had revealed to the prophets that which He had commanded him to say. Moreover, Jesus, as a man, was sent by God, and he acted as a representative of God on earth. This is because He who sends is greater than the one who is sent. This is why Jesus said, "My Father is greater than I. I of myself can do nothing. The Father does it." (John 8:38)

29. JESUS' METHOD

And whatsoever ye shall ask in my name, that will I do,
that the Father may be glorified in the Son.
If ye shall ask any thing in my name, I will do it.
John 14:13–14

Beshimi, "in my name," means "according to my method,
my way of doing things." Jesus' way was different from that of
any other religious man in that he taught people to pray to
God and ask His blessings while thinking of Him as a loving
Father and not as an earthly ruler whom the people feared
and worshiped as God.

In many lands, members of various religions mention the
names of their patron saints when petitioning God. The Jews
invoked the names of their patriarchs, Abraham, Isaac and Jacob,
who had been close to God.

Jesus' way was meekness, forgiveness and loving-kindness.
The turning of the other cheek and the going of another mile
were a new idea, a new approach to God. Moreover, Jesus had
the power, from God, to grant favors; all power in heaven and
on earth were his.

Even today, great inventions and discoveries are credited to
and are known by the names of their authors. Jesus was the
author of the simplest, yet most practical, method of praying
and seeking God's blessings ever discovered.

The disciples and followers of Jesus were assured of greater
miracles and wonders than those Jesus himself had performed.
Anything they would ask of God, believing in Jesus' teaching,
using his method, and knowing that God had sent him, would
be granted for the glory of God. Jesus' method was simple and
sure; a father would do anything for his children. (Matt. 7:7–8,
John 15:7–8)

30. THE COMFORTER

> But the Comforter, which is the Holy Ghost, whom the
> Father will send in my name, he shall teach you all things,
> and bring all things to your remembrance, whatsoever I
> have said unto you.
>
> John 14:26

The term *parekleta* is an Aramaic word: *parek* means "to
save"; *porkana,* "salvation"; *paroka,* "savior." *Leta* in Aramaic
is spelled with the letter *thet,* which is not found in Western
alphabets. *Leta* means "the accursed ones," those who have
gone astray from the way of God and reject the truth of the
gospel. Such people in Jesus' day were called the accursed
ones, that is, those who did not know the law. *Parekleta,*
"Holy Spirit," was to strengthen, comfort and gather the disciples together.

Since the gospel of Jesus Christ reached the Western world
through the Greek language, the term *parekleta* is supposed to
be Greek. But we know that the gospel was preached in Aramaic
to the Aramaic-speaking people. And *parak* is an Aramaic
word. No scholar doubts this today.

Jesus could not have used a Greek theological term. His
simple and illiterate disciples and followers would not have
understood it, nor did he know any Greek.

The Greeks borrowed many Aramaic words and changed their
form into Greek expressions, just as the English and Germans
borrowed hundreds of Latin words, and Latins borrowed from
the Greek. Both Armenians and Arabs also borrowed this
Aramaic word. The Arabs used the Aramaic word *porkana*
for "salvation"; they call it *porkan,* while the Armenians call it
perqueton.

The Holy Spirit was to guide and strengthen the apostles and
their followers, who were soon to be bereaved, and comfort
them for their great loss. Moreover, it would enlighten those
who were living in darkness and bring them to the Christian
truth. (Luke 24:49)

31. JESUS' PEACE

Peace I leave with you, my peace I give unto you: not
as the world giveth, give I unto you. Let not your heart
be troubled, neither let it be afraid.

John 14:27

The peace of Jesus Christ is the just, sure and everlasting
peace, that is, the peace of God which passes human understanding. It is not the kind of unconditional and unjust peace
which the kings and princes of this world offer to one another,
after the one has defeated the other. Such unconditional peace
does not endure, because when the defeated become strong
again, they avenge themselves.

Jesus was not only leaving his peace with his disciples to
protect them. No, it was peace of mind, peace of soul he left
with them; the peace which caused them to surrender themselves to God. Indeed, all the disciples were sooner or later to
suffer for the sake of the gospel because they had surrendered
their bodies and their souls to God. The Aramaic word *shalam*
and the Hebrew word *shalom* means "I surrender," that is,
"I place everything under the care of God."

The peace of God is hard to understand simply because the
strong make peace with the weak, the great become servants.
Men pray for their enemies and bless those who hate them.
Such a simple way of life is practical, but difficult for the proud
rulers of this world to accept.

32. POLITICAL AND RELIGIOUS POWER

> Hereafter I will not talk much with you: for the prince
> of this world cometh, and hath nothing in me.
>
> John 14:30

The "prince of this world," the Roman Emperor, had nothing against Jesus, who had committed no crime and broken no state law. But the princes of this world, the political and religious authorities, were accustomed to persecute and even put to death any person who opposed them, regardless of any guilt or crime, just as King Herod did to John the Baptist. The King had nothing against John, but had him beheaded in order to please his wife.

Jesus was to be crucified for no crime. An innocent man was to suffer at the hands of the sinful. As Pilate said, he had done nothing worthy of death.

33. LIFE ETERNAL

> And this is life eternal, that they might know thee the only
> true God, and Jesus Christ, whom thou hast sent.
>
> John 17:3

Jesus, in this instance, states that the only way to secure everlasting life is to believe that God, his Father, is the only true God, and there is no other god beside Him; moreover, to believe in Jesus Christ, whom God has sent to bring people to the way of God. The first of the old commandments is, "Hear, O Israel, the Lord our God is one Lord . . ." (Deut. 6:4, Mark 12:29)

To believe in Jesus Christ is to believe in his way, his method of prayer, his religion, salvation and worship of God.

All other ways and the false philosophies which people sought as a means of salvation were misleading and destructive. Jesus had been leading the people to the religion which God had revealed to the prophets. (Isa. 53:11)

34. JESUS PROMISES A PLACE

Father, I will that they also, whom thou hast given me, be with me where I am; that they may behold my glory, which thou hast given me: for thou lovedst me before the foundation of the world.

John 17:24

The reference here is to the Day of Resurrection and the life hereafter. Jesus here implies that God would grant a place in His heavenly kingdom for the men who had accepted him, left everything, and had believed in him. This is because these disciples and followers were called by God and guided to follow Jesus. To be where he is means to be in heaven, so that they might see his glory and know how God loved him before the world was created.

In the East, a good lord who loves his faithful servants always sees that they are treated as he is; they sleep where he sleeps and eat what he eats.

35. BORN TO DIE ON THE CROSS

Pilate therefore said unto him, Art thou a king then? Jesus answered, Thou sayest that I am a king. To this end was I born, and for this cause came I into the world, that I should bear witness unto the truth. Every one that is of the truth heareth my voice.

John 18:37

Jesus, prior to his entry into the holy city, knew that he would suffer death on the cross. He knew that he would be rejected by the people of Jerusalem and be betrayed by one of his own disciples, arrested, judged and condemned to die on the cross.

But Jesus also knew that the cross was his destiny and the crown of victory. The Hebrew prophets had foreseen his rejection and death. The cross was the only means whereby he could change the sword into meekness and hatred into love, and thus save mankind. In other words, his death on the cross was to reveal to humanity the new way, the way of meekness and love.

Naturally, Jesus' humanity wanted to escape the horrible death on the cross, but his spirit was aware that death on the cross was his destiny. The Scripture must be fulfilled, and the cross must be given a new meaning.

A few days later, when Jesus stood before Pilate in the judgment hall, he said to the governor that he had come into the world that he might bear witness concerning the truth, that is to say, suffer death for the sake of the truth.

While he was on the cross he cried out, "My God, my God, for this purpose you have kept me or spared me." That is to say, the cross was his destiny. (See Matt. 27:46, Mark 15:34.)

Peter in his first Epistle says, "Who [Jesus Christ] verily was foreordained for this very purpose before the foundation of the world, and was manifest in these last times for your sakes." (I Pet. 1:20, Eastern text)

Moreover, Jesus had said, "Now my soul is disturbed, and what shall I say? O my Father, deliver me from this hour; but for this cause I came to this very hour." (John 12:27, Eastern text)

36. PILATE HAD NO POWER

Jesus answered, Thou couldest have no power at all against me, except it were given thee from above: therefore he that delivered me unto thee hath the greater sin.

John 19:11

The reference here is to the high priest, for it was he who delivered Jesus to Pilate. Therefore, his sin was greater than that of Pilate and the men who were to crucify him. Moreover, the high priest had access to the Scriptures, but the governor was not acquainted with Jewish theology. In the eyes of the high priest, Jesus was guilty unto death, but in the eyes of Pilate he was innocent.

All governments are of God. It is He who gives them power and glory, and He who sends them away empty.

Pilate was a military governor. He had to comply with the imperial policy and the wishes of the people over whom he was ruling, or answer to the emperor. According to Jesus, God had given the authority to Pilate. It was prophesied that the Messiah must die on the cross. Peter says it was preordained from the foundation of the world that the Messiah must suffer these things. (I Pet. 1:20)

37. THE HOUR OF THE CRUCIFIXION

And it was the preparation of the passover, and about the
sixth hour: and he saith unto the Jews, Behold your King!
John 19:14

The authors of three Gospels agree on the hour of the
crucifixion, but the author of the fourth, St. John, does not. "It
was Friday of the Passover, and it was about the sixth hour;
and he [Pilate] said to the Jews, Behold your king!" says John.
The sixth hour would be twelve o'clock our time. The authors
of other Gospels say it was the third hour. The third hour would
be nine o'clock in the morning, our time. (See Mark 15:33,
Luke 23:44.)

We must remember that all of Jesus' disciples, except John,
had fled. John was the only one present when Jesus was crucified. The other disciples received their information from others
who had been in Jerusalem on that fatal Friday. We must also
remember that in those days there were no watches or clocks.
Time was measured by the slant of the shadows of the cliffs and
trees and the crowing of the cock.

Then, too, Easterners are not concerned with exact time.
We know that during such a great tragedy no one would be
mindful of time, or even care to know the exact hour or
minute of the crucifixion, but all the apostles one way or another
agree that it was on Friday, after the passover. Some of the
disciples may have counted the time from the hour when Jesus
was delivered to Pilate; others from when he was crucified.
There is no theological point in this.

tion of the passover, and about the
.ch unto the Jews, Behold your King!

John 19:14

Erota means "weekend day," that is, Friday. The Jews
called it the sixth day. According to Jewish custom, at 6:01 P.M.
the Sabbath dawns. The Hebrew week, like that of the Chaldeans, starts with the first day, Sunday, and ends with the sixth
day, Friday. Sabbath, or the seventh day, is the holy day.

According to the Mosaic laws, bodies of victims who had been
crucified must not remain on their crosses on the Sabbath, but
must be lowered from the cross and buried.

Jesus and his disciples ate the passover on Thursday, and not
on Friday, as some scholars erroneously teach. This error is
caused by the fact that Friday at times is also called the preparation day, that is, preparation for the Sabbath. This is because
the Jews cannot cook food or do any other work on the Sabbath.

Jesus died on the cross on Friday, and rose up early Sunday
morning, while it was dark. (John 20:1)

39. SINS FORGIVEN

Whose soever sins ye remit, they are remitted unto them;
and whose soever sins ye retain, they are retained.

John 20:23

The disciples, after Jesus had given them courage and they
had received the Holy Spirit, were empowered to heal the
sick and to forgive sins. According to the Jewish concept of

God's way in the Old Testament, God can forgive through intermediaries, such as the high priests. But New Testament, the new order, the disciples and their cessors were granted the power to forgive sins and even raise the dead.

The term "sin" means "transgression against the law," or "deviation from truth or justice." Any human act which causes harm to other men and women around us is sin. Nevertheless, some sins are offenses which can be easily forgiven and forgotten; others are mortal sins, such as murder, blasphemy and adultery. These can be forgiven, but only providing that those who have committed them are willing to repent and make restitution. Offenses are mere faults, misdemeanors which are often committed unknowingly and are therefore forgivable.

According to Jesus' teachings, one does not have to offer animal sacrifices and other offerings in order to seek forgiveness of sins. This power was already granted Jesus' disciples and their followers by means of the Word, just as Jesus himself did when he said, "Your sins are forgiven, go and sin no more." A sincere penitent will be forgiven and restored. (Matt. 16:19)

40. PETER'S LOYALTY

So when they had dined, Jesus saith to Simon Peter, Simon, son of Jonas, lovest thou me more than these? He saith unto him, Yea, Lord; thou knowest that I love thee. He saith unto him, Feed my lambs.

John 21:15

The Aramaic word *khoba,* "love," is derived from *khob,* "debt." In Aramaic the word "love" has a different meaning than in other languages. It means a debt, but also love. When used for "love," it is used in a spiritual sense, and has no connection with physical love or sex. Love is a debt we owe to God our Creator and to our fellow man. It is a debt that one generation owes to another.

All epistles in Aramaic start with the phrase, "My beloved." Jesus spoke these words to Peter after his resurrection. When Peter had returned to his old occupation, he had seemingly forgotten that he had traveled for three years with Jesus, whom he had called the Christ, the son of the living God.

While the large pile of fish which they had just caught was lying on the seaside, Jesus looked at Simon Peter, then pointed his right hand at the fish and said, "Do you love me more than this large catch of fish?," implying, "You have deserted your mission and resumed your old business." Jesus did not say, as some translators hint, "Do you love me more than these other disciples?" What he meant was, "Do you love me more than these material things?" Simon Peter affirmed his loyalty to his master, and understood what was being said.

This verse is misunderstood by Western scholars. They maintain that Jesus said, "Do you love me more than the other disciples?" Jesus had admonished them to love one another, that is, never to quarrel among themselves or resort to rivalry. (Matt. 26:33)

41. OTHERS WILL TIE YOUR GIRDLE

> Verily, verily, I say unto thee, When thou wast young,
> thou girdedst thyself, and walkedst whither thou would-
> est: but when thou shalt be old, thou shalt stretch forth
> thy hands, and another shall gird thee, and carry thee
> whither thou wouldest not.
>
> John 21:18

"Another shall gird thee" means, "You will lose your liberty, and you will be in prison; your hands will be tied."

In the East, prisoners were usually chained and their hands tied. Today only the more dangerous prisoners are chained. Moreover, when prisoners are taken to court for trial, the jailer puts their girdles on them. This custom prevailed in many parts of the East until World War II, and is still practiced in some of the backward countries, where the government authorities are trying hard to stop crime.

Jesus predicted that the day would come when Simon Peter, the shepherd of his flock, would be arrested and, with his hands tied behind him, be thrown into prison. On the other hand, he hinted that John would live long and see Jesus' kingdom established. Evidently Peter died before John. Peter's death was foretold symbolically by Jesus.

42. JOHN LIVED A LONGER LIFE

Jesus saith unto him, If I will that he tarry till I come, what is that to thee? follow thou me.

John 21:22

Jesus loved John so much that he wished John would live until his coming. "Till I come" means Jesus' second coming, and also the coming of his kingdom. (Matt. 16:27)

Jesus was repudiated as the Messiah, Christ, judged, convicted and crucified as a malefactor. Humanly speaking, he died a defeated man, but he was soon to come to power and glory. In Aramaic, when a defeated man recovers from his losses and regains his strength and glory, we say, "He has come back," or, "He has risen." Moreover, when a political leader loses his power we say, "He is dead." When he returns to power, we say, "He has risen," or, "He has made a return," which means he has succeeded.

Jesus did not mean that John would be living when he returned. Such a remark is generally mere wishful thinking. We often say, "I pray you will live a thousand years." Jesus said that no one would know the hour and the day of his coming, but that his coming would be like that of a thief who comes in the night.

John saw the Christian religion spreading in many lands. He saw the Gospels written. He died in the year A.D. 90, but Peter had died before him.

Peter took Jesus' words literally, and wondered why he was not included. What Jesus means by "What is that to you?" is, "I am talking to John," and that is all. Prior to Jesus' death there was some rivalry among the disciples over leadership. They wondered who would succeed him. He even upbraided some of them because of this.

The Acts of the Apostles

1. JESUS' SECOND COMING

Which also said, Ye men of Galilee, why stand ye gazing up into heaven? this same Jesus, which is taken up from you into heaven, shall so come in like manner as ye have seen him go into heaven.

Acts 1:11

The second coming of Jesus will be a spiritual coming, that is, he will come in a spiritual body, free from all physical limitations. Moreover, the people's consciousness will be raised to a spiritual level, so that every eye will see nothing but good. In other words, it will be a spiritual life and a spiritual kingdom.

The apostles saw Jesus' ascension with their human eyes. In other words, he appeared to them in a manner whereby they would recognize him. Jesus rose in a spiritual body, but appeared to the disciples in the way they had known him formerly. Spirit can manifest itself in any form or manner. The prophets conversed with God in spirit and in visions.

At Jesus second coming the whole world will recognize him. His kingdom will be established, and the world will be ready to receive him. Jesus assured his disciples of his triumphant return. On the other hand, he also told them he would remain with them until the end, and that whenever two or three were gathered in his name he would be there among them. (See John 14:3, I Tim. 1:10, and Rev. 1:7.)

2. UNIVERSE MOURNS

And I will shew wonders in heaven above, and signs in the earth beneath; blood, and fire, and vapour of smoke: The sun shall be turned into darkness, and the moon into blood, before that great and notable day of the Lord come.

Acts 2:19–20

"Darkness," in this instance, means mourning," "disaster," and "calamity." The term "blood" means "death and destruction." The ancients believed that nature shared in man's joys and tragedies.

Even today these terms of speech are very prevalent in Semitic languages. When kings, princes, or men of nobility die, professional mourners, in their songs of mourning and lamentation, portray the sun and the moon as refusing to give light, sharing in the tragedy. The people do not take these terms literally. They know they are written to reveal the magnitude of the calamity. (See Joel 2:30, Matt. 24:29.)

3. GOD RAISED JESUS

Whom God hath raised up, having loosed the pains of
death: because it was not possible that he should be
holden of it.

Acts 2:24

The Aramaic text reads, ". . . having destroyed the pains
of death, because it was not possible for the Sheol to hold him."
Sheol is a powerful place from which no one has ever been able
to escape. But Jesus through his resurrection destroyed the
power of sin, death and Sheol, and gave to life a new synthesis,
and to religion a new meaning.

Death was painful to those who did not know that God has
power over it and over Sheol. But death holds no fear for
those who live in the realm of the spirit, and believe that God
is the only power in the universe. When we understand death as
a function of nature and life eternal, death and the grave lose
their power.

4. ACCORDING TO THE FLESH

Men and brethren, let me freely speak unto you of the patriarch David, that he is both dead and buried, and his sepulchre is with us unto this day.

Therefore being a prophet, and knowing that God had sworn with an oath to him, that of the fruit of his loins, according to the flesh, he would raise up Christ to sit on his throne . . .

Acts 2:29–30

The term "according to the flesh" means "carnal, earthly and terrestrial." Jesus the man was supposed to be a descendant of David. (Ps. 132:11)

The promise made to David was also a spiritual promise. The term "seed" in Aramaic also means "teaching." For example, Abraham is called the father of all believers in God, and yet not all of his descendants were heirs of the promise. Only those who believed in the faith of Abraham were known as the children of Abraham. (See article on Seed, *Old Testament Light,* Gen. 17:7.)

King David was the symbol of the highest loyalty to God. David, though he sinned and committed many crimes, always repented and turned to God. Jesus' loyalty to God was even greater.

These promises are spiritual, for David's dynastic line ceased in 586 B.C., when Jerusalem was destroyed by the Chaldean Army. Since that time there has never been an heir of the flesh of David to sit on his throne. The term in this instance is spiritual. On the other hand, the term "son of David" was also commonly used, meaning "like David." In the East, a great warrior is often called the son of a great and famous warrior who might have lived many centuries before. This is the greatest honor that can be bestowed upon him.

Moreover, David lived a thousand years before Jesus. The Messiah was expected to be a great conqueror like David, and to deliver the Jews from their oppression. Christ, the Spirit, is the Son of God, and he existed even before Abraham.

Luke tells us, "He will be great, and he will be called the Son of the Highest, and the Lord will give him the throne of his father David." (Luke 1:32) Meanwhile, Luke does not trace Jesus through the royal line of the kings of Judah; he traces him through Nathan, a son of David. Jesus Christ was greater than David; the latter called him "Lord."

5. FAITH IN HIS NAME

And his name through faith in his name hath made this man strong, whom ye see and know: yea, the faith which is by him hath given him this perfect soundness in the presence of you all.

Acts 3:16

In the Eastern text this passage reads, "Faith in his name has healed this man, whom you see and know . . . it is faith in Jesus which has granted this healing before you all."

The term "faith in his name" in this instance means belief in his teaching, his way, or his method of approach to God. In other words, we must pray to God as Jesus prayed, and look to God as a Father, as Jesus did, and love our enemies as Jesus loved.

Moreover, "faith in his name" means to believe that Jesus Christ is the promised Messiah, who was sent by God. The apostles used the same method of healing which they had learned from their master. They did what they had seen him do. (I Peter 1:21)

6. REPENTANCE

> Repent ye therefore, and be converted, that your sins may
> be blotted out, when the times of refreshing shall come
> from the presence of the Lord;
> And he shall send Jesus Christ, which before was preached
> unto you.
>
> Acts 3:19–20

When their sins are blotted out, sinners are relieved of the
heavy burdens they have been carrying. Thereafter they find
themselves in a state of harmony and tranquility. After they
have repented and cleansed their hearts, then Christ, God's
truth, dwells in them.

As long as evil forces dominate man's heart and mind, truth
cannot come, for truth and error cannot dwell together. Even
as fire and water are contrary to one another, truth and error,
evil and good, cannot be placed in the same container.

When truth comes in, error destroys itself.

7. ANGEL OPENED THE DOOR

> But the angel of the Lord by night opened the prison
> doors, and brought them forth, and said.
>
> Acts 5:19

The term "angel" means "God's messenger," "a pious man,"
"an ambassador," "an innocent man."

In the East, miraculous acts are generally attributed to higher
powers. Angels are seen in dreams and visions. They appear at
night or in a trance.

Angels are spirits. They have no physical bodies, but in a dream they appear like men and converse like men. They appeared to Mary, to Joseph, to Gideon, to Daniel, and to many other holy men.

The apostles were helped by God. The door was opened in a mysterious, miraculous way. God, Truth, must have intervened. The host of the angels of the Lord encompass round about them that worship Him, and deliver. (Ps. 34:7, Eastern text)

8. HELLENTISTIC JEWS

And in those days, when the number of the disciples was multiplied, there arose a murmuring of the Grecians against the Hebrews, because their widows were neglected in the daily ministration.

Acts 6:1

The term "Greek," in this instance, means "Hellenistic Jews," that is, the Jews who were Greek-minded. In those days, all Jews who did not live strictly by the Mosaic law and its ordinances were called Greeks, or foreigners. In Turkey, all Moslems who drink liquor and eat forbidden foods are called either *Aleman, Fransai* or *agnabi,* that is to say, "German," "French," or "foreigner."

At this early time, Christianity was restricted to the people of the Jewish religion and to the members of the ten tribes. These people for centuries had been expecting the coming of the Messiah, the great deliverer. On the other hand, the Greeks knew nothing about the Messianic promises, nor had they heard of the Hebrew prophets and patriarchs. The Greeks, like the Romans, were aliens, and enemies of the Jews.

One of the men whom the apostles chose to administer food supplies and other help was Stephen, a Jew. A great many

157

Jews used Greek and Roman names, as today they use English, German and Russian names.

Stephen started his address with the calling of Abraham. (Acts 7:1–12) He also addressed the Jews as "men, brethren," that is, members of the same religion and race.

Today, the Arab Christians in Palestine, who are members of the Greek Orthodox Church, call themselves Greeks, that is, Greek by religion. They do this in order to distinguish themselves from Christian Arabs who call themselves Roman Catholics, and from others who call themselves Monophysites and Maronites. Converts to the Congregational Church call themselves "Americans." The Hellenistic Jews were considered pagans by some of the strict Jews.

Even today it is hard to administer relief in Palestine. The members of some religions and sects complain, charging that there is discrimination against their people.

9. STEPHEN WAS A JEW

And Stephen, full of faith and power, did great wonders and miracles among the people.

Then there arose certain of the synagogue, which is called the synagogue of the Libertines, and Cyrenians, and Alexandrians, and of them of Cilicia and of Asia, disputing with Stephen.

Acts 6:8–9

Stephen was a Jew who, like many other Jews, had become a convert to Christianity. At this early time, nearly all of Jesus' disciples and followers were members of the Jewish religion. Jesus had come first to the Jews. The reformation of religion was to take place, and the seeds of the Christian gospel were to be sown in the Jewish soil. This is because Jesus was following in the footsteps of the Hebrew prophets who had hailed him as the Prince of Peace, the Messiah. Jesus had come to fulfill the law and the prophets.

The charges against Stephen were these: "We have heard him say blasphemous words against Moses and against God." (Acts 6:11) Had Stephen been a Greek by nationality, the Jewish council could not have condemned him for blaspheming against the Mosaic law. But Stephen was a faithful Christian and a strict Jew. He was also a learned man. This is why the priests and scribes were alarmed at his utterances, which they construed as blasphemy.

Stephen in his wonderful defense before the council gave the Jewish leaders a concise outline of Hebrew history, their fathers and their Messianic hopes. (Acts 7)

It is obvious that the Jews could not put a Greek to death by stoning. Only Jews who were found guilty of breaking the Mosaic law were thus punished. Even Jesus, being a Galilean, could not be put to death by the Jews. All races and people other than the Jews were under the jurisdiction of the Roman imperial government. But the high priest, as an ethnarch, had political authority over the Jews in Judea. Thus, Stephen was stoned without consulting the Roman authorities.

10. A GREATER PROPHET

This is that Moses, which said unto the children of Israel, A prophet shall the Lord your God raise up unto you of your brethren, like unto me; him shall ye hear.

Acts 7:37

The Christians believed this prophecy was fulfilled in Jesus of Nazareth, who was the greatest prophet since the days of Moses, and whose coming Moses had predicted. (Deut. 18:15)

159

The term "of your brethren" is somewhat difficult to explain. Some people wonder why Moses did not say, "from among you." Moses was addressing the Israelite people. The term "brother" was often used to mean "people who are kindred of the Jews." For example, Abraham said to Lot, his nephew, "We are brothers." The Edomites, the descendants of Esau, were also brothers of the Jews.

Some people are led to believe that the term "brothers" in this instance means the Galileans and the Arabs, who are kindred of the Jews. The Moslems maintain that this reference was to their prophet Mohammed, a descendant of Ishmael, son of Abraham. (Gen. 17:20)

Be that as it may, Jesus is generally acclaimed as the greater prophet. He performed greater miracles and wonders than any who had preceded him or who came after.

11. THE TABERNACLE OF MALCOM

Yea, ye took up the tabernacle of Moloch, and the star of your god Remphan, figures which ye made to worship them: and I will carry you away beyond Babylon.

Acts 7:43

The term *mashkna*, or in Arabic, *maskan*, "tabernacle" or "tent," refers to the dwelling place of Malcom, the god of the Ammonites. This god, like the God of the Israelites, had a tabernacle in which he was worshiped by the tribal peoples who migrated from one place to another, carrying the tabernacle and the god with them. This temporal sanctuary was made of goat hair. Even today, the Emirs of Arabian nomadic tribes have such a sanctuary for worship and for assembly which they carry with them wherever they go.

In the wilderness, the Israelites at Sinai carried the tabernacle of God from one place to another for a period of forty years, but when they departed from the true God, they carried the tabernacles of Malcom and other strange gods.

Now the Israelites had left their God and were worshiping Malcom, the god of the Ammonites, thus carrying his tabernacle. They also were worshiping the star of the god of Derphan.

12. JESUS OF NAZARETH

And he said, Who art thou, Lord? And the Lord said, I am Jesus whom thou persecutest: it is hard for thee to kick against the pricks.

Acts 9:5

When Paul wondered who was talking to him, Jesus said to him, "I am Jesus of Nazareth whom you persecute." (See Eastern text Peshitta.) Other versions for some unknown reason have omitted "of Nazareth." Jesus would not have said, "I am Jesus," for Jesus is a very common name, and in the East when a man's name is common, his village is mentioned.

Moreover, Jesus was known as "the prophet from Nazareth in Galilee." He was also called "the Galilean." (Luke 23:6) Matthew tells us that Jesus will be called "a Nazarene." (Matt. 2:22–23) Moreover, the Pharisees and scribes called him a Galilean; they said, "No prophet shall arise from Galilee." Philip also used "of Nazareth," as we read, "Philip found Nathanael, and said to him, we have found that Jesus, the son of Joseph, of Nazareth, is the one concerning whom Moses wrote in the law and the prophets." (John 1:45–46) Jesus never denied his town and the region wherein he was reared.

13. WORSHIPING PETER

And as Peter was coming in, Cornelius met him, and fell
down at his feet and worshipped him.
But Peter took him up, saying, Stand up; I myself also
am a man.

Acts 10:25–26

According to Eastern custom, when people meet a holy
man or a high government official, they bow down to him as a
token of respect. The Aramaic word *saghad,* and the Arabic
word *sagada* mean "to bow down in respect." The more important the person, the lower the bow. For example, for a king
or a prince, the people bow until their foreheads touch the
ground. Moreover, Nestorian Christians and Moslems, when
they pray, bow on their knees until their foreheads touch the
ground. This is the reason that Cornelius fell down at Peter's
feet.

Cornelius was not really worshiping Peter as he would worship God; he was paying homage to the man of God who had
been a disciple of Jesus. But Peter, a true follower of Jesus
Christ, did not want this high government official to bow to
him. Jesus had told his disciples that the greatest among them
should be their servant, in order to show his humility. Therefore,
Peter declined the honors and the glory which were sought by
religious and political men in his day.

Other religious men demanded such homage from their followers, especially in the religions which recognized an emperor
as their god. This is why Cornelius bowed to the ground as
though he was worshiping a human god.

14. JUDGE OF THE LIVING
AND THE DEAD

And he commanded us to preach unto the people, and to
testify that it is he which was ordained of God to be the
Judge of quick and dead.

Acts 10:42

Jesus, on the last day, will judge both the living and the
dead. The dead will rise and, together with the living, will come
before the judgment seat to answer for their works. Jesus said,
"For the Father judgeth no man, but hath committed all judgment unto the Son." (John 5:22)

The Scripture tells us that the good and the bad will be
separated, as a shepherd separates the sheep from the goats and
as a farmer separates the tares from the wheat. At the end,
truth will expose the forces of evil, and evil will destroy itself.
(See Rom. 14:9.)

15. SIMON THE CARPENTER

Now there were in the church that was at Antioch certain
prophets and teachers; as Barnabas, and Simeon that was
called Niger, and Lucius of Cyrene, and Manaen, which
had been brought up with Herod the tetrarch, and Saul.

Acts 13:1

Simon Niger is an Aramaic name which means "Simon the
carpenter." *Niger* in colloquial speech is often pronounced
najjar, that is, "one who works with wood." Some biblical authorities, not knowing Aramaic or Arabic, think that *Niger* means
"Negro" or "nigger." Today there are many preachers who use

this word in their sermons, stating that a Negro helped Jesus carry his cross to Golgotha. These men do not even realize that "Negro" is derived from a Latin word, not Semitic.

James the junior in Mark 15:40 is called James the less. A commentator states that he was a very short and small man. *Zora* in Aramaic means "younger," that is, "junior." Even today, two men with the same name are called *zora*, "the younger," and *gora*, "the older." Moreover, at times we call men by the name of their occupation or their village or some other association, like Simon the tanner, Simon the leper, Mary of Magdala, James the junior, Simon the elder, and so on.

16. PAUL'S NAME CHANGED

Then Saul (who also is called Paul) filled with the Holy Ghost, set his eyes on him,

Acts 13:9

The name *Saul* in Semitic languages means "to ask." Evidently, Paul was named for King Saul, who like himself was of the tribe of Benjamin.

In the Book of Samuel we are told that when Jesse, Saul's father, had lost his donkeys he sent his son, Saul, to find them. And while Saul was searching for the donkeys he came to Rama and asked the prophet Samuel to help him find them. This name might have been given to Saul after this event. This is because Samuel told him that he would be king over Israel.

In the East, when a general triumphs in battle, he is generally given a new name. General Inono, the former President of the Turkish Republic, was first known as Ismit Pacha, but when he defeated the Greek Army he was given the name Inono, the namesake of the place of battle.

On the other hand, many biblical names indicate a great event that had taken place at the time the person was born.

This is not all. In the East, when people change their religion, they frequently also change their names. For example, when a Christian in the Holy Land becomes a Moslem he is given a new name, usually the name of a great Moslem, and often the name of the prophet Mohammed.

Paul (Pul) is the name of an Assyrian King who invaded Israel in 771 B.C. No doubt Paul changed the name under which he had persecuted the Christians to another name.

(This practice prevails today in America. When a Christian Negro becomes a Moslem, his name is changed to a Moslem name.)

17. BY HIM

For in him we live, and move, and have our being; as certain also of your own poets have said, For we are also his offspring.

Acts 17:28

In this instance, the Aramaic word *Beh* means "by him." We often say, "He does these things by the command of the king," or, "The governor stands by him," that is, supports him.

The term "in him" literally means "by him"—that is to say, by God's grace, his power, his method, or through him.

Through Jesus Christ we become the children of the living God, because our origin is of God, who created us in His image and likeness. This spiritual sonship was lost, but Jesus rediscovered it. Thus, through him or by means of him we call God our Father, and all of us become brothers.

18. BREAKING OF BREAD

And upon the first day of the week, when the disciples came together to break bread, Paul preached unto them, ready to depart on the morrow; and continued his speech until midnight.

Acts 20:7

Khad-beshaba, in Aramaic, means "the first day of the week." The last day of the week is called the Sabbath, the seventh day. This is the day the Lord God ordained as the day of rest. (Ex. 20:10)

Jesus and his disciples and their followers kept the Sabbath. They fasted and went to the temple to pray like other Jews.

The Christians broke bread on their first day of the week, Sunday, because they could not meet for instructions on the Sabbath, which was a holy day. The Jews rested from all their labors on that day. Some of them even refused to walk, or to answer a call. Their food was prepared on Friday, so that they need not do any manual work on the Sabbath.

The Christians met on the first day of the week not only to worship but also to teach. At this time, a few Scriptures were available, but most of the people were illiterate. The disciples and their followers met for instruction at the homes of certain converts. They brought their food with them, and after the instruction they broke bread together. The Eastern term "breaking bread" means "eating together." In the East, bread is baked in round, thin loaves. The people break it into pieces with their hands, and dip it into the dish while eating. They could not do this on the Sabbath, as such an act would have been considered labor, and hence, the breaking of the Sabbath.

19. NAZARENES

For we have found this man a pestilent fellow, and a
mover of sedition among all the Jews throughout the world,
and a ringleader of the sect of the Nazarenes.

Acts 24:5

Prior to Paul's conversion and the expansion of Christianity among the Gentiles, the Aramaeans, Assyrians and Arabs,
the followers of Jesus were called Nazarenes. (Matt. 2:22–23,
Mark 14:66)

In the East, the followers of a teacher are called by their
teacher's name, and often the teacher is known by the name of
his town, especially when there are several teachers with the
same name—for example, Jesus of Nazareth, Joseph of Ramtha,
Simon of Cyrene, and Mary of Magdala. Even today, many
Easterners use the name of their towns as surnames.

The term "Christian" was used later, at Antioch. (Acts 15)
In Aramaic, it is *mashikaye*, which means "anointed with oil."
The term "Christ" means "the anointed one." "Christians" is a
direct translation of the term *mashikaye*. The Arabs called the
Christians *nossara*, and the Turks, *nosrani*. The followers of
Islam were nicknamed "Mohammedans," that is, followers of
the prophet Mohammed.

Paul was accused by his enemies of being ringleader of the
sect of the Nazarenes, the followers of Jesus of Nazareth.
Jesus was also accused as a revolutionary and disturber of the
peace in Palestine. He had told his disciples in advance that
they would be persecuted and reviled. (Matt. 5:11, John 15:20)

20. BRIBES WERE COMMON

> He hoped also that money should have been given him
> of Paul, that he might loose him: wherefore he sent for him
> the oftener, and communed with him.
>
> Acts 24:26

In the olden days, governorships, judgeships and other high positions were obtained by paying a large sum of money, which was called a present. This custom prevailed in many lands until World War I. High government officials and judges expected gifts before performing their duties or extending favors. Some people sent gifts a few days before seeing the official. These bribes were always called gifts. (Ex. 23:8, Ps. 26:10)

Jesus told his disciples the parable of the poor widow whom the judge refused to see because she had nothing to offer him, but she persisted until she compelled him to see her. (Luke 18:2–3) The Roman governor, knowing that Paul had a great many followers, expected a large sum of money from him, but Paul had no money to bribe him, so he stayed in jail until a new governor arrived.

21. PAUL EXHORTS THE PASSENGERS

But after long abstinence Paul stood forth in the midst of them, and said, Sirs, ye should have hearkened unto me, and not have loosed from Crete, and to have gained this harm and loss.

And now I exhort you to be of good cheer: for there shall be no loss of any man's life among you, but of the ship.

Acts 27:21–22

Paul was a prisoner on board the ship. In such emergencies, the prisoners are not chained, especially those who are imprisoned for minor offenses. Paul was not a criminal. He had appealed to Caesar, and he was on board a ship which was sailing for Rome, where he was to appear before the emperor.

Paul was free to mix with other people, and, being a preacher of the gospel of Jesus Christ and a believer in God, he tried to encourage the people during the shipwreck, assuring them that they would be safe. He had warned the sailors not to leave Crete. Moreover, Paul had been assured by an angel of God in a dream that he would stand before Caesar, and that no one would be lost in the shipwreck.

22. ANGEL COMMUNED WITH PAUL

For there stood by me this night the angel of God, whose I am, and whom I serve,

Saying, Fear not, Paul; thou must be brought before Caesar: and, lo, God hath given thee all them that sail with thee.

Acts 27:23–24

The Eastern (Aramaic) text reads, "For there has appeared to me this night the angel of God to whom I belong and whom I serve."

Paul in his vision saw the angel of God, who gave him counsel and encouragement. The Aramaic word *malahka* means "an angel," "God's counsel," "minister" or "messenger." In other words, God communed with Paul.

In the East, people believe that an angel rests upon the right shoulder of a man to protect, guide, and admonish him, which in reality means that Gods counsel is constantly available to those who trust in him and worship him. This is because God is the Father, who always loves, protects, and cares for His children.

23. PAUL AT APPII FORUM

Where we found brethren, and were desired to tarry with them seven days: and so we went toward Rome.
And from thence, when the brethren heard of us, they came to meet us as far as Appii forum, and The three taverns: whom when Paul saw, he thanked God, and took courage.

Acts 28:14–15

Apparently the Christians in Italy had established a center of Christianity in Rome. No doubt, most of these people were servants and slaves, Christians and Jews, who had been sold in Roman markets.

When Paul landed in southern Italy, at Puteoli, he was met by these Christian brethren. (Acts 28:13) Moreover, there was a Jewish synagogue and a Christian group in Rome, the imperial city.

Paul had been very eager to see these Christians and to lay his hands upon them, thus imparting to them the Christian gifts—the gifts of healing, prophesying, teaching, and preaching. (Rom. 15:29)

24. PAUL A HOUSE PRISONER IN ROME

And Paul dwelt two whole years in his own hired house, and received all that came in unto him.

Acts 28:30

Paul, before his arrival in Rome, met a number of Christians at Rhegium and Appii forum who had come to greet him and undoubtedly to assist him. Moreover, there were a great many Christians and Syrian Jews in Rome. Some of them were brought from Palestine as captives, some were merchants, and others were in the Roman Army.

Paul lived in a house which he had rented. The house was guarded by a soldier, who sat at the door or at the gate, as is the custom in the East when a political prisoner is made a house prisoner.

Paul was free to communicate with the Jews and receive callers. It must be remembered that Paul, in the eyes of the Romans, was not a criminal. He was delivered to the Romans by the Jews because of religious matters, in which the Romans had no interest or concern. The Romans could even have helped Paul. Today, in the East, if a Christian should be imprisoned because of his controversial beliefs, and delivered into a Moslem jail, the Moslems would assuredly be sympathetic toward him, and vice versa.

Tradition says that Paul was freed from jail and had left for Spain. There were many Jewish colonies in that country, and it was Paul's custom to visit the Jewish communities which were scattered throughout the Roman Empire, to preach to them the gospel of Jesus Christ. As we learn from his epistle to the Romans, he had planned to visit Spain. (Rom. 15:24-28) We know nothing more about Paul.

The Epistle of Paul the Apostle to the Romans

1. CHURCH IN ROME

For I long to see you, that I may impart unto you some
spiritual gift, to the end ye may be established.

Rom. 1:11

The first church in Rome was made up of captives,
servants, and soldiers. Thousands of Jews had been taken captive and sold in the slave markets. Among these Jews were
many devout Christians, the same Christians whom Paul himself had previously persecuted. When the Romans persecuted
the Jews and took them captive, they did not distinguish between
Jews and Christians. After all, the members of both religions
were Jewish by race; they were dressed alike, they looked alike;
and the Romans were not interested in what religion they belonged to.

Moreover, there were in Rome some Jewish and Aramaean
merchants who supplied Roman markets with fabricated ma-
terials, dry goods, hardware, and other products which were
produced in Damascus and other ancient and highly civilized
centers in the East.

Some of these Christians continued to worship at the Jewish synagogue for a long time. As far as they were concerned,
Christianity was a reformation of Judaism, and Jesus Christ
had come first for the Jews. This is why, whenever Paul spoke
in synagogues, some of these Jews immediately followed him.
They were the Jewish Christians. At this early time there were
few Aramaeans in the Church. Christianity was opposed by the
Greeks and the Romans.

Paul was eager to meet the church in Rome so that he might
impart to them spiritual gifts, knowledge, and the Christian
doctrine. After all, Paul was a great Jewish scholar and was
well versed in the Scriptures and in the Jewish religion and
law.

2. JUDGING ONE'S NEIGHBORS

Therefore thou art inexcusable, O man, whosoever thou art
that judgest: for wherein thou judgest another, thou con-
demnest thyself; for thou that judgest doest the same
things.
But we are sure that the judgment of God is according to
truth against them which commit such things.

Rom. 2:1-2

Paul admonishes the Roman Christians not to judge, that
is, criticize, one another unless the one who judges is free from
the things he condemns in the other. In Aramaic, the term
"judge" often means "to criticize others," even though the one
who judges does the same thing.

Paul, in this instance, is quoting from the Gospel of Matthew:
"Judge not, that you may not be judged," which in Aramaic
means, "Criticize not, that you may not be criticized." (Matt.
7:1-5) For example, how can one criticize another for smoking
cigarettes when he himself smokes cigars; or say to someone,
"Why do you drink wine?" when he himself is an alcoholic.
Indeed, one has to see and correct these evil habits first in
himself, before he can point them out in his neighbors. Jesus
said, "O hypocrites, first take out the beam from your own eye,
and then you will see clearly to get out the splinter from your
neighbor's eye." (Matt. 7:5)

3. HYPOCRITICAL TEACHERS

. . . An instructor of the foolish, a teacher of babes, which
hast the form of knowledge and of the truth in the law.
Rom. 2:20

The Eastern text reads, "An instructor of the foolish, a
teacher of children, you are the pattern of knowledge and of
truth as embodied in the law."

Paul here upbraids the teachers of religion, and in particular
the Jews who were reared in the Jewish Christian religion and
who knew the law of Moses and its ordinances, and yet acted
as blind guides.

These teachers of religion were the instructors of folly and
the teachers of children; that is, the teachers of the unlearned
men and women who were easily misled from the gospel of
Jesus Christ. These instructors tried to teach others, but they
themselves had failed to learn the truth of the gospel. Moreover,
instead of emphasizing the new religion, the gospel of Jesus
Christ, they exhorted the people to obey all the laws and
ordinances of Moses. But they themselves dishonored God and
Moses by breaking the same laws they taught others. (See Rom.
2:21–24, Matt. 7:1–5.)

4. NO ADVANTAGE IN CIRCUMCISION

> What advantage then hath the Jew? or what profit is there
> of circumcision?
>
> Rom. 3:1

There is no spiritual advantage in circumcision or in uncircumcision. The uncircumcision would not affect the faith of
believers in God or in Jesus Christ. Abraham believed in God
and was considered a righteous man before he was circumcised.
Circumcision was an ordinance which was given only to the
Jews. All the laws and ordinances could not make a person
perfect.

Christian believers are justified by their faith and good works.
God looks into the hearts of men and sees their good works,
not into the customs and rituals which they observe. No matter
how strictly a person may observe the law, he cannot be justified,
or reach perfection. (Job 3:33)

5. THE RIGHTEOUSNESS OF GOD

> God forbid: yea, let God be true, but every man a liar;
> as it is written, That thou mightest be justified in thy say-
> ings, and mightest overcome when thou art judged.
> But if our unrighteousness commend the righteousness of
> God, what shall we say? Is God unrighteous who taketh
> vengeance? (I speak as a man)
>
> Rom. 3:4–5

The Eastern (Aramaic) text reads, "Far be it; only God is
true and no man is wholly perfect; as it is written, That you

may be justified by your words, and triumph when you are judged. Now if our iniquity serves to establish the righteousness of God, what then shall we say? Is God unjust when he inflicts his anger? I speak as a man."

Unfortunately the translators of the King James version, from the Latin and Greek, were unable to understand what Paul meant here. The apostle, in this instance, tries to express many things at once. Peter tells us that there are certain things in Pauline epistles very difficult to understand. (II Pet. 3:16)

What Paul is trying to say is that no matter what a man does he cannot be justified, that is, declared righteous or sinless. We know this from the Book of Job. The men who argued with Job tried to convince him that he was not as righteous as he thought, because there is no one just or holy but God. Even Jesus, when he was called a good or wonderful master, said, "Why do you call me good? there is no one who is good except God." (Matt. 19:17, Eastern text)

Our iniquities reveal the righteousness of God and His abundant love. Just as darkness is compared with light, righteousness and iniquities are compared. It is because of our iniquities that we speak of God as a righteous judge. (See Ps. 7:11–17.) God is justified in His reproof. (Ps. 51:4)

6. OPEN SEPULCHERS

Their throat is an open sepulchre; with their tongues they have used deceit; the poison of asps is under their lips.

Rom. 3:13

This saying is a quotation from Psalm 5:9—"For there is no justice in their mouth; there is wickedness in them; their throat is an open sepulcher; they deceive with their tongues." (Eastern text)

177

"Their throat is an open sepulcher" means that they are full of evil things. In the East during wars and revolutions, sepulchers and graves are opened by enemies seeking treasures in the coffins of the princes and the rich, just as they do today in Egypt and other places. Some corpses are newly buried, and have a dreadful odor when the graves are opened. Such places were shunned by pious men, because they could not look at dead bodies.

Evil men and hypocrites are likened to open and bad-smelling sepulchers.

7. RECONCILIATIONS

For if, when we were enemies, we were reconciled to God by the death of his Son, much more, being reconciled, we shall be saved by his life.

Rom. 5:10

The term "enemies," in this instance, means "unbelievers in God's way." An unbeliever is one who rejects the truth and fights against it, and persecutes those who believe in it.

Jesus through his death on the cross reconciled us to God. Man had gone astray from God, but Jesus, through his death, revealed God's abundant love towards His children and reminded them that God was always seeking them as a shepherd seeks a lost sheep.

Now, having made peace with God, we will be saved by the life of Jesus Christ. That is to say, Jesus' life should be exemplified in our lives. (John 14:19, II Cor. 5:18)

It is not those who merely confess the name of Jesus Christ who will be saved, but those who hear his voice and then, turning to God, live the way Jesus Christ lived. That is, to say that Jesus died on the cross and that we believe in him and have faith is not enough. One has to do the works of Jesus. Christians will be known by their works, as a good tree is known by its fruits. (Rom. 5:17)

8. THE GIFT OF GOD

And not as it was by one that sinned, so is the gift: for the judgment was by one to condemnation, but the free gift is of many offences unto justification.
For if by one man's offence death reigned by one; much more they which receive abundance of grace and of the gift of righteousness shall reign in life by one, Jesus Christ.

Rom. 5:16–17

The Eastern text reads, "And the effect of the gift of God was greater than the effect of the offense of Adam; for while the judgment from one man's offense resulted in condemnation of many, the gift of God in forgiveness of sins resulted in righteousness to many more."

The reference here is to the physical death which was caused by transgression of the law at Eden (the moral law). Transgression of the moral law brought sin into the world, and the result of sin was death.

It was by one man, Adam, that sin and death reigned, so by one man and the grace of God through Jesus Christ shall salvation come to man. That is to say, as Adam and Eve brought sin into the world, so Jesus Christ will destroy sin by crushing the head of the serpent, devil or error.

9. SIN HAS NO POWER

For sin shall not have dominion over you: for ye are not
under the law, but under grace.

Rom. 6:14

When there was no law there was no sin. Sin came as the
result of breaking the law. The law said, "Do this" and "Do
not do that." Then, as the result of transgression of the law, sin
came into the world. Therefore, those who were without law
were not under sin, because for them sin was dormant.

Jesus by his death on the cross destroyed the power of sin
and death and brought salvation into the world by means of
obedience to God's way and by forgiveness of sin. As long as a
man was under the law, sin had dominion over him. This is
because he could not keep the whole law. One may abstain
from committing adultery, but he may lie against his neighbors,
or covet something which is not his. Man can only keep the
law in part; no one can keep all of it. Therefore man is saved
by the grace of God, Who, being the Father, saves His children
through His love. (I Cor. 9:21, Titus 2:14)

10. SPEAKING PLAINLY

I speak after the manner of men because of the infirmity
of your flesh: for as ye have yielded your members servants to uncleanness and to iniquity unto iniquity; even
so now yield your members servants to righteousness unto
holiness.
For when ye were the servants of sin, ye were free from
righteousness.

Rom. 6:19–20

"I speak after the manner of men" is an Eastern expression
which means, "I speak as a man," or, "humanly speaking." The
term "infirmity" is a mistranslation. It should read, "weakness of
your flesh," that is, human weakness, which is evidenced in
every phase of life.

11. FREED FROM THE LAW

Wherefore, my brethren, ye also are become dead to the
law by the body of Christ; that ye should be married to
another, even to him who is raised from the dead, that
we should bring forth fruit unto God.

Rom. 7:4

The term "law" in this instance means the Ten Commandments, the law which God gave to Moses on Mount Sinai.
(Ex. 20) This law has authority over a person as long as he
lives, just as a woman is bound by her husband as long as he is
alive.

When the people were under the law, sin had the power to

181

cause death. Now they were no longer under the law, but under the grace of God. That is to say, since the people died believing in Jesus Christ and rose up with him into a new life, the law had no more power over them, just as a dead husband has no more power over his wife.

The Christians are admonished to bear good fruits and live a new and spiritual life. (Rom. 6:14, Gal. 2:19)

12. LAW OF NATURE

But I see another law in my members, warring against the law of my mind, and bringing me into captivity to the law of sin which is in my members.

O wretched man that I am! who shall deliver me from the body of this death?

I thank God through Jesus Christ our Lord. So then with the mind I myself serve the law of God; but with the flesh the law of sin.

Rom. 7:23–25

Paul in this instance speaks of the law of nature, which is our physical body. This law constantly wars against the law of the mind, or the law of the spirit. This is because the physical body seeks things of its own, that is, physical desires. In the Garden of Gethsemane this law warred against the law of the spirit in Jesus Christ. Jesus' spirit was willing, but his body was weak and unwilling to die on the cross. Therefore, Jesus had to submit the interests of his physical body to the spirit. In other words, he rejected what the body was demanding, and left everything in the hands of God, his Father. The mortal body is always governed by physical laws and dominated by physical desires.

Spiritually, we are the servants of the law of God through Jesus Christ, but physically we are the servants of the law of sin. Whenever we break the law, sin becomes operative; and the result of sin is death. We attain our freedom from physical forces through our complete surrender to God through Jesus Christ. God is the author of both spiritual and natural laws, and has power over both. Jesus, while praying in Gethsemane, surrendered his human will to His divine will.

13. THE SPIRIT IS LIFE

And if Christ be in you, the body is dead because of sin; but the Spirit is life because of righteousness.
But if the Spirit of him that raised up Jesus from the dead dwell in you, he that raised up Christ from the dead shall also quicken your mortal bodies by his Spirit that dwelleth in you.

Rom. 8:10–11

Paul here explains that if the bodies of those who are Christians are dominated by Christ, then the physical, or the sinful, body is dead, because sin is dead.

The spirit continues to live because of the righteousness attained by Christians through the teachings of Jesus Christ. God will raise the bodies of the believers through the spirit of Jesus Christ, which is in them. And when the evil is destroyed, the spirit of Jesus Christ and the spirit of God will reign. Through the Christian gospel and the death of Jesus on the cross, both sin and the forces of evil have been subdued by the spirit of Jesus Christ. Neither sin nor death has power over those who live according to the gospel of Jesus Christ. (Rom. 8:4–5)

14. THE NEW MAN

For the earnest expectation of the creature waiteth for
the manifestation of the sons of God.

Rom. 8:19

The whole objective of Christianity is to restore man to
his former dignity and find his rightful place in the universe.
Man was created in the image and the likeness of God, but
transgression against the law, and sin, caused him to lose both
his divinity and his dignity. All mankind was earnestly expecting
a change in man, from evil to good and from unrighteousness
to righteousness.

The term *gilyana* means "revelation." When the sinful man is
gone, the true man will be revealed—the son of the living
God, endowed with all powers. Man's restoration will be
accomplished when evil forces are completely eradicated, and
when truth supplants error. Then there will be a new world,
a new Adam, and a new creation; the old creation will disappear. (II Pet. 3:13)

15. FIRST FRUITS OF THE SPIRIT

And not only they, but ourselves also, which have the first
fruits of the Spirit, even we ourselves groan within ourselves, waiting for the adoption, to wit, the redemption of
our body.

Rom. 8:23

The Eastern (Aramaic) text reads, "And not only they,
but ourselves also, who have the first fruits of the Spirit, even

we groan within ourselves, waiting for the adoption, that is, the salvation, of our bodies."

The Christians in Rome were the first fruits, or the first Jewish Christians in Italy to receive the gospel of Jesus Christ. Evidently, most of these Jews were brought in captivity to Rome. But having lived in a pagan land, they had not succeeded in reaching the perfection, as true Christians, to be called the sons of God. They had failed to destroy their sinful desires and the lusts of this material world completely. Therefore, they were waiting to know more about the gospel of Jesus Christ and to be adopted as the children of God through him.

Some of these Christian Jews, having been far away from their land and culture, had fallen victim to the corrupt teaching of pagan cults. Many of them were destroying their bodies with immorality and sensual pagan practices. In other words, they had fallen short of their goals as a Christian community living in a pagan city. They had not become a light to the pagan people around them.

Paul includes himself in the groan for the salvation of the body from the forces of evil; therefore, the Christians in Rome were not completely free from the strong desires of the flesh.

Jesus conquered the physical forces when he overcame the alluring rewards that Satan had offered him in the wilderness.

The Christians in Rome were to rise above the members of other religions and cults in order to prove their superiority over the pagan world, and to become examples of Jesus Christ. Jesus said, "By their works you shall know them."

16. THE HEIRS

Not as though the word of God hath taken none effect.
For they are not all Israel, which are of Israel.

Rom. 9:6

Jacob, whose surname is Israel (Prince of God), was the
father of many people. At the time Paul wrote this epistle,
the descendants of Judah, the son of Jacob, were heirs of the
promise. This is because they had remained loyal to Mosaic
law and the temple worship, and were therefore expecting the
coming of the promised Messiah. Most of the other descendants
of Jacob from his other sons had gone astray from the true
religion of their forefathers, into Baal worship, many years before
the captivity of Judah. Moreover, because of their disloyalty
to God's commandments and His religion, they had been taken
captive to Assyria. Now they were considered the lost sheep
from the house of Israel.

Therefore, even though these Israelites were descendants of
Israel in the flesh, they were not qualified to be his heirs in
the spirit, that is, heirs of the divine promises. The Word of
God was effective in that a remnant remained loyal to God's
way and His divine promises. And this remnant was called
the seed of Abraham. In Aramaic, the term "seed" also means
"teaching," "faith," or "religion." In Genesis we are told that
Abraham's descendants were to come through Isaac. (Gen.
21:12) In other words, the heirship is of the flesh but also of
the spirit.

Paul tells the Jewish Christians in Rome that not all the
descendants of Abraham are the children of Abraham and heirs
of the promise. Only the descendants of Isaac were heirs of
the promise; the descendants of Ishmael and Esau were not
heirs. Yet God blessed both Ishmael and Esau, because they
were the descendants of Abraham in the flesh.

The Aramaic term *zara*, "descendant," also means "seed,"
that is, "teaching." This is why Jesus said the kingdom of God

is like a mustard seed. Paul in this instance is proving that the only true descendants of Abraham are those who are loyal to his teaching, and not the descendants of the flesh.

We know from the Scriptures that Esau disqualified himself as an heir to his father, and also sold his birthright to his brother Jacob. The apostle tells us that the term "seed" does not always mean an offspring or descendant, but "an heir of the promise." Today many Arab, Syrian, Assyrian and other Christians call themselves the children of Abraham, simply because they believe in the teaching of Abraham and in that of the holy prophets who came after him. The Moslems also claim they are children of Abraham. All believers in the faith of Abraham are heirs of the promise. (Col. 6:16)

17. ESAU PUT ASIDE

As it is written, Jacob have I loved, but Esau have I hated.

Rom. 9:13

The Aramaic *saney*, "to put aside," is written exactly like the word for "hate." The meaning of such words is only ascertained by the context, the pronunciation of the word, and the facial expression of the speaker. Today in Aramaic we say *snila shraga*, "remove the wick from the lamp or candle." It is written exactly as though we were saying, "Hate the wick in the lamp," but a native Aramaean would understand the meaning of it, as Americans understand the meanings of many words which are written alike but have different meanings. (For example, a *fair* woman, a *fair* judge; a *fresh* person, a *fresh* fruit.) Then too, in these ancient Semitic languages, often a slight difference in pronunciation or in emphasis changed the meaning of the word.

God did not hate Esau. God is love, and there is no hatred in Him. But God put Esau aside, simply because he disqualified himself as an heir to his forefathers. Esau was more interested in the materialistic world than in religion and racial traditions. This is why God chose Jacob, who was the younger son by only a few minutes. Jacob was deeply interested in the history of his grandfather Abraham, his calling and his code of morals.

18. GOD DOES NOT HARDEN HEARTS

For the scripture saith unto Pharaoh, Even for this same purpose have I raised thee up, that I might shew my power in thee, and that my name might be declared throughout all the earth.

Rom. 9:17

Since Pharaoh refused to let the Israelites leave Egypt, the author of the Book of Exodus felt that God had hardened His heart in order to perform miracles and wonders in Egypt. (Ex. 9:16) "God had hardened Pharaoh's heart so that He may perform more miracles and wonders in Egypt" is a footnote. In other words, this is what some later writer thinks. The footnote was originally written on the margin, and was later incorporated into the text by the scribe or copyist. This still happens today. There are hundreds of passages in the Bible where a footnote has become an integral part of the text. God didn't have to harden Pharaoh's heart in order to show His power; He never acts in this manner. If He had hardened Pharaoh's heart, how could He blame Pharaoh for not obeying His orders?

Many Bible students have wondered why a good and just God would do such a thng to Pharaoh, that is, send His emissary to him to ask him to let the Israelites leave Egypt, and then to harden his heart to refuse the request. Pharaoh in such a situation would be helpless and blameless. He would have had no other choice but to refuse God's commands. Some scholars believe it would have been more miraculous if Pharaoh had complied with God's commands and done the right thing, without causing so many hardships, suffering, death and destruction to innocent people in Egypt.

In reading the account of the miracles and wonders, we find that Egyptian magicians performed all the wonders which Moses and Aaron had performed, and this is one reason that Pharaoh was not convinced by Moses and Aaron.

God does not have to rely on miracles and magical performances in order to show His power. Jesus refused to show signs and wonders and to perform magical acts to astonish the people. And as we see from the Gospel, the people did not believe in the miracles which he performed. They said to him, "What miracles have you performed, to believe in you?" (John 6:30) The Hebrew prophets wrought miracles and healed the sick, but most of them were put to death by the people.

The most important reason for Pharaoh's refusal to let the Israelites leave Egypt was political and economic. Pharaoh was using the Hebrews as slave workers in building large palaces, vast fortifications and other projects near the Suez. Then again, Pharaoh was afraid to let the Israelites go, thinking they might join an invading army and return to occupy Egypt. The Israelites were of the Semitic race. Egypt had been, off and on, invaded by Semitic people.

Some people cannot believe that God would bring plagues and calamities, which destroy cattle and little children, just to show His power. It is interesting to note that in the East everything is blamed on God or on the Devil. Jesus never quoted any of these wonders, nor did he say that God ever ordered the destruction of women and children. In those days, we must not forget, every act was attributed to God. When these events were recorded, man's concept of God was different from that which was later crystallized by the Hebrew prophets.

19. THE RIGHTEOUS BELIEVE

But the righteousness which is of faith speaketh on this wise, Say not in thine heart, Who shall ascend into heaven? (that is, to bring Christ down from above)
Or, Who shall descend into the deep? (that is, to bring up Christ again from the dead).

Rom. 10:6–7

The righteous, or pious, men who believed in the gospel of Jesus Christ did not question his coming into our world. They accepted everything by faith.

There were, however, many Jews in Rome, including Christians, who questioned the validity of the gospel. These men asked this question: Who had gone to heaven to verify these things, or who had ascended to heaven and brought down Christ? Who had descended into the depths of Sheol and brought out Christ? In other words, these people did not believe in the resurrection of the body and in eternal salvation. Probably they subscribed to the teachings of the Sadducees. They ridiculed the message of the gospel. Even today, men say, "How do I know that these things are true?"

Only by faith can we accept many things which are in the gospel. The mysteries of God are beyond human comprehension. It was by faith that Abraham left his country and went to Palestine; and by faith that Moses led the Israelites in the vast wilderness.

20. GENTILES

For I speak to you Gentiles, inasmuch as I am the apostle
of the Gentiles, I magnify mine office.

Rom. 11:13

All unbelievers in Jewish thought were called *ammey*,
"Gentiles." The term "Gentile" was originally given to the people of the Semitic race or the kindred of the Hebrews who were
not Jewish by religion—for example, the Edomites, who were
descendants of Esau, and the Ishmaelites, who were descendants
of Abraham. They were called *ammey* in Aramaic, meaning
"uncles." *Lo ammi*, "not my people." (Hos. 1:9)

The term *ammey* also means "people," and *ammi*, "my people."
(See Hos. 2:1.) Paul was apostle to the Gentiles, who were
mostly Aramaeans (Syrians), Edomites, Ammonites, Moabites,
and other races kin to the Jews. All of these peoples were of
one race and one culture and spoke the same language, but
their religious beliefs differed.

Even the descendants of the ten tribes who had forsaken the
God of Israel were looked upon as Gentiles. Paul was proud to
be an apostle to these people of Hebrew race and to the
Aramaeans, or Syrians.

The Aramaic word *khanpey* means "unbelievers," "pagans,"
"those who do not believe in God." Some of the Gentiles
believed in the God of Israel who was the God of their forefathers.

21. CHASTITY

I beseech you therefore, brethren, by the mercies of God,
that ye present your bodies a living sacrifice, holy, acceptable unto God, which is your reasonable service.

Rom. 12:1

"Present your body a living sacrifice" means to keep your
body pure and unblemished. All sacrifices offered to God must
be unblemished. Some Roman Christians had been disloyal to
the gospel and had gone astray, following the teachings of
pagan gods. Some of them had reverted to paganism.

Paul was not asking too much in warning them not to conform
to the things of this world, but to be chaste, unspoiled and
sincere Christians, in all things acceptable to God, and to become citizens of the new kingdom.

22. TIME TO AWAKE

And that, knowing the time, that now it is high time
to awake out of sleep: for now is our salvation nearer than
when we believed.
The night is far spent, the day is at hand: let us therefore cast off the works of darkness, and let us put on the
armor of light.

Rom. 13:11–12

Paul here places emphasis on the present. The Christian
must be aware that now is the hour to awake from a long
sleep. The present was so important, because the people knew

more about the fresh teachings of Jesus Christ than at the time when they were converted from paganism. Therefore, the time of salvation was at hand.

Salvation comes through Christian knowledge and understanding. Most Roman Christians were brought to the imperial city as captives from Judea, and some of them were children of captives and slaves. All these Jews in the Roman Empire were looking for a day of deliverance and the establishment of the overdue Messianic kingdom, which was to free the world from oppression, slavery and misery.

23. THE LIVING AND THE DEAD

For to this end Christ both died, and rose, and revived, that he might be Lord both of the dead and living.
Rom. 14:9

Jesus Christ, through his death and resurrection, triumphed over death and the grave. He also united the living and the dead by preaching to both, therefore becoming the Lord and Savior of both.

Moreover, through his death on the cross, Jesus demonstrated that life is eternal and indestructible, for God is eternal and indestructible. Death is a temporary separation. On the resurrection day, the departed ones will join the living. (Acts. 10:36, II Cor. 5:15)

24. CONFESSING

For it is written, As I live, saith the Lord, every knee shall
bow to me, and every tongue shall confess to God.

Rom. 14:11

The Aramaic word *nawdey* means "to give thanks," but
also, "to confess." The term "confess" means "to acknowledge,"
that is to say, in this passage, that every person would acknowledge God's blessings and give thanks to Him, for He is the
Lord of this world.

The time will come when the whole world will accept God
as the Creator of this world, and they will offer thanks to Him
and acknowledge Him as the Lord of all.

Thousands of early Christians were put to death by pagan
rulers simply because they confessed that God was the ruler
of the world and Jesus Christ was the Prince of Peace. Their
testimony, that is, dying for Christ, caused many pagans to accept the teaching of Jesus Christ and helped to spread Christianity throughout the pagan world.

25. THE CHRISTIANS

For I will not dare to speak of any of those things which
Christ hath not wrought by me, to make the Gentiles
obedient, by word and deed.

Rom. 15:18

Many of the Christians in the Roman Empire had left the
Jewish religion. The Christians in Judea for some time continued
to worship in the temple and to keep the Mosaic law and its

ordinances, but when the temple was destroyed by Titus in A.D. 70, Christians slowly but surely divorced themselves from Jewish tradition and some of its institutions. Hitherto they had come to Jerusalem for worship, but now they held their meetings at the homes of some of the believers. Thus, they became a separate organization, known as the Nazarenes, followers of the prophet from Nazareth.

The term *ammey,* "Gentiles," refers to the people who were kindred of the Jews, such as the Aramaeans, Edomites, Moabites, and other Semitic races. Many of these people were intermarried with the Jews, as in the case of Titus and Timothy, whose mothers were Jewesses and whose fathers were Aramaeans. All the members of these Gentile races in the large cities in Greece, Rome, and other lands clung together, for they all spoke the same language, ate the same foods, and their culture and way of life, with the exception of their religion, was the same.

The same is true today in New York, Chicago, London, and other large cities. When they are far away from their own lands, people's racial antipathy seemingly disappears, and they are friendly toward one another.

26. CRUSH SATAN

And the God of peace shall bruise Satan under your feet shortly. The grace of our Lord Jesus Christ be with you. Amen.

Rom. 16:20

"Crush Satan" means "destroy error and all evil works which are caused by it." The term "Satan" is derived from the Aramaic word *sata,* "to miss the mark," "to slip," "to mislead."

Evil was to be defeated and trampled under the feet of the faithful. As the sun melts ice, truth destroys error. In the East, when people reject a teaching or a thing, they generally spit upon it and trample it under their feet. Even abstract things, such as Satan, they trample upon; this signifies that they have rejected them. The people portray the abstract thing in figurative speech, then trample or spit upon it, so that the simple people can understand. Then again, when religious laws are broken, people often say, "They have trampled upon the laws."

The First Epistle of Paul the Apostle to the Corinthians

1. THE INVITED

Unto the church of God which is at Corinth, to them that are sanctified in Christ Jesus, called to be saints, with all that in every place call upon the name of Jesus Christ our Lord, both theirs and ours . . .

I Cor. 1:2

The Aramaic word *kraya* means "the called ones" or "the invited." In this case it means "invited," as in the story of the rich man who invited many guests to the wedding feast, but some of them refused to come.

The Jewish and Aramaean Christians in Corinth were invited, or called, by the grace of God to come into the Church of Jesus Christ. They had been sanctified, that is, set aside for the ministry of the gospel of Jesus Christ. Thousands of Jews in Greece were children of the promise and had been expecting the coming of the Messiah, the great deliverer who would gather the scattered children of Israel.

2. SIMPLE GOSPEL

For after that in the wisdom of God the world by wisdom
knew not God, it pleased God by the foolishness of preaching to save them that believe.

I Cor. 1:21

The Aramaic word *shatiotha*, "folly," has other meanings,
including "beside himself," "simple," and "stupid."

Paul used colloquial speech when he referred to the simplicity of the gospel and compared it with the complicated
teachings of the rabbinical school—the learned rabbis. Jesus
simplified the teaching of the prophets and the laws, and thus
made it look like folly in the eyes of the learned Jews who
valued literary style and obscure terms of speech more than
they valued the truth. Teachers who spoke in a simple
language so that the common folk could understand them were
often described as being "beside themselves," or foolish and
crazy. Jesus also was called crazy; his brothers said that he
had lost his mind.

The gospel of Jesus is so simple that it sounded like foolishness to the learned men of his day, but the term "foolishness"
is wrong. It should read, "a simple gospel," a gospel that even a
child could understand.

This is why the Gospels are read more than any other portion
of the Scriptures. Jesus spoke to both the learned and the unlearned; so his followers preached and wrote in a simple, colloquial language.

3. THE UNLEARNED

For ye see your calling, brethren, how that not many
wise men after the flesh, not many mighty, not many noble, are called:
But God hath chosen the foolish thngs of the world to
confound the wise; and God hath chosen the weak things
of the world to confound the things which are mighty;
And base things of the world, and things which are despised, hath God chosen, yea, and things which are not, to
bring to nought things that are.

I Cor. 1:26–28

The Aramaic term *sakhla* in this instance means "stupid,"
"foolish" or "devoid of understanding." The words Paul uses here
are of the common, or vernacular, speech. In Hebrew, the people
without understanding, or the uneducated, are called *ammey ha
aratz*. On one occasion the high priest, while belittling Jesus,
asked who had followed him but the uneducated and common
people, who are unlearned.

In Aramaic the word for "prudent," "wise" and "intelligent"
also means "stupid." *Sakal* means "the people of understanding."
The difference between the two words is the position of a dot,
placed over or under the word, but the letters are exactly the
same. (See I Cor. 1:20–25.)

God chooses the unlearned to embarrass the learned, who
rely on human wisdom. He also chooses the weak to humble the
strong and mighty. The gospel of Jesus in Aramaic is a simple
gospel and needs no exposition.

Eusebius, the church historian, tells us that all the writings
of the apostles were called *pshetta*, or *peshitta*, the simple,
pure and direct.

4. THE MIND OF GOD

For who hath known the mind of the Lord, that he may
instruct him? But we have the mind of Christ.

I Cor. 2:16

What Paul tries to say here is that, humanly speaking, no
one can understand the mind of God or His mysteries. We can,
however, understand the mind and thoughts of Jesus Christ,
because Jesus lived in this world. He appeared in the flesh, and
preached a simple gospel which his followers understand.

We can only understand the mind of God through the simple
and true gospel of Jesus Christ, for Christ and God are of one
accord. Jesus kept God's commandments and carried out His
wishes while he was on earth. He tells us that God, his Father,
showed him everything. Moreover, he states that he of himself
could do nothing, but God did everything through him. Therefore, he who sees Jesus Christ and understands his thoughts will
see God and understand His mind. Jesus Christ was a perfect
demonstration of God on earth.

5. HUMAN TEACHERS

Therefore let no man glory in men. For all things are
yours;
Whether Paul, or Apollos, or Cephas, or the world, or
life, or death, or things present, or things to come; all are
yours.

I Cor. 3:21–22

Paul in this instance says, "Let no man glory or boast in
human teachers. The glory and honor belong to Jesus Christ,

for everything was revealed by him." Therefore, no one could say, "This is my own teaching." Jesus' teaching belongs to all believers in the gospel.

Christians in Corinth were following certain rival teachers who gloried in their own teachings and philosophies. Some of them claimed to belong to Paul, some to Apollos, and others to Cephas (in Aramaic, Kepa), Peter. But all these teachers were members of the Church of Jesus Christ or belonged to him by the grace of God who had sent them. Therefore, no member of the congregation was indebted to them. Jesus' teaching was a revelation from God—a direct revelation which had formerly been given to the holy prophets.

The Christians who remained loyal to the gospel and suffered for it were to possess everything in life. Even death would have no power over them. (II Cor. 4:5)

6. WORDS WITHOUT ACTION

For the kingdom of God is not in word, but in power.

I Cor. 4:20

What Paul means here is that the kingdom of God cannot be brought on earth just by mere words, or by talking about it. Christians must labor hard, produce good fruits and let their light shine in order to hasten its coming. They must also use their energies and their material means to reach all the people of the world, and to let the gospel of Jesus Christ be known to all races and colors.

The Jews, at the time of the apostle, talked about the kingdom, but they thought it would come without any effort or sacrifice on their part. Jesus said, "It is not he who says Lord, Lord, but he who hears my words and does them."

In the Christian religion it is action that counts, and words without action are like hot winds—they come and go. But when words are put into action, they live forever. This is why the words of the prophets, of Jesus and his apostles, are living words, but the words of others are soon forgotten.

Even today, Christians teach the gospel of Christ and admonish people to accept it, but they do little or nothing to demonstrate it. Jesus said, "If you love me, keep my commandments."

7. NEAR IN SPIRIT

For I verily, as absent in body, but present in spirit, have judged already, as though I were present, concerning him that hath so done this deed.

I Cor. 5:3

Paul had already judged the evildoers, or those who caused disturbances in the church at Corinth, as though he had been present. He had been with the Christians in spirit, even though in body he was far away from them. Assuredly, the apostle had heard about the un-Christian conduct and evil deeds of some of the converts, and had already classified them as unbelievers.

True Christians can always be together in spirit and be concerned about one another. This is because in spirit there is no space and no time, and in Jesus Christ we are all one.

The prophet Ezekiel visited Jerusalem and saw the evil done by the Jews in the Holy City; he also measured the temple in spirit while his body was at a camp on the River Chabor, in Mesopotamia, or Iraq.

8. SUFFERING FROM EVIL

. . . To deliver such an one unto Satan for the destruction of the flesh, that the spirit may be saved in the day of the Lord Jesus.

I Cor. 5:5

"To deliver such ones to Satan" is an Aramaic idiom which means "to let them suffer with their own evil devices," or, as we say in English, "Let them stew in their own juice." When people suffer they find out that evil does not pay. Paul in this instance is talking about some evil which the Christians at Corinth had done, because of which they could not be brought into the fold of Christ without first suffering or paying the penalty for their evil deed. Note: Corinth was well known for its riotous living, immorality, etc., and many Christians had become the victims of pagan practices.

Many evildoers, after suffering, repent from their evil and thus save their souls. St. Francis, in the early part of his life, lived a riotous life. Paul himself, before his conversion, committed evil acts, but when he saw the light of the truth, he repented and gave his life to preach the gospel of Jesus Christ and to save men's souls. Many people suffer for their evil deeds and learn their lesson the hard way.

9. JUDGING ANGELS

Know ye not that we shall judge angels? how much more
things that pertain to this life?

I Cor. 6:3

To "judge angels" does not mean "to judge the spirits
who minister before God and are sent by him to assist us." In
Aramaic, the term "angel" also means "God's counsel," "pious
men," or "innocent persons."

Angels have no physical bodies and are not like human beings. They do not have wings; they were portrayed with wings
to indicate omnipresence, for God's counsel is present everywhere. The angels, being spirits, would not come under judgment, but good men are often called angels.

Jacob said to his brother Esau, "I have seen you in my vision
as an angel." Jacob was afraid of Esau, thinking he would try to
avenge the wrong which had been done to him, but when
Jacob met him, he found Esau as innocent as an angel of God.
(Gen. 33:10)

In the East, pious men are often addressed as angels, because they live a pure life. The Christians were to judge pious
men of other religions; Jesus said that his disciples were to
judge the ten tribes of Israel. True Christians had a higher
revelation of God's truth, and thus could judge others.

Jesus will come in a spiritual body so that all people in the
world can see him. We will all arise in a spiritual body, and
those who are living at the time of resurrection will be
transformed into spiritual bodies just as Jesus' body was transformed. Then *pious* Christians could judge even the fallen
angels. (See I Cor. 15.)

Paul says we die in a physical, or corruptible, body, but we
will rise in a spiritual body.

10. MODERATION

All things are lawful unto me, but all things are not expedient: all things are lawful for me, but I will not be brought under the power of any.
Meats for the belly, and the belly for meats: but God shall destroy both it and them. Now the body is not for fornication, but for the Lord; and the Lord for the body.

I Cor. 6:12–13

All things are lawful for Christians, but not all things are advisable. All things were lawful for Paul, but he did not want to be enslaved by them. This is because when certain things, such as eating or drinking, are done without moderation, they cause men and women to form habits which sooner or later become destructive to them.

The reference here is to eating and drinking. As we have said, all things are lawful, but in moderation. Nevertheless, some people eat and drink to excess. Jesus said that nothing that goes into a man defiles him, but that which comes out of him.

The Jews were too strict in their observance of dietary laws. Some of them, even though they had become Christians, were still bound by their ancient rituals and ordinances. They abstained from certain foods, and some of them even refused to eat with the Gentile converts.

11. HUSBAND AND WIFE

And unto the married I command, yet not I, but the Lord,
Let not the wife depart from her husband:
But and if she depart, let her remain unmarried, or be
reconciled to her husband: and let not the husband put
away his wife.

I Cor. 7:10–11

The reference here is to husband and wife. Paul in this
instance refers to that which his Lord, Jesus Christ, had said.
This is why he says, "I command you, yet not I, but the Lord."
Jesus prohibited divorce, except on the grounds of adultery.
(Matt. 5:32, Mal. 2:14–15. See also comment in the *Gospel
Light,* Matt. 5:32.)

12. PAST EXAMPLE

Now all these things happened unto them for ensamples:
and they are written for our admonition, upon whom the
ends of the world are come.

I Cor. 10:11

Paul reminds the Corinthian Christians that the same
Scriptures which were revealed and preached to the Israelite
people in the past now serve as an admonition to us.

Many misfortunes that happened to the Israelites during their
wanderings in the desert were the result of their disobedience
to God, and serve as examples to us.

The fulfillment of the Scriptures has come in our days. The
Israelites heard about the Messiah, the Prince of Peace, and

looked for his coming, but they did not see him. Our condemnation is even greater, because though Jesus Christ is the light of the world, we still walk in darkness and follow false saviors, the gods of this material world. (Rom. 15:4)

13. TRIALS IN THIS LIFE

There hath no temptation taken you but such as is common to man: but God is faithful, who will not suffer you to be tempted above that ye are able; but will with the temptation also make a way to escape, that ye may be able to bear it.

Wherefore, my dearly beloved, flee from idolatry.

I Cor. 10:13–14

The Aramaic word *nisyona*, "temptation," also means "trials" or "tests." Paul in this instance states that all men, one way or another, go through some trials in this life; there are no exceptions. But this does not mean that God tempts us, or places on us heavier burdens than we can carry. No, God's burdens are light, and His yoke pleasant. Temptations often serve as examples which strengthen us. On the other hand, God always guides those who trust in Him, and helps them not to enter into temptation.

For example, Joseph was tempted by his master's wife, but God gave him strength and understanding to resist the temptation. God tempts no one. This is because He knows both our strength and our weakness, and He knows the depths of our hearts. All of our acts are open before His eyes; there is nothing hidden from Him.

The apostle James says, "Let no man say when he is tempted, I am tempted of God; for God cannot be tempted with evil, neither does he tempt any man; but every man is tempted by his own lust; he covets, and is enticed." (James 1:13–14) When we are tempted we are tempted with the physical forces which are within us, and with our own wrong inclinations.

14. FALSEHOOD

> But I say, that the things which the Gentiles sacrifice, they sacrifice to devils, and not to God: and I would not that ye should have fellowship with devils.
>
> I Cor. 10:20

The term "devil" in this instance means "falsehood," or "deviation from the truth of God." It does not mean that the devil is a person. Often evil is personified to make it understandable, but evil is not a person.

The pagans worshiped images and devilish—crazy—things. They believed that there was some power behind the images and the oracles, for they did not know how they were devised by cunning priests and craftsmen. All the priests were magicians. Moreover, pagan religions, being immoral cults, offered alluring rewards to their adherents, permitting them to practice immorality as a virtue in order to lure more people into the cults.

Christians were warned to shun these pagan, immoral practices and vile rituals. (See I Cor. 10:21.) Christian truth could not be contaminated with evil, pagan rituals, nor could good Christians participate in them.

15. COVERING OF THE HEAD

For this cause ought the woman to have power on her
head because of the angels.

I Cor. 11:10

The Eastern text reads, "For this reason the woman ought
to be modest and cover her head as a mark of respect to the
angels."

The Easterners believe that when they pray, the angels,
"God's counsel" or "ministers," are present around them to carry
their prayers and supplications before God. On the other hand,
saintly, or pious, men and women are addressed as angels of
God.

In the East, women always cover their faces in the presence
of holy men not as a token of fear, but of reverence and dignity.
This is still done today. Rebecca covered herself, when she saw
Isaac coming to greet her, as a token of respect to him. (Gen.
25:65)

Jesus ignored all these man-made Jewish ordinances and
racial customs. According to Jesus, men and women are equal,
because they are both created in the image and likeness of God.
Paul was brought up very strictly in Judaism, and he was a
faithful observer of Mosaic ordinances and rabbinical doctrines
which he had learned at the school in Jerusalem. In other
words, this admonition is Paul's own idea, and is not based on
Jesus' teaching.

16. PAGAN JEWS

Ye know that ye were Gentiles, carried away unto these
dumb idols, even as ye were led.

I Cor. 12:2

The Hebrews often left their pure religion and reverted to
paganism, that is, to sensual Baal worship. Many Jews who were
living in Greece and Egypt had forsaken the true way, the
religion of their forefathers, and had followed pagan deities.
The pagan Jews, like Baal worshipers, sacrificed their children
to images.

It is interesting to note that all the Pauline epistles which
contain admonitions and warnings were written to the people
of the dispersion, that is, to the Jews who had been taken
captive to far-off lands, and who were living among the Gentiles
and pagans. This is because these Jews, being away from their
homeland, were exposed to temptations and dangers. This
is why Paul says, "Our forefathers crossed the Red Sea," or,
"They were sheltered under the cloud," or "They ate manna."
(I Cor. 10:1-9) Greeks would not have understood these terms,
because their forefathers had not experienced these things in
Egypt and the Sinai Desert.

This epistle was written because some of the Christian converts were tempted by pagan rituals and other evils. Moreover, morality was very low in Greece and other pagan lands.

17. WE KNOW THINGS IN PART

For we know in part, and we prophesy in part.

I Cor. 13:9

All that we know about God, His laws, His ordinances, and the life hereafter is only in part. That is, we have not yet grasped the full meaning of God's revelation. But when the perfect teaching, the gospel of Jesus Christ, was given to the world, that which was imperfect became perfect, and that which was in part was fully revealed.

We grow in wisdom and understanding like children. Even Jesus grew in wisdom and understanding. When we were children, we saw things as children see them, but when we grew older, we saw them as mature men do. In other words, truth is revealed according to our human capacity to grasp it and understand it. ·

Therefore, the rituals and human ordinances were nothing but the shadow of the truth which was to be revealed in the fullness of time, that is, the gospel of Jesus Christ.

18. PERFECTION

But when that which is perfect is come, then that which is in part shall be done away.

I Cor. 13:10

The reference here is to the Jewish religion, the temple worship and rituals, which even though imperfect served as a shadow or a reminder of a perfect religion which was to be revealed through the prophets and through Jesus Christ.

Humanly speaking, when an imperfect gadget or machine is improved, the old one is discarded and replaced by the new and better one. All that we now know was known in part by the people in the past, but when the truth is revealed we know them as the whole. For example, the idea and the design of the wheel, which was invented thousands of years ago, is the same, but the wheel as we know it now has been perfected.

The teaching of Jesus Christ revealed to us the abundant love of God, His fatherhood, His forgiveness, and His divine care for us. That is, religion as preached by the Hebrew prophets and by Jesus and his disciples is a perfect religion, which will meet all the needs of the world, regardless of race or color.

19. UNKNOWN TONGUES

If any man speak in an unknown tongue, let it be by two, or at the most by three, and that by course; and let one interpret.

I Cor. 14:27

There were many Jews who spoke diverse dialects of Aramaic, which was the vernacular in Palestine. In those early days even the distance of two or three miles between towns made a difference between the dialects. Some of the words were pronounced differently, just as they are today in English, Spanish, and other languages. This is still true today of the Aramaic and Arabic languages. Each area has its own peculiar pronunciation, idioms, and mannerisms of speech, but all the people read and write the same language.

Apparently there were a few learned Jewish men who tried to speak in the ancient Hebrew dialect, which had been dead since the Babylonian captivity, 586 B.C. Moreover, there were many Jews who had come to the feast who could not speak well in Semitic languages, so they spoke in Arabic, Greek, Persian, and the dialects thereof. Evidently, when these men rose up to express themselves on religious matters, they had to speak in different tongues, or dialects, and had to have interpreters. (See I Cor. 14:27.) But Paul admonished the speakers to keep silent if there were no interpreters.

The term "an unknown tongue" means a language not understood by the listeners. Even today, when people pray in ancient languages such as Hebrew, Aramaic, or Latin, the masses do not understand what the priests say. Today, some churches use two or even three languages during the services so that they may be understood by all. Moreover, the Scriptures are always interpreted in the vernacular, so that the simplest people can understand.

20. WOMEN KEEP SILENT

Let your women keep silence in the churches: for it is not permitted unto them to speak; but they are commanded to be under obedience, as also saith the law.

I Cor. 14:34

In the East even today women keep silent and do not participate in worship. They stand behind the congregation and watch with much admiration the services which the men perform.

In the Jewish and Moslem religions the women have their own places of worship, which are separate from the rest of the temple or mosque. Nevertheless, women generally do not attend the services, but the pious pray and study the Scriptures at home, and learn from their husbands, brothers, and sons, and the priests and teachers of their religion.

Paul was a strict Jew and upheld many Jewish teachings, traditions, and doctrines of the elders. He did not want women to speak, sing or teach in churches, but rather to keep silence and listen. Jesus did not exclude women. He did not uphold some of the Mosaic ordinances which discriminate against women, seemingly making them inferior to men.

Paul also prohibited women from uncovering their faces, adorning themselves with jewelry and speaking or teaching in the churches. This was an ancient custom; many men would resent seeing strangers looking upon the faces of their wives or sisters. This custom is still upheld among the Moslems and some Christians.

Mary, the sister of Moses and Aaron, and other women sang and praised the Lord with timbrels. (Ex. 15:20–21) Moreover, women were always supporters of religion, and this is still true.

21. INTERPRETERS

What? came the word of God out from you? or came it unto you only?
If any man think himself to be a prophet, or spiritual, let him acknowledge that the things that I write unto you are the commandments of the Lord.

I Cor. 14:36–37

The reference here is to the men who interrupted the speaker or the teacher, stating that they had had a revelation and that they must declare it before the speaker could continue. Some men overdo this just to show themselves and thus become noticeable before the eyes of the congregation.

In the East, unlearned men may try to speak just to be noticed by members of the congregation and to prove that they are not inferior to those who can read. Paul is upbraiding these people because many of them spoke without knowing what they were saying. Moreover, there were many who prophesied but who were not prophets.

Paul is not against the men who really had a message and wanted to share it, or who were inspired. Moreover, the apostle wanted these meetings to be conducted in an orderly way, every person knowing his place and every teacher his vocation. (See I Cor. 14:40.)

Paul admonishes the Christians in Corinth to prophesy and not to prohibit those who prayed or spoke in unknown tongues, that is, in the languages which could not be understood by most of the members of the congregation. Even today, some Near-Eastern Christians pray in Turkish, even though only a few understand that language. (See I Cor. 14:18–40.)

22. GOD'S KINGDOM

Then cometh the end, when he shall have delivered up the kingdom to God, even the Father; when he shall have put down all rule and all authority and power.

I Cor. 15:24

Truth will ultimately triumph over the powers of this world and the evil forces. Then the kingdom of heaven, the universal kingdom, the church of Christ, will become the kingdom of God, wherein there will be no evil. (See the parable of the tares and the wheat, Matt. 13:24–25.)

When the whole world is converted to the true teaching of Jesus Christ, he will deliver his kingdom to God, his Father. Jesus will continue to reign until he subjugates his enemies. (Heb. 1:13) The last enemy is death, that is to say, the fear of death, and the death of the soul. (Heb. 2:14)

In the olden days, when a man went astray from God, he was automatically cut off from the living God and from life to come. (Matt. 28:18, Rev. 17:14) When Jesus has attained his mission and eradicated the forces of evil, he himself will be subject to God, so that everything will be under the control of God. According to Paul, Jesus was commissioned by God to restore His kingdom. Jesus himself said that he had been sent by his Father.

23. BAPTISM FOR THE DEAD

Else what shall they do which are baptized for the dead, if the dead rise not at all? why are they then baptized for the dead?

I Cor. 15:29

In the first century of the Christian Era, Christian relatives had themselves baptized for their dead who had not been baptized and had died without hearing the gospel of Jesus Christ. People thought that the dead could not be saved without being baptized. They also were baptized when they had committed a sin, for baptism was a form of cleansing, like some of the other Jewish ceremonies. But Christian baptism is symbolic of the inner baptism, and baptism of the spirit, which removes sin.

Apparently baptism for the dead was abolished at the time of the Nicaean Creed, A.D. 325. This is why we read in the Creed, "I believe in one baptism. . . ."

The dead live in the living, or in their posterity. On the other hand, the dead could not come under condemnation for their failure to be baptized, for there was no baptism in their day, nor did their pagan religion practice it.

Jesus Christ, through his death on the cross, wrought a complete salvation for both the living and the dead. He also preached to the souls of the dead while he was in Sheol.

In the Church of the East even today we pray for the dead, and we believe that we still have communion with their souls. God is not the God of the dead but of the living—the souls of the dead are living.

24. THE FIRST ADAM

And so it is written, The first man Adam was made a living soul; the last Adam was made a quickening spirit.

I Cor. 15:45

The first Adam is the first man who was created by God, into whose nostrils God breathed his spirit, making him a living being. (Gen. 2:7)

The last Adam is Jesus Christ, to whom God granted power to save the world and bring life to those who had been dead. As by the fall of the first man, Adam, sin entered into the world, so by one man, Jesus Christ, was sin destroyed and death abolished. Thus, Jesus is the new Adam, free from sin. The first Adam died because of transgression against God's law; the second Adam was obedient to the law and lives forever because he triumphed over sin and death.

25. JESUS' SUDDEN RETURN

Behold, I shew you a mystery; We shall not all sleep, but
we shall all be changed,
In a moment, in the twinkling of an eye, at the last trump:
for the trumpet shall sound, and the dead shall be raised
incorruptible, and we shall be changed.
For this corruptible must put on incorruption, and this
mortal must put on immortality.

I Cor. 15:51–53

In Paul's day, many Christians were expecting the immediate return of Jesus Christ. His coming was to be so sudden
that some would have no time to put off their worldly bodies.
(See Matt. 24:31.)

The news of a sudden coming of Jesus was a mystery. Jesus
himself had told his disciples that no one but God knows when
he will return. (See Matt. 25, the parable of the virgins.) He
also told his followers that there will be wars and rumors of
wars before the end.

The gospel must be preached all over the world before the
end will come. Jesus knew that his gospel of good news would
meet with stern opposition from pagan religions and from worldly
men, and that it would take many centuries before his true
teaching was accepted and understood.

At this time the Christian converts of Corinth were looking
for the sudden coming of Jesus, and his coming was to be so
unexpected that they would not have enough time to change
this corruptible body into an incorruptible body. This may happen at the second coming, but as Jesus has said, no one knows
the day and the hour but God Himself.

The Second Epistle of Paul the Apostle to the Corinthians

1. CHRISTIANS SUFFER

For as the sufferings of Christ abound in us, so our consolation also aboundeth by Christ.

II Cor. 1:5

The apostle and his companions as well as many of the believers were constantly harassed because of the gospel of Jesus Christ. This was because Jesus' teaching was contrary to pagan institutions and to Jewish rabbinical teachings. In other words, the converts had inherited the suffering of Jesus Christ and the opposition he had faced. He had told them that if they wished to follow him they must take up their crosses and, if necessary, be ready to die for the sake of the gospel.

The new way, the religion of Jesus Christ, was not an easy way. The Christian workers of the gospel were constantly meeting opposition from pagan priests and philosophers, and from kings and emperors, who were worshiped as gods.

Nevertheless Paul and his companions were happy to suffer for the sake of the gospel which brought salvation and eternal rewards. Jesus Christ had blessed those who would be reproached and persecuted for the sake of the gospel, and had assured them of joy, consolation, and eternal rewards in the life hereafter. (See Acts 19:23–37.)

2. DIANA OF EPHESUS

For we would not, brethren, have you ignorant of our trouble which came to us in Asia, that we were pressed out of measure, above strength, insomuch that we despaired even of life:

But we had the sentence of death in ourselves, that we should not trust in ourselves, but in God which raiseth the dead:

Who delivered us from so great a death, and doth deliver: in whom we trust that he will yet deliver us.

II Cor. 1:8–10

When Paul was at Ephesus, Demetrius, a silversmith, and some other artisans who belonged to the guild of silversmiths who made silver shrines and images for the goddess Diana rose up against Paul and his companions. And as the result of this uprising, the whole city was in tumult and confusion. Rumors had spread that Paul had attacked the pagan deity and the worship of the image. (Acts 19:23–37)

The silversmiths and other craftsmen, members of the guild, were afraid that they would lose business if Paul was permitted to preach the doctrine of one God and the gospel of Jesus Christ. Thousands of people came to Ephesus to worship Diana, and took with them to their homes images of Diana in gold, silver and brass. A great many people were engaged in this trade, so a guild, or union, had been organized. The city officals were obliged to listen to their complaints. After all, Diana was the goddess of Asia Minor; consequently, Paul was punished for his utterances against this ancient goddess.

Truth has always been opposed by those who worship the gods of the material world, and make of religion a lucrative business. Ephesus is gone and forgotten; both the city and the temple are in ruins. But there are other Dianas that are much more powerful and much more revered. Nevertheless, the truth is indestructible, and the fire of God is still burning, and will continue to burn until the forces of evil are consumed.

3. PAUL'S SINCERITY

When I therefore was thus minded, did I use lightness? or the things that I purpose, do I purpose according to the flesh, that with me there should be yea yea, and nay nay?
But as God is true, our word toward you was not yea and nay.
For the Son of God, Jesus Christ, who was preached among you by us, even by me and Silvanus and Timotheus, was not yea and nay, but in him was yea.

II Cor. 1:17–19

The Eastern (Aramaic) text reads, "When I, therefore, was considering this, did I consider it lightly or are the things which I am considering wholly worldly? Because the answers should have been either yes yes, or no no. But as God is true, our word to you was not yes and no. For the Son of God, Jesus Christ, who was preached among you by us, even by me and Silvanus and Timotheus, was not yes and no, but with him always yes."

Paul is assuring the Corinthian Christians of his sincerity and devotion toward them. Just as he is their joy, so they are his. (See II Cor. 1:12.) In verse thirteen, he answers them that what he writes them comes from his heart, and that even though they might not understand some of the things he writes, he is sincere. He assures them that everything he considered or proposed was not done lightly, but that he meant well in all his letters.

Paul wrote at length. He did not reply to the Corinthians yes yes, or no no, but he went on to explain what he wanted to say, and this made his epistle harder to understand for the simple readers who knew so little about the background of Christianity and Judaism, and whose main interest was in Jesus Christ. In other words, Paul could not answer them the way Jesus answered his followers and critics. (See II Cor. 10:23.)

4. CHRISTIANS AT CORINTH

So that contrariwise ye ought rather to forgive him, and comfort him, lest perhaps such a one should be swallowed up with overmuch sorrow.
Wherefore I beseech you that ye would confirm your love toward him.

II Cor. 2:7–8

There were many faithful Christians in Corinth, some of whom later turned against Paul and his teaching. Some of these ungrateful men had given the apostle considerable trouble, and they also had become a grievance to the Christian congregation at Corinth. (Most of the Christian converts in Corinth were formerly Jews.) Paul had preached in Corinth, as in other cities, at the Jewish synagogue, and made many converts, but there were also a few Aramaeans (Syrians) in the congregation.

The term "him" in this instance is used collectively, meaning "anyone who had turned against Paul and against the gospel of Jesus Christ." Paul exhorts the members of the congregation to forgive and to comfort such men, hoping that they might repent of the evil they had done.

Immorality was rampant in Corinth, and many so-called Christians were living like pagans, men with men and women with women. (See I Cor. 5:1–12.)

5. A SWEET SAVOR

Now thanks be unto God, which always causeth us to triumph in Christ, and maketh manifest the savour of his
knowledge by us in every place.

For we are unto God a sweet savour of Christ, in them
that are saved, and in them that perish:

To the one we are the savour of death unto death; and
to the other the savour of life unto life. And who is sufficient for these things?

II Cor. 2:14–16

The true Christian converts were newly born. Now they
were tasting the fruits of a new religion which had changed
their lives and given them hope of life hereafter. They had
become like Jesus Christ because they were witnessing him
before those who opposed the Christian gospel. Moreover, they
were demonstrating Christ, not only through their words, but
also through their good deeds. Such Christians were a sweet
savor to God through Jesus Christ. Even those who rejected
the gospel and persecuted the Christians felt the fragance of
this savor, and saw the light of God through these faithful men,
who were ready to give their lives for Him.

Indeed, even the wicked see the light of God in holy men,
but still they reject the truth and choose the material world
and its fleeting pleasures.

6. OPEN FACE

Now the Lord is that Spirit and where the Spirit of the Lord is, there is liberty.
But we all, with open face beholding as in a glass the glory of the Lord, are changed into the same image from glory to glory, even as by the Spirit of the Lord.

II Cor. 3:17–18

An "open" or "uncovered face" is an idiom in the Aramaic which means "innocent," "unafraid." Guilty people generally cannot look straight. In court or in any other situation, they either hide their faces or look down.

In biblical days, when a man was found guilty of treason or blasphemy, when the sentence of guilt was pronounced, his face was covered, for Easterners would be disgusted even to see the face of such a one. When Haman incurred the wrath of the King of Persia, they covered his face: "And the word went out of the king's mouth, they covered Haman's face." (Esther 7:8) And when Jesus was convicted in the court of the high priest, they covered his face. (Luke 22:64)

What Paul means here is this: The true believers on the Judgment Day will stand straight and face their God with their faces uncovered, and without flinching or fear.

7. GOD OF THIS WORLD

In whom the god of this world hath blinded the minds of
them which believe not, lest the light of the glorious gospel
of Christ, who is the image of God, should shine unto
them.

II Cor. 4:4

The Eastern (Aramaic) text reads, "To those in this world
whose minds have been blinded by God, because they did not
believe, lest the light of the glorious gospel of Christ, who is the
likeness of God, should shine on them."

The term "god of this world" metaphorically means the material world. That is to say, when men love money and worldly
possessions, they make gods of them. And therefore they are
reluctant to accept the way of the true God, the God of heaven.

God, being the light of the world, blinds no one's eyes. But
since man is created with a prerogative to choose either good
or evil, God, after warning him, lets him do what he pleases.
Paul here refers to the people who had rejected the gospel of
Jesus Christ. They were lost because of their disobedience.

In biblical days, every action was attributed to God. For
example, when Pharaoh refused to let the Israelites leave Egypt,
a scribe noted on the margin of the law, "God hardens his
heart." This is because God did not interfere. Pharaoh did
not want the people to leave Egypt, because they were working
for him as slaves. His refusal was based on economics.

8. LIFE OF JESUS MANIFESTED

Always bearing about in the body the dying of the Lord
Jesus, that the life also of Jesus might be made manifest
in our body.
For we which live are alway delivered unto death for Jesus' sake, that the life also of Jesus might be made manifest in our mortal flesh.

II Cor. 4:10–11

"Bearing about in the body the dying of the Lord Jesus"
is interpreted to mean that the trials and sufferings of Jesus
are reproduced in the bodies of those who believe in him
and practice his teaching. Jesus told his disciples that if they
were to follow him sincerely, they must take up their crosses
and be ready to die for the cause of his gospel.

"The life also of Jesus made manifest in our body" means
that the light of the gospel of meekness will be manifested
in our lives. As Jesus was persecuted and crucified for the
sake of truth, our mortal bodies may suffer the same fate so
that the teaching of Jesus Christ may triumph and the kingdom
of heaven be established on earth.

9. EARTHLY HOME

> For we know that if our earthly house of this tabernacle were dissolved, we have a building of God, an house not made with hands, eternal in the heavens.
>
> II Cor. 5:1

The Aramaic term *beta*, "a dwelling place," also means "worldly gains," such as possessions, money, land, and other things which men acquire in this life. Indeed many people have houses but no possessions. Some nomadic people have neither houses nor tents, but the ground on which they live is called a house, and they call the sky their roof.

The house, whether built of stones or other material, is a temporal house—a shepherd's tent. On the other hand, the heavenly home, which is not made or built by human hands, is built of good works, which endure forever. This earthly house, being made by the hands of mortal man, is temporal and destructible.

10. NAKED

> . . . If so be that being clothed we shall not be found naked.
> For we that are in this tabernacle do groan, being burdened: not for that we would be unclothed, but clothed upon, that mortality might be swallowed up of life.
>
> II Cor. 5:3–4

Paul here compares our everlasting and heavenly life with our earthly life. Indeed such a comparison is difficult because whatever we try to do we still find ourselves lacking, or naked. This is because the garments we wear in this life wear out, and the earthly rewards we receive perish, but the eternal rewards are lasting.

Therefore, Christians should strive to work for the things which do not perish, and for the life which is eternal. (I Cor. 15:53)

11. JUDGMENT BEFORE CHRIST

For we must all appear before the judgment seat of Christ; that every one may receive the things done in his body, according to that he hath done, whether it be good or bad.

II Cor. 5:10

What Paul hints at here is the judgment of men who had departed from their true religion and returned to paganism. These men defiled their bodies with immoral practices which exceeded even the pagan immorality. (See I Cor. 5:1.)

These men were to answer before the throne of Christ for their evil deeds. Their bodies were the temples of the Holy Spirit, but they had been polluted through sensuality, homosexuality, drunkenness and other evils.

The whole tone of these epistles is a warning against the Christians who backslid. (See Rev. 22:12.)

These sinners did not have to wait until the Judgment Day to be punished by Jesus. They had already punished themselves by destroying their bodies, the temple in which God dwelt. God and Jesus punish no one. People bring punishment upon themselves through their own evil deeds.

We gather what we scatter, and we reap what we have sown. This is an immutable law, that no one can either rescind or alter. When the Prodigal Son returned home, his father did not punish him but received him with open arms, because he had already punished himself and had learned his lesson.

12. JESUS DIED TO SAVE ALL

And that he died for all, that they which live should not henceforth live unto themselves, but unto him which died for them, and rose again.

II Cor. 5:15

Jesus died for the sake of everyone, for the oppressed and for the oppressor, for the good and for the bad. This he did so that those who live may not try to live for themselves alone, but for him who died for their sake, so that through his death he might bring them from darkness into the light.

Jesus, through his death, became an everlasting example of meekness and loving-kindness, and the finder of a new way which leads men unto the kingdom of God.

13. THE DEATH OF A SINNER

For he hath made him to be sin for us, who knew no sin; that we might be made the righteousness of God in him.

II Cor. 5:21

Jesus did not make himself sin, but he was willing to die the death of a sinner. That is to say, the one who was

228

sinless died in order to save those who were sinful. We do not mean that Jesus died to pay a price to the forces of evil for the sins of the people, but that he risked his life to rescue them from sin. For example, suppose a man was walking by the bank of a river and saw a person drowning, and he jumped in to save him, but lost his own life. He saved the other without paying any ransom.

Had Jesus been a sinner, his death would have been a punishment for his own sins. This is because a sinful or guilty man can die only for his own sin. But a righteous man may expose his life to danger and die to save others. "Hardly would any man die for the sake of the wicked; but for the sake of the good, one might be willing to die. God has here manifested his love towards us, in that while we were yet sinners, Christ died for us." (Rom. 5:7–8)

14. THE RIGHT TIME

(For he saith, I have heard thee in a time accepted, and in the day of salvation have I succoured thee: behold, now is the accepted time; behold, now is the day of salvation.)

II Cor. 6:2

The Eastern (Aramaic) text reads, "For he said, I have answered you in an acceptable time, and I have helped you on the day of salvation; behold, now is the acceptable time; and behold now is the day of salvation."

Paul here refers to Isaiah, who predicted the coming of the Messiah Christ, who would be a light to the Gentiles. (Isa. 49:8)

God has answered the people at the acceptable time, which means the right time, or the time of need. Jesus Christ came into the world at the acceptable time, when the world was tired of wars and oppressions, and needed a universal brotherhood. He also became a savior to those who had fallen and a light to the Gentiles who had been walking in darkness.

15. SORROW CAUSES DEATH

For godly sorrow worketh repentance to salvation not to be repented of: but the sorrow of the world worketh death.

II Cor. 7:10

When we are sorry about the blunders which have caused us to go astray from the truth, we receive spiritual benefits, because the things of God endure forever and bring eternal rewards. In such cases, we must sincerely repent and forget the past. But this is not true when we feel sorrowful over the ephemeral things of this world. In such cases, instead of receiving relief and consolation, we bring more unhappiness and destruction upon ourselves.

This is because in such cases we do not repent, but regret, and try to regain what we have materially lost.

Death in this sense means destruction. Many people have destroyed themselves by their excessive acts of evil.

16. FILTHINESS OF SPIRIT

Having therefore these promises, dearly beloved, let us
cleanse ourselves from all filthiness of the flesh and spirit,
perfecting holiness in the fear of God.

II Cor. 7:1

"Filthiness of the spirit" is an Aramaic saying which means
"an evil inclination." The term "spirit" in Aramaic has many
meanings, such as "the Holy Spirit," "pride," "rheumatism," "inclination," and "wind."

Paul here admonishes the Corinthian Christians to beware
of pagan practices, which at times had lured many Christian
converts into destruction.

The term "spirit" cannot be contaminated. This is because
there is nothing in the spirit to be affected by any uncleanliness.
But our human inclinations or thoughts can be polluted with
worldly desires.

17. OBEDIENCE TO JESUS CHRIST

. . . And having in a readiness to revenge all disobedience,
when your obedience is fulfilled.

II Cor. 10:6

When our own obedience to Jesus Christ is put into
practice, we open the eyes of those who are disobedient and
living in darkness, for through our obedience and good works
we let our light shine. Those who are disobedient see the light
of God in us and know that they have been wrong. We do

not bring any condemnation upon them; they themselves confess their own evil deeds and seek forgiveness from God who is the Father of all, and Who has compassion upon those who return to Him.

18. SIMPLE TEACHING

But I fear, lest by any means, as the serpent beguiled Eve through his subtilty, so your minds should be corrupted from the simplicity that is in Christ.

For if he that cometh preacheth another Jesus, whom we have not preached, or if ye receive another spirit, which ye have not received, or another gospel, which ye have not accepted, ye might well bear with him.

II Cor. 11:3–4

The Aramaic word *peshitta* is derived from *pashat*, "to be straight, simple, sincere, plain and true." This word has other meanings, such as "to extend," "to reach out," "to give a helping hand." Nevertheless, in this instance, the apostle Paul uses it to mean "simple, true, straightforward." In Aramaic we often say, "He is *nashapeshitta*," that is, "He is a simple, or a true, man."

It is interesting to know that Eusebius, the first Christian historian, states in his book that all the writings of the apostles were called *peshitta*, or *pheshitta*, "simple." This is because not one of the disciples of Jesus had attended a higher school; most of them were illiterate. Their virgin minds were free from man-made doctrines and dogmas, which instead of helping the people obstruct the truth. We can see this from their simple epistles.

Paul warns the Corinthians against false teachers who beguiled many of the faithful with their corrupt and complicated teachings. The gospel of Jesus Christ is simple and direct, and it needs no commentaries in its original setting.

19. WARNING AGAINST FALSE TEACHERS

For if he that cometh preacheth another Jesus, whom we have not preached, or if ye receive another spirit, which ye have not received, or another gospel, which ye have not accepted, ye might well bear with him.

For I suppose I was not a whit behind the very chiefest apostles.

But though I be rude in speech, yet not in knowledge; but we have been throughly made manifest among you in all things.

II Cor. 11:4–6

The Eastern (Aramaic) text reads, "For if he who has come to you preaches another Jesus, whom we have not preached, or if you have received another spirit, which you had not received, or another gospel, which you had not accepted, you might have listened to him.

"For I think that I am not in the least inferior to the most distinguished apostles.

"But though I am a poor speaker, I am not poor in knowledge; but we have been thoroughly made manifest among you in all things."

Paul here warns against other Christian teachers who came from time to time to visit these congregations. Some of these teachers were false; some were enemies of Paul and tried to undermine his work wherever they went.

Paul states that a Corinthian should not accept any other gospel besides that which he had given them.

"Received another spirit" is an Aramaic saying which means, "received another revelation." Paul wanted the Corinthians to shun all these teachers and their teachings. In another instance, he states that even if an angel should come from heaven preaching another gospel, they should not accept it.

Many teachers who came from Judea had known Paul as a persecutor of the Church of Jesus Christ. They also knew that he had never been with Jesus. Thus they easily turned some of the Jewish converts against him. Other apostles had seen Jesus; they had walked with him and sat at his feet, but Paul had not.

Nevertheless, Paul was a graduate of the Jewish theological school at the temple in Jerusalem and therefore esteemed himself superior to the other apostles.

20. PAUL'S RANK

And when I was present with you, and wanted, I was chargeable to no man; for that which was lacking to me, the brethren which came from Macedonia supplied; and in all things I have kept myself from being burdensome unto you, and so will I keep myself.

II Cor. 11:9

The needs of the other apostles who presided over the Church of Christ were met or supplied by the converts. Paul himself raised money from Christians in Macedonia and other places for the church in Jerusalem, that is, for the poor people.

We must realize that Paul was sent forth by other apostles, who were his superiors. Paul was not commissioned by Jesus Christ like the twelve upon whom he laid his hands, giving them the Holy Spirit and the power to heal the sick and restore the insane.

Nevertheless, Paul, because of his superior education, believed that he should have the same respect given to the other apostles because he did not consider himself inferior to them in knowledge, in hard work or in suffering. Moreover, Paul made his living by his own hands, embroidering trappings for saddles. He was a saddle maker, not a tent maker. (Acts 18:3)

Paul, not having seen Jesus, faced many problems. This is the reason he uses the Aramaic idiom "thorn in my flesh," which means "a grievance." But as we have said before, Paul was a hard worker, Hebrew by race, an Israelite and a descendant of Abraham. He considered himself to have qualifications equal to those of the other apostles, who were Galileans. (See II Cor. 11:23, 12:11, Eastern [Aramaic] text, Lamsa.)

21. IN A VISION

It is not expedient for me doubtless to glory. I will come to visions and revelations of the Lord.

I knew a man in Christ above fourteen years ago, (whether in the body, I cannot tell; or whether out of the body, I cannot tell: God knoweth;) such an one caught up to the third heaven.

II Cor. 12:1–2

Paul saw Jesus in a vision while he was on his way to Damascus to persecute the Christians and to close their churches. This happened fourteen years before he sent his epistle.

When a man is in a vision, everything seems familiar and real to him. He is not aware that he is in a vision or trance. Moreover, in a vision, time and space seem to vanish. In other words, when a person sees a vision, he is momentarily in the world of spirit, and not in the physical world. Therefore, everything is revealed to him in a symbolic manner.

Paul in his vision was carried to the third part of heaven, that is, one third of the distance between earth and heaven. He was so overcome by the phenomenon that he could not understand the meaning of the vision, the whole of which occurred as a flash of light.

22. CAUGHT UP INTO PARADISE

. . . How that he was caught up into paradise, and heard unspeakable words, which it is not lawful for a man to utter.

II Cor. 12:4

Paul in his vision does not know where he is, nor can he understand whether he is in the flesh, in a physical body, or not. The vision, or the heavenly words which were spoken to him, came from the other world in a mystical way which only a prophet or seer could interpret. Moreover, Paul boasts the gift of divine revelations, but he does not glory in any of his gifts.

In the olden days, the people thought that heaven, or paradise, was above the clouds, and many still do. God and the angels are supposed to reside there. This is because in the olden days clouds were considered the highest things in nature. But today we know this is not true. We also know that clouds could not contain God, who is spirit and all in all.

Paul spoke and wrote to people in that day whose concept of science and religion was different from ours. Jesus also preached in language which the people could understand.

23. SATAN'S ANGEL

And lest I should be exalted above measure through the
abundance of the revelations, there was given to me a
thorn in the flesh, the messenger of Satan to buffet me,
lest I should be exalted above measure.
For this thing I besought the Lord thrice, that it might depart from me.

II Cor. 12:7–8

"The messenger of Satan" means "tribulation," "sickness
and hindrances." Paul calls these things "the messenger of
Satan" because they came upon him through man, who had
strayed from God's truth. The term "Satan" means "to miss the
mark," "to go astray," "to slip," "to deviate from the truth."
The term "angel" means "God's counsel." "Thorn in the flesh" is
an Aramaic idiom which means "grievance."

Paul might have suffered from fever and colds, as many
people do, but he was far from being an invalid, as some
commentators think. Moreover, Paul suffered hunger and other
privations which at times weakened his body, but God always
strengthened him.

The term "three" is used figuratively, meaning "many times."
Many of Paul's enemies were false Christian brothers who under-
minded his work and caused him many tribulations.

24. MIRACLES OF PAUL

Truly the signs of an apostle were wrought among you in
all patience, in signs, and wonders, and mighty deeds.

II Cor. 12:12

Several miracles have been attributed to Paul. Peter and
John healed the lame man who was begging at the entrance

of the temple at Jerusalem, when they said to him, "Gold and silver have I none; but what I have I give to you. In the name of our Lord Jesus Christ of Nazareth, rise up and walk." (Acts 3:6) Peter also raised Tabitha, which means "gazelle," from the dead. (Acts 9:40) There are several other wonders which occurred in Peter's life, such as when he was released from prison by an "angel of the Lord." (Acts 5:19) The only miracles, or wonders, which Paul performed are these:

In a town in Cyprus, while he was placing fuel on the fire, a deadly viper was hanging on his hand. (Acts 29:3–6) The Eastern text says that Paul was bitten by the deadly viper, but the miracle or wonder is that the poison of the reptile did not cause him to die. This is why the pagans were surprised.

The other miracle occurred when he was preaching at Troas, and a young man named Eutychus fell down from the balcony and was injured. Paul came down and told the people that the young man was not dead; his life was still in him, and the young man was healed. On this occasion, Paul spoke until midnight. (See Acts 20:7–10.)

Paul, like Peter, was also released from prison and the prison warden was converted. All the true believers in Jesus Christ had power over disease.

Be that as it may, there was some rivalry between Paul and the other apostles.

25. CORINTHIANS ADMONISHED

Therefore I write these things being absent, lest being present I should use sharpness, according to the power which the Lord hath given me to edification, and not to destruction.

II Cor. 13:10

Paul wrote these things to the Corinthians as an admonition and not as a rebuke. As an apostle in charge of churches, he had the authority to deal harshly with those who were disloyal to the teachings of the gospel of Jesus Christ, which he had preached to them. And now they were living like pagans.

What Paul wrote to them was for their discipline and edification. Paul wanted the Corinthian Christians to bring forth the fruits of the Christian gospel, so that when he came to see them he would rejoice in them. Paul had heard many rumors about the evil conduct of some of these so-called Christians, who lived as pagans, practicing immorality and disobeying the law of God.

The Epistle of Paul the Apostle to the Galatians

1. TURNED TO ANOTHER GOSPEL

I marvel that ye are so soon removed from him that called
you into the grace of Christ unto another gospel:
Which is not another; but there be some that trouble you,
and would pervert the gospel of Christ.

Gal. 1:6–7

Apparently, some Christian Jews from Judea had come to Galatia and told the Christians there to keep the Mosaic law and its ordinances. These Christian converts were so zealous toward the Mosaic law that they wanted not only the Jewish Christians but even the Gentiles to observe it. They told Paul's converts that Paul was not an apostle or a disciple of Jesus Christ but that he was sent by the apostles. These men preached a different gospel from that preached by Paul to the Galatians.

The Jewish Christians believed that no one could transgress the law of God and not receive punishment. Even Jesus himself had obeyed the Sabbath, the Ten Commandments, and most of the Jewish religious ordinances and rituals. He said, "Do not suppose that I have come to weaken the law or the prophets; I have not come to weaken but to fulfill." (Matt. 5:17)

2. THE TRUE GOSPEL

But though we, or an angel from heaven, preach any other gospel unto you than that which we have preached unto you, let him be accursed.

Gal. 1:8

Paul in this instance means that Christians must not depart from the true teaching of the gospel of Jesus Christ, which the apostles had preached to them. He also warns them not to accept anything new which is contrary to the gospel which he and the other apostles had received; not even the teaching of an angel should be accepted if that teaching is contrary to the gospel they had preached to them.

Some of the Christian converts from Judaism and some Aramaeans were influenced by the pagan doctrines and practices, and had fallen prey to the new teachers. The Christians, after the conversion of the Emperor Constantine, accepted other teachings which were contrary to the teaching of the Hebrew prophets, the Mosaic law and that of Jesus Christ. For the sake of honor, glory, and material things, they broke the stern command which was given by the apostle Paul.

There was no need to add to the gospel of Jesus Christ and the teaching of the prophets, which was dictated by God Himself. This is because no one could improve on a revelation which came from God, or could make twice five to be anything

240

more or less than ten. Indeed the true pattern of religion is like science and physics, based on actual truths which cannot be changed or altered.

The term "angels" in this instance means "teachers of religion," who would appear to be like angels. In the East, teachers of religion are looked upon as angels of God and His ministers, because they guide the people as a shepherd guides his sheep. God's angels would not try to teach or preach anything contrary to God's truth.

3. A REVELATION

But I certify you, brethren, that the gospel which was preached of me is not after man.
For I neither received it of man, neither was I taught it, but by the revelation of Jesus Christ.

Gal. 1:11–12

Paul confesses that his gospel is not based on the human understanding of the rabbinical teachers, whose words were final; but on the revelation which he had received directly from Jesus Christ, like the Hebrew prophets, whose teachings came through revelations which they received directly from God.

Such teaching as that which was taught by Jesus Christ must have come through a revelation and therefore must be understood by means of a revelation. Jesus' teaching was based on the teaching of the prophets, but was contrary to the teaching of religious men of his day. It was based on meekness, loving-kindness, sharing, forgiving one's enemies, going another mile, not resisting evil—new things which the world had never experienced before. Therefore, it had to be revealed in order to be understood in human language.

4. TITUS AN ARAMAEAN

> But neither Titus, who was with me, being a Greek, was
> compelled to be circumcised.
>
> Gal. 2:3

Titus was an Aramaean, or Syrian, though his mother
was a Jewess. The term "Greek" is used wrongly; I believe
it was done purposely to show that some of the early Christians
were of Greek origin.

The Aramaeans were not only geographically adjacent to
Judea but also related to the Jews. Titus was brought up in
the Jewish religion and by his mother's teachings. It is interesting to note that Jewish women who marry Gentile husbands
always remain loyal to their religion, tradition and customs
and try to bring up their children in the religion in which
they themselves were reared, the religion of their forefathers.

5. LAW CANNOT SAVE

> For I through the law am dead to the law, that I might
> live unto God.
>
> Gal. 2:19

No one can be justified by the law, for no one can keep
the whole law. One may observe the Sabbath day strictly, but
he may covet another man's vineyard, wife, or property, or he
may lie. Thus, when one law is broken, the whole law is
broken.

In other words, there is no salvation by mere observance

of the law; and since no one can keep the whole law, man continues to be subject to sin and hence to death, because the wages of sin are death.

Christians live by faith, grace, good works, and the teachings of Jesus Christ. Nevertheless, faith must be demonstrated by good works. Just to believe in Jesus or his teaching is not enough. One has to live up to it in order to let his light shine so that men may know that he is a child of God.

6. GENTILES DECLARED RIGHTEOUS

And the scripture, foreseeing that God would justify the heathen through faith, preached before the gospel unto Abraham, saying, In thee shall all nations be blessed.
So then they which be of faith are blessed with faithful Abraham.

Gal. 3:8–9

When these Gentiles were living in paganism, they did not know God. Therefore, they worshiped images which were supposed to be gods. But now they knew God; therefore they had no excuse to revert to paganism and pagan practices, which were contrary to the teachings of the prophets and Jesus Christ.

Paul upbraids the Galatian Christians for not having remained loyal to the teachings of the gospel which he had imparted to them. Paul's work was often beset by his enemies, who told his converts that he had never seen Jesus and therefore he was not an apostle. This charge remained a thorn in Paul's flesh.

7. PROMISE MADE TO ABRAHAM

Now to Abraham and his seed were the promises made.
He saith not, And to seeds, as of many; but as of one,
And to thy seed, which is Christ.

Gal 3:16

This promise was made to Abraham and his descendants, or seed, which in the singular, means "teaching." It was not to his descendants but to his descendant; therefore, not all the people who were the descendants of Abraham were the heirs of the promise, but only those who believed in his teaching. (See Gal. 3:8.)

Abraham had many descendants, including Ishmaelites, Edomites, Medionites and many others, but these were not included in the promise, and therefore were not the heirs. Jacob became the only rightful heir, and through him the teaching of Abraham was handed down from one generation to another. Nevertheless, all other descendants of Abraham were blessed by God, Who had blessed them before He blessed Isaac. Before Isaac was born, God had blessed Ishmael and assured Abraham that his descendants would multiply and would become a great people.

Esau was also blessed. All the descendants of these two were called *Ammey*, "Gentiles." *Ammey* means "our uncles" or "kindred." Those descendants of Abraham who accepted his faith became heirs through Jesus Christ.

8. TRANSGRESSION

Wherefore then serveth the law? It was added because of
transgressions, till the seed should come to whom the
promise was made; and it was ordained by angels in the
hand of a mediator.

Gal. 3:19

Paul tries to explain that the law was given because of
the transgression. If there had been no transgression there would
have been no law.

The law was a necessity until the truth and grace were
revealed by Jesus Christ, whose coming was preordained by
God. (See Ex. 20:19.)

9. DESCENDANTS THROUGH CHRIST

And if ye be Christ's, then are ye Abraham's seed, and heirs
according to the promise.

Gal. 3:29

The phrase *zarey di Abraham*, in this instance, means
"the teachings of Abraham"; therefore it refers to the heirs of
the promise made to Abraham when God had said to him,
"By your seed, your faith, will all the people of the earth
be blessed."

Paul here includes all believers in Jesus Christ, regardless
of their race or color, as the heirs of Abraham. Even the
Aramaeans, who were kindred of Abraham but not his descendants, had now become the descendants of Abraham because

they had accepted the teachings of Jesus Christ, who is the spiritual heir of the promise.

Note: at this time, Greeks were not yet converted to Christianity. The first Christian converts were Jews, Aramaeans and Arabians, who were a kindred people and spoke the same language. Moreover, there were many intermarriages between them, as there are today in the Near East.

It was difficult for the apostles to sell the idea of the cross and its strange meaning and saving power to the Aramaeans, because most of them were concerned about life and its pleasures on this earth rather than in the hereafter. They had sought the wisdom of this world. Jesus had died on the cross as a malefactor. They could not see any success in the grave.

At the same time, the cross was a stumbling block to the Jews, and foolishness to the Aramaeans. (I Cor. 1:22–23)

10. HAGAR AND SARAH

For this Agar is mount Sinai in Arabia, and answereth to Jerusalem which now is, and is in bondage with her children.

Gal. 4:25

Paul in this instance is using an allegory, the two sons of Abraham: Ishmael, his son by the bondswoman, and Isaac, the son of Sarah, a free woman. (See Gen. 16:15 and 21:2.)

Now Ishmael, the son of Hagar, the bondswoman, was born before the promise, before the Lord said to Abraham, "By your seed all the nations of the world will be blessed." ("Seed," in Aramaic, also means "teaching.")

Thus, Hagar is symbolic of Mount Sinai, where the law was given by God to Moses, and she is the mother of the Ishmaelites.

The Eastern text reads, "For this Hagar is Mount Sinai in Arabia, and surrenders to Jerusalem which now is, and is in bondage with her children." Jerusalem was under the Romans. The Jews had lost their political freedom, but were still heirs of the promise.

The Epistle of Paul the Apostle to the Ephesians

1. THE GOSPEL WILL TRIUMPH

That in the dispensation of the fulness of times he might gather together in one all things in Christ, both which are in heaven, and which are on earth; even in him:

Eph. 1:10

In the fullness of time the gospel of Jesus Christ will ultimately supplant all other teachings which are contrary to the truth of God. In other words, there will be a new creation; the old Adam will give way to the new Adam, which is Jesus Christ; and the old law of the flesh to the law of the spirit.

Paul here gives hope of a universal salvation of mankind. The new teaching inspired and inaugurated by Jesus Christ will usher in the long-coveted heaven on earth—the kingdom of God. Jesus said, "The kingdom of God is within you, that is, within your reach."

Time is element. It takes some time for the leaven to leaven the dough, and for the seed to spring up and mature.

2. JESUS' NAME

. . . Far above all principality, and power, and might,
and dominion, and every name that is named, not only in
this world, but also in that which is to come.

Eph. 1:21

After his resurrection and his triumph over death and
sin, Jesus' name became the greatest in this world and in the
world to come. This is because Jesus was the first man to
defy death, the forces of evil, and the grave. Therefore, God
made him great, and set all things under his authority.

3. THE PRINCE OF THE AIR

. . . Wherein in time past ye walked according to the
course of this world, according to the prince of the
power of the air, the spirit that now worketh in the children
of disobedience.

Eph. 2:2

Paul in this instance refers to the former way of life
of the Ephesians—the way in which they walked, or conducted
themselves, prior to their conversion to Jesus Christ. Not having
seen the light of God, they did as the other pagans did.
Resh shultana means "the head of the government," or "the
prince of pride and glory, and of the forces of evil, who is
called the prince of this world." The term "spirit" in this instance
means "inclination toward evil," which always leads men to
disobedience to God and His way of life.

4. RESTING IN HEAVEN

. . . And hath raised us up together, and made us sit
together in heavenly places in Christ Jesus.

Eph. 2:6

Jesus, through his resurrection, saved all mankind in that
he gave to man an assurance of life hereafter. Prior to his
resurrection, death was feared and looked upon as a sinister
end. But when Jesus triumphed over death and the grave he
became the first fruits of a new and everlasting life.

Jesus' followers were to be in heaven together. (The term
"sit" means "to rest.") Jesus promised his followers he was
going to prepare a place for them in heaven. Heaven means
a place of peace, harmony, tranquility, and understanding, where
war, persecutions, and hatred will end, and man will become
cognizant of himself as a son of God.

5. SAVED BY GRACE

Wherefore remember, that ye being in time past Gentiles
in the flesh, who are called Uncircumcision by that which
is called the Circumcision in the flesh made by hands;
That at that time ye were without Christ, being aliens from
the commonwealth of Israel, and strangers from the covenants of promise, having no hope, and without God in
the world . . .

Eph. 2:11–12

The reference here is to the Aramaeans, or Syrians, who
had become converts to the gospel of Jesus Christ. These people

were formerly alien to the promises which had been made to Israel. In other words, they were not the heirs of the covenant, nor were they circumcized according to the ordinance which God had given to Abraham. Before they became Christian, they were called "the uncircumcized." They had had no hope, no law, and no scriptures—the light of God—but now they were saved by the grace of God and their belief in Jesus Christ. (See Gal. 4:8.)

These people were Semitic in origin but not members of the Jewish religion. This is the reason they had not been circumcized. For instance, the Aramaeans were the same race as the Hebrews but were not circumcized. This is because the law of circumcision came after Abraham's tribe had crossed the River Euphrates into Syria and Palestine. On the other hand, the Moslems were circumcized, because circumcision was introduced when Ishmael was thirteen years of age, and Isaac only eight days old. So it became the custom for Moslems to circumcize at the age of thirteen years, and the Jews at the age of eight days.

6. PREACHER AMONG THE GENTILES

Unto me, who am less than the least of all saints, is this grace given, that I should preach among the Gentiles the unsearchable riches of Christ.

Eph. 3:8

Paul was not one of the twelve disciples of Jesus Christ, nor had he seen Jesus while he was on earth. Paul came late into the fold of Christ and he was sent by Peter, John, and James, the three great pillars of the Church, as an apostle to preach to the Jews and later to the Gentiles. In other words, he was the apostles' apostle.

Nevertheless, Paul was called to preach the gospel among the Gentiles, the Aramaeans, or Syrians, the Moabites, Ammonites, and Edomites, who were dispersed throughout the Roman Empire. "Gentiles" means "people who were kindred of the Jews but not members of the Jewish religion."

Paul was looked upon as one of the least of the apostles, simply because he did not belong to the ranks of the Twelve. But he was a hard worker, and ready to suffer for the cause of the gospel of Jesus Christ.

Note: No one could belong to the ranks of the Twelve without having actually been with Jesus. (Acts 1:21)

7. GOD'S WISDOM HIDDEN

. . . To the intent that now unto the principalities and powers in heavenly places might be known by the church the manifold wisdom of God . . .

Eph. 3:10

The Eastern (Aramaic) text reads, "to the intent that through the church [the gospel of Jesus Christ] the manifold wisdom of God may be made known to the angels and powers which are in heaven."

Arcus is the name of the seventh order of the angels. In other words, even the rulers and principalities were to be affected by the power of the gospel.

The wisdom of God and His salvation had been hidden from the world, but they were now made manifest through Jesus Christ and his simple gospel of meekness and loving-kindness. "And that I might enlighten all men that they may see what is the dispensation of the mystery which for ages had been hidden from the world by God who created all things." (Eph.

251

3:9) That is to say, salvation was hidden from men until it was revealed through the grace of God by Jesus Christ.

God was always mindful of the Gentiles and pagans, because they also were His children, who in the fullness of time would be brought into His fold.

8. DIVINE GIFTS

And he gave some, apostles; and some, prophets; and some, evangelists; and some, pastors and teachers.

Eph. 4:11

"Gave," in this instance, means "assigned" or "appointed"; that is, gave them power to exercise their gifts, as the apostles and prophets were given power to become teachers of the Word of God.

All the workers for the gospel were endowed with these diverse gifts which were, and are still, needed in the work of the Church of Christ.

The apostles were engaged in prayer and in healing the sick, and were active as guardians in all spiritual matters. The prophets, like the prophets of old, acted as counselors and advisers in matters of conduct and guidance. The evangelists were engaged in preaching the gospel and in teaching and training the faithful.

9. STRUGGLE AGAINST EVIL

For we wrestle not against flesh and blood, but against principalities, against powers, against the rulers of the darkness of this world, against spiritual wickedness in high places.

Eph. 6:12

Paul states that all the powers of darkness, the forces of evil, were in opposition to Christian teaching. The wicked rulers of this world were unwilling to change their evil way of life and to accept the true way, but the light of the Christian gospel exposed evil.

"Evil spirits" in this instance means "evil people," or "those who were possessed by wrong thinking." The term "spirit" also means "a person." In the East, we often ask one another, "How many spirits, or souls, are there in your house?" The term "angel" does not mean angels of God, but "evil people who pretend to be innocent, like angels." This term was used sarcastically by Paul. In Aramaic, when we point our finger at an evil man, we often say, "He's an angel," which means he pretends to be one. Such remarks can only be interpreted by facial expression, the movement of the hands, and the tone of voice.

The phrase "spiritual wickedness" is a mistranslation, as there is no such things as spiritual wickedness. The Eastern text reads, "the evil spirits under the heavens," that is, persons with evil and destructive inclinations.

Christians must always be armed with truth in order to combat the forces of evil, for Christianity is a challenge, and the conflict between good and evil will continue until they are finally separated, as illustrated in the parable of the wheat and the tares.

10. THE ARMOR OF GOD

Wherefore take unto you the whole armour of God, that
ye may be able to withstand in the evil day, and having
done all, to stand.
Stand therefore, having your loins girt about with truth,
and having on the breastplate of righteousness.

Eph. 6:13–14

The Aramaic word *zena,* "weapon," is used metaphorically
to mean "truth." This is because truth is stronger than any
armor forged by human hands.

The Christians are admonished to manifest their true Christian
qualities in order that their light may shine in the pagan world.
In Ephesians 6:14, Paul uses the term "truth."

Easterners always wear a girdle over their clothes, and soldiers
are also girded, with their weapons upon their bodies. The
Christians are told to be like armed men, girded with the
truth and ready for combat against evil forces. (See Eph. 6:15.)

11. HELMET OF SALVATION

Above all, taking the shield of faith, wherewith ye shall
be able to quench all the fiery darts of the wicked.
And take the helmet of salvation, and the sword of the
Spirit, which is the word of God.

Eph. 6:16–17

The shield of faith is the truth of the Christian gospel
which will ultimately overcome the forces of darkness. The
term "truth" in Aramaic means "something unbreakable," like

a hard rock. When one possesses the truth, he shields himself with unpierceable armor and the helmet of salvation.

Fiery arrows were used by the enemy to burn cities. The arrows were dipped in oil and then ignited before they were fired.

All the earthly opposition against God's way—God's religion —can be overcome by means of the simple gospel, meekness, forgiveness, loving-kindness, the spirit of God and faith in Jesus Christ.

The Epistle of Paul the Apostle to the Philippians

1. INSINCERE TEACHERS

. . . The one preach Christ of contention, not sincerely, supposing to add affliction to my bonds . . .

Phil. 1:16

The Eastern (Aramaic) text reads, "For they know that I am appointed for the defense of the gospel."

Some people were preachers of the gospels, but they were not sincere in their hearts, nor were they true believers in Jesus Christ. Therefore, their preaching caused dissension and strife among the Christians. Moreover, the evil conduct of these men caused Paul much suffering and added to his burdens.

In Philippians 1:17, we read, "But those who preach Christ out of contention do it not sincerely, but do it expecting to increase the hardship of my imprisonment." Unfortunately, the contention and rivalry between preachers of the gospel has continued to this day.

2. CONFESSING JESUS CHRIST

. . . That at the name of Jesus every knee should bow,
of things in heaven, and things in earth, and things under
the earth;
And that every tongue should confess that Jesus Christ is
Lord, to the glory of God the Father.

Phil. 2:10–11

"Under the earth" means "in Sheol." The Hebrews believed
that the souls of the departed were underground. Sheol is a
place of inactivity for the resting of souls. We are told that
Jesus preached to the departed souls in Sheol, that they might
become partakers of the gospel.

The gospel was to be preached in every tongue to every
nation and people. This is being witnessed today as the gospel
of Jesus Christ has been published in hundreds of languages.
Nevertheless, owing to mistranslations and diverse theological
concepts, and rivalry among the followers of Jesus, the progress
of the gospel has been retarded, and in some lands Christianity
has been supplanted by other faiths.

3. PARTAKER OF HIS SUFFERING

. . . That I may know him, and the power of his resurrection, and the fellowship of his sufferings, being made
conformable unto his death;
If by any means I might attain unto the resurrection of
the dead.
Not as though I had already attained, either were already
perfect: but I follow after, if that I may apprehend that
for which also I am apprehended of Christ Jesus.

Phil. 3:10–12

The Eastern (Aramaic) text reads, "So that through this
righteousness I may know Jesus and the power of his resurrection, and be a partaker of his sufferings, even to a death
like his, that I may by any means attain the resurrection from
the dead. Not as though I had already attained or were already
perfect; but I am striving that I may reach that for which
Jesus Christ appointed me."

The righteousness which Paul had gained by means of the
Mosaic law was not sufficient to attain resurrection from the
dead. Paul wanted to follow Jesus Christ even to death on
the cross so that he might attain resurrection just as Jesus
had. This was Paul's goal in life, to work and even to die
for the sake of the gospel. He had left most of the teachings
of Judaism behind him, and now he was striving to attain
salvation and life hereafter through Jesus Christ. Judaism had
not given him a complete assurance of resurrection from death.

4. YOKEFELLOWS

And I entreat thee also, true yoke-fellow, help those
women which laboured with me in the gospel, with Clem-
ent also, and with other my fellow-labourers, whose names
are in the book of life.

Phil. 4:3

The term "yokefellows" means "co-workers." They are so
called simply because they shared the difficulties of preaching
the gospel, as two oxen under the same yoke share the weight
and pull the plow equally.

A great many converts, men and women, helped the apostles
with money, food, clothing, and even in preaching the gospel.
The names of these men and women co-workers were written
in the book of life. They were to receive rich rewards for their
good deeds. (See Rom. 16:3.)

Jesus said, "But do not rejoice in this that the demons submit
to you; but rejoice because your names are written in heaven."
(Luke 10:20) John says, "He who overcomes, the same shall
be clothed in white robes; and I will not blot his name out
of the book of life, but I will confess his name before my
Father and before his angels." (Rev. 3:5)

Paul also exhorts the Philippians to show their humility before
all men.

The Epistle of Paul the Apostle to the Colossians

1. WITH YOU IN SPIRIT

For though I be absent in the flesh, yet am I with you in the spirit, joying and beholding your order, and the stedfastness of your faith in Christ.

Col. 2:5

Paul, in the flesh, or physically, was far away from the Christians in Colossae, but he was with them in spirit, for spirit knows no time or distance. In English, we often say, "I haven't seen you for a long time, but you have been in my thoughts."

Paul was implying that even though he did not visit the Christians in Colossae, they were always in his mind and heart, and that he was greatly concerned over their welfare. Paul rejoiced to hear that they had been sincere and faithful to the gospel.

Paul was eager to visit all of the Christian churches, or centers, both large and small, but it was difficult to do so. Travel was beset with many difficulties, and the Christians were hated by the non-Christians.

2. THE MYSTERY

> Even the mystery which hath been hid from ages and from
> generations, but now is made manifest to his saints:
> To whom God would make known what is the riches of
> the glory of this mystery among the Gentiles; which is
> Christ in you, the hope of glory.
>
> Col. 1:26–27

The reference here is to the saints, or the Christians, to
whom the mystery of the coming of the Messiah, his death on
the cross, and his resurrection, had been revealed.

Jesus Christ is the hope of glory to the Jews and to the
Gentiles. The term "hope of glory" in this instance means "the
glorious resurrection," which was attained through Jesus' death
on the cross, and his triumph over death and the grave.

God had from the very beginning devised a means of salvation
for all His children throughout the world. But the mystery of
this salvation and triumph over death were to be revealed in
the fullness of time through Jesus Christ, who revealed the
true God to both the Gentiles and the pagans.

3. CHRIST THE MAIN OBJECTIVE

> Let no man therefore judge you in meat, or in drink, or
> in respect of an holyday, or of the new moon, or of the
> sabbath days:
> Which are a shadow of things to come; but the body is of
> Christ.
>
> Col. 2:16–17

The disturbances were due to the Jewish ordinances or
rabbinical doctrines relative to the eating of certain meats and

abstaining from others. These statutes were primarily based on the Mosaic law, which was strictly observed by the scribes and Pharisees, who had given it different interpretations, thus making it hard for the people to agree on it. Moreover, at times, the alteration of a single letter or dot changed the meaning of the law or obscured the truth. Indeed, Mosaic laws were written in a simple language without any of the added qualifying clauses—ifs, buts, providings, unlesses, etc.—which served to confuse the people and weaken the law or the ordinance.

There were also some difficulties over the observance of the feast days and the beginnings of months, or the moon. It was difficult to determine the exact minute and hour of the Sabbath, the distance walked on that day, and other man-made laws, such as the washing of hands, cups and dishes. Jesus had called these rules the doctrines of the elders.

Paul calls these Jewish laws and ordinances the shadow of the true interpretation of the law which was to come through the Messiah, Christ. The law and the prophets were fulfilled by the coming of the Messiah Christ who was the main objective and the hope of the world. This is because the Messiah's teaching became a light to the Gentiles and a hope for Israel.

4. CHRIST IS THE HEAD

. . . And not holding the Head, from which all the body
by joints and bands having nourishment ministered, and
knit together, increaseth with the increase of God.

Col. 2:19

Paul warns the faithful not to be deceived by men who by their cunning and intellectuality would cause them to go astray from the teaching of Jesus Christ. Manifestly, such teachers were not upholding Jesus Christ, who is the head of the Church.

Therefore they could not stand, not having a head, just as no member of the body can stand without the head.

Jesus Christ is the foundation of the Christian teaching. He is the stone which the builders rejected, which became the foundation of a new order—a new and universal kingdom. Therefore, no Christian teacher should try to build upon any other foundation.

5. LOYALTY TO CHRIST

And whatsoever ye do in word or deed, do all in the name of the Lord Jesus, giving thanks to God and the Father by him.

Col. 3:17

Paul admonishes the Colossian Christians that everything they do should be done according to the teaching of Jesus Christ. Nothing should be done which is contrary to the Christian gospel and the example set forth by Jesus Christ. They should even refrain from the Mosaic ordinances which they had hitherto observed, if they were contrary to the teaching of Jesus Christ, for all these past things were but shadows of truth which was revealed by Jesus Christ.

The light of Christianity was to shine through the Christian teaching, backed by humility and good deeds. (See Col. 2:17.)

The First Epistle of Paul the Apostle to the Thessalonians

1. DEAD TO MEET CHRIST

For this we say unto you by the word of the Lord, that
we which are alive and remain unto the coming of the
Lord shall not prevent them which are asleep.

I Thess. 4:15

Paul is so sure of the resurrection of the dead that he
writes to the Thessalonians and assures them by the word of
our Lord Jesus Christ, that the dead will rise again and greet
the coming of our Lord before the living.

At that time, there were rumors and expectations of the sudden early return of Jesus. The Aramaic text correctly reads *eta,*
"he has come," instead of, "he is coming." In other words, Paul
was trying to prove to the Jews in Thessalonica that Christ
had come in the person of Jesus of Nazareth, who had been
crucified in Jerusalem. (Note: These Jews in Greece had not
yet heard of Jesus' death. In those days it took a long time
for news to travel.) Evidently, it was this mistranslation into
the Greek which caused the Christians to expect an early return. The gospel was not yet preached, and Jesus himself had
warned his disciples against any rumors of an early second
coming. He had told his followers that no one knows the day
and the hour of his coming but the Father. Moreover, Jesus
assured his disciples that he would be with them always, and
that whenever two or three are together he is always with them.

2. CAUGHT IN THE CLOUDS

For the Lord himself shall descend from heaven with a shout, with the voice of the archangel, and with the trump of God: and the dead in Christ shall rise first: Then we which are alive and remain shall be caught up together with them in the clouds to meet the Lord in the air: and so shall we ever be with the Lord.

I Thess. 4:16–17

In biblical days, people's concept of heaven was different from ours. Heaven was supposed to be above the clouds, a few miles above the earth. The firmament and the clouds separated the heaven and the earth. Thus it was easy for angels to ascend and descend. (See John 1:51.) Then again, the disciples had seen Jesus ascending into heaven in a cloud, and clouds were supposed to be the highest thing above the earth. (Acts 1:9–11)

In the Old Testament we are told that God rode on the clouds; He made clouds His chariot. (Psalms) Jesus was expected to return in the same manner in which his disciples had seen him ascend. Even though Jesus had never set a date for his return or his second coming, some Christian teachers have predicted the day, but so far there has been no "coming"; he is already here.

The Eastern text reads, *etha*, "has come," instead of *atey*, "is coming."

Jesus will come in a spiritual body, so that all the world will see him. And according to Paul, those who are living will be transformed into a spiritual body just as Jesus' body was transformed. (See I Cor. 15.)

The phrase "meet him in the air" is an Aramaic idiom which means that we will hasten to meet him before he sets his foot on the ground, as a president is greeted before he alights from his plane.

The Second Epistle of Paul the Apostle to the Thessalonians

1. CHRIST STANDS BY YOU

That the name of our Lord Jesus Christ may be glorified in you, and ye in him, according to the grace of our God and the Lord Jesus Christ.

II Thess. 1:12

"In you" means "by you," that is to say, by or through the things you do. In the East we often ask a man by what authority he does things. The Pharisees asked Jesus by what authority he was performing miracles.

Then again, in Aramaic we often say, "He is backed by the king," or, "The king stands by him," which means, "He has the support of the king." This preposition is difficult to translate. We have another word for "in," which is *begaw*, but this is not the case here. In other words, in these ancient Semitic languages we do not say, "One man is in another"; we say, "I stand by you."

This indicates that when one works for the Christian gospel, Christ upholds him and becomes one with him. On the other hand, Christ, being spirit, cannot be contained. When Christ stands by a man or woman they become one with him in the spirit.

2. MAN OF SIN

> That ye be not soon shaken in mind, or be troubled,
> neither by spirit, nor by word, nor by letter as from us,
> as that the day of Christ is at hand.
> Let no man deceive you by any means: for that day shall
> not come, except there comes a falling away first, and
> that man of sin be revealed, the son of perdition.
>
> II Thess. 2:2–3

Paul here reminds the Thessalonians not to be deceived by the teachers who had set the day of the coming of the Lord. Many of these teachers were constantly preaching about the second coming of Christ and the destruction of the world. They had little else to say. Some preachers are doing it today.

Even Jesus himself warned his disciples not to believe anyone who set forth the day of his coming. This is because no one but God knows that day and that hour. His coming will be like that of a thief at night. (See parable of the virgins, Matt. 25:1–13, and that of the servant who watched for the coming of his lord, Luke 12:39.)

Jesus' coming will be preceded by wars, revolutions, and much suffering. The man of sin, that is, the forces of evil, must be revealed and defeated. Christianity, from its very inception, has faced opposition from false philosophies and false religions which have deceived the people and led them astray from the way of God. In other words, Christ will come when the world is ready for him and his gospel is accepted universally.

3. HUMAN DEITIES

... Who opposeth and exalteth himself above all that
is called God, or that is worshipped; so that he as God
sitteth in the temple of God, shewing himself that he is
God.

II Thess. 2:4

The Eastern text reads, ". . . who opposes and exalts
himself above all that is called God or that is reverenced; so
that even in the temple of God he sits as a god, and shows
himself, as though he were a god."

Paul is speaking in a metaphorical manner. In the East, when
people speak unfavorably of kings, princes, or religious authorities, they use numerical speech. For example, when John referred to the persecutor of the Church, Nero Caesar, he called
him "the beast," and gave his number, 666. (See New Testament
commentary, Rev. 13:17–18.)

The reference here is to kings and religious authorities who
posed as deities and promoted deceptive and evil doctrines.
Paul hated both pagan and Jewish religious authorities because
they opposed and persecuted him.

During the time of Paul, every Roman Emperor was looked
upon as a god. On the other hand, the Jewish high priests, who
were supposed to represent God in the temple, had become
kings and were revered by some people more than God.

The apostle said the time was coming when these men would
be exposed by opposition and rebellion. The time came when
the deity of the Roman Emperor was ended and the Christian
cross triumphed over pagan religions. The temple was destroyed
and the high priest lost his power and glory.

4. EVIL FORCES AT WORK

And now ye know what withholdeth that he might be revealed in his time.
For the mystery of iniquity doth already work: only he who now letteth will let, until he be taken out of the way.

II Thess. 2:6–7

The Eastern (Aramaic) text reads, "And now you know what has prevented him from being revealed in his time. For the mystery of iniquity is already at work, until he who now is the obstacle is taken out of the way."

Paul had predicted changes both in the imperial systems and the religious order of his day. The forces which were to bring about these changes were already at work. There was growing opposition to the empire and to religion in Palestine and other Eastern countries, where people were heavily laden with taxation and tributes, and were being crushed under a heavy burden. Judaism had failed to free the people. Many religious and political leaders were eager to free their countries from the foreign yoke and pagan influences.

All strong religions were opposed to Christianity because Jesus' teaching of meekness, loving-kindness and nonresistance was contrary to pagan institutions. It was also opposed by the Jewish hierarchy. These evil hindrances were to be overcome, and the gospel of Christ was to triumph and become more powerful than paganism and Judaism. Later on, Constantine declared it the religion of the Roman Empire.

Christianity is ultimately to triumph over the political and religious systems of the world in order to inaugurate the reign of righteousness and hasten the kingdom of God.

5. THE ANTI-CHRIST

And then shall that Wicked be revealed, whom the Lord
shall consume with the spirit of his mouth, and shall destroy with the brightness of his coming:
Even him, whose coming is after the working of Satan
with all power and signs and lying wonders . . .

II Thess. 2:8–9

The "wicked" here is the Anti-Christ, that is, the deceiver
who would perform wonders and thus cause many to go astray
from the way of Christ.

The reference here is to the new and destructive philosophies
which had already come. (See Matt. 24:24.)

The false teachers and teachings were soon to be exposed by
the words of truth which came from the mouth of Jesus Christ.

Jesus, through his triumphant coming, will do away with all
evil forces which have stood in the way of his gospel. His
glorious coming will not only be witnessed by his own followers,
but also by those who have opposed his gospel, and when they
see him they will stand bewildered and shamed.

6. DELUSION

And for this cause God shall send them strong delusion,
that they should believe a lie.

II Thess. 2:11

God does not send evil to the world, that is, anything
which is harmful to His people. But He lets the people bring
evil upon themselves if they wish. In other words, when they

refuse His counsel they do not receive His guidance. These evil men—the Anti-Christ—had rejected the truth of Jesus Christ, and hence they were not guided by the Holy Spirit which guided the true believers and guarded them from impending disasters. In due time, they were to perish by their own evil devices and acts. (Matt. 24:5, Rom. 1:24)

The First Epistle of Paul the Apostle to Timothy

1. PAUL'S TRIALS AND SUFFERING

Howbeit for this cause I obtained mercy, that in me first Jesus Christ might shew forth all long-suffering, for a pattern to them which should hereafter believe on him to life everlasting.

I Tim. 1:16

The apostle in this instance speaks of his trials and suffering for the cause of the gospel. Paul met opposition everywhere he went, for many people doubted his apostleship and his sincerity as a Christian convert. Also, some of the Jewish Christians hated him because of his sympathy with the Gentiles.

Paul had obtained his salvation, not by means of the law and the Mosaic ordinances, but by the grace of God and the mercies of Jesus Christ. This is because the God that Jesus Christ preached to the people is a loving Father Who constantly forgives His children and gladly receives them when they return to Him. But Mosaic laws and ordinances were very difficult to keep, and there was no forgiveness such as that taught by Jesus.

Paul, during all his tribulations, remained calm, faithful and long-suffering, and thus became an example for the martyrs who were to come after him.

Jesus Christ never complained about his hardships, suffering and death, because he knew that his death on the cross was preordained and that the people could not comprehend his teaching. He forgave his enemies and those who crucified him because they did not know what they were doing. The Hebrew prophets had predicted his suffering and death centuries before his birth.

2. TRANSGRESSION OF MORAL LAW

Notwithstanding she shall be saved in childbearing, if they continue in faith and charity and holiness with sobriety.

I Tim. 2:15

The reference here is to the fall of man. Paul quotes the Book of Genesis and therefore blames woman for the fall of man, or the transgression of the law. (See I Tim. 2:13–14.)

The woman, Eve, the mother of life, will be restored through her posterity; that is to say, if her children remain faithful in the religion of Jesus Christ she will continue to live through them. God promised Eve that one of her offspring would bruise the head of the serpent, that is, destroy the devil, or temptation. Jesus, through his death on the cross, destroyed the power of sin and death. In other words, Jesus is the new Adam. An Eastern theologian states that, as by one man sin entered into the world, by one man sin and the power of Satan and death were destroyed.

3. A MINISTER'S CONDUCT

. . . Not given to wine, no striker, not greedy of filthy
lucre; but patient, not a brawler, not covetous . . .

I Tim. 3:3

People who went astray from their faith were condemned
to punishment by pagan priests and other higher authorities.
Jewish priests ordered guilty men to be stoned, punished or
rebuked, according to their guilt. They were harsh in their
dealings with those who broke the law or its ordinances, for
they were living under a harsh law—an eye for an eye, a tooth
for a tooth.

The Moslems punished those guilty of breaking the law very
severely, by cutting off their hands, legs, or other members of
their bodies to serve as an example to others. There is more
mercy and forgiveness in the Christian religion than in any
other. This is largely due to the fact that Jesus forgave sinners
and stated that he had come to call sinners rather than the
righteous, and to find those who were lost.

Paul admonishes the elders and priests to be meek, gentle,
kind and forgiving, so that pagans and members of other religions might know that they were the followers of Jesus Christ,
the exponent of a gospel based on meekness, forgiveness, and
loving-kindness.

By living a chaste and faithful life, they would become examples of Christian conduct, not only to their congregations,
but to people round about them. Indeed, just as the success of a
flock of sheep depends upon the character and faithfulness of
their shepherd, so does a congregation depend on the virtues of
its minister, for he is their example.

4. MINISTER TO BE ABOVE REPROACH

Let no man despise thy youth; but be thou an example
of the believers, in word, in conversation, in charity, in
spirit, in faith, in purity.

I Tim. 4:12

Timotheus is admonished to act as a Christian convert
and to conduct himself so well that no one could despise him
or reject his teaching. Paul wanted him to become an example
of Christian conduct above reproach, so that the new converts
to the Christian religion could emulate his life. Easterners judge
a preacher not by his sermons and his words, but by his actions
and his way of life.

Jesus said that a good tree is known by its good fruit, but
a bad tree is known by its bad fruit. True Christian men and
women are known by their good lives.

5. YOUNG WIDOWS

But the younger widows refuse: for when they have
begun to wax wanton against Christ, they will marry.

I Tim. 5:11

The elders of the churches were admonished by Paul
to differentiate between the older and younger widows, for
the older widows remained loyal to the work which the church
assigned to them, but the younger ones often changed their
minds and remarried—leaving the work assigned to their care
by the church.

In those early days of Christianity when the church was in

its infancy, widows played an important part in the work of the church. They cared for the poor and the strangers who found no lodging place except the church, and spent considerable time in prayer and in teaching the women students who could not attend the church meetings. Thus many of them became excellent examples for other women and girls. (See Luke 2:30–37.)

In the Jewish religion, such pious women worked in the temples, cleaning, washing and cooking for the priests. The Church of the East also had devout widows who were constantly engaged in prayer and in church work. And this is not all. Women have always played an important part in all great religions. Women ministered to Jesus and to the Hebrew prophets, and they played a great part in the Islamic religion.

6. WIDOWS' BEHAVIOR

For some are already turned aside after Satan.

I Tim. 5:15

Evidently some of the younger Christian widows were not behaving as Christian widows should. They were negligent in their prayers and fasting, and in the work of charity. Some of them had strayed from the true way of life, and like pagan widows, had become immoral, thus giving occasion for unbelievers to speak against them. In other words, these widows were bad examples for the Christian church over which Timotheus was ministering.

7. TRUE CHRISTIAN DOCTRINE

If any man teach otherwise, and consent not to whole-
some words, even the words of our Lord Jesus Christ,
and to the doctrine which is according to godliness . . .

I Tim. 6:3

Paul states that any teaching which is not based on the
words of Jesus Christ is preached for pride, dispute, and division in the church. In other words, such teachings are destructive and not edifying. Such teachers were under the impres-
sion that religion was a business rather than the worship of
God. Timotheus is warned to keep away from such false teachers and destructive doctrines.

There were many Christian teachers who were influenced
by Neo-Platonism and other false doctrines which were ad-
vanced from time to time in the Western world. Then again,
there were Christian teachers who were formerly Jewish. These
men tried to introduce Jewish teachings and the doctrines of
the elders into the Christian faith. Jesus had discarded many
of these man-made doctrines.

8. THE CHRISTIAN CHALLENGE

Fight the good fight of faith, lay hold on eternal life,
whereunto thou art also called, and hast professed a good
profession before many witnesses.

I Tim. 6:12

"Fight the good fight" is an idiom which means "to defend
the faith which has been entrusted to you and continue to up-

hold the true religion of Jesus Christ which promises eternal life and heavenly rewards."

Christians were always exposed to dangers and persecutions from pagans and other worldly people who were opposed to the new way of life, the way of human brotherhood.

Timotheus was called by God to become the minister or bishop of the church in Cyprus. Paul exhorts him to remain faithful and steadfast, unblemished and loyal to the true doctrine which he had received, for there were too many backsliders. Pagan religion offered abundant material and carnal rewards to its followers which were a temptation to the new converts. (See Eph. 6:10–18.)

The Second Epistle of Paul the Apostle to Timothy

1. CHRISTIANS MUST REMAIN FAITHFUL

For the which cause I also suffer these things: nevertheless I am not ashamed: for I know whom I have believed, and am persuaded that he is able to keep that which I have committed unto him against that day.
Hold fast the form of sound words, which thou hast heard of me, in faith and love which is in Christ Jesus.

II Tim. 1:12–13

Paul states that whether the converts believe in Jesus or not, he himself will remain faithful to his teaching regardless of any opposition or persecution.

That is to say, Paul would not consider changing or compromising the teaching, or even altering it in order to make it easy so that people might believe in it. Jesus' teaching was set once and for all. It is like a mathematical equation—it cannot be altered.

2. SUFFERING FOR THE GOSPEL

If we suffer, we shall also reign with him: if we deny him, he also will deny us:
If we believe not, yet he abideth faithful: he cannot deny himself.

II Tim. 2:12–13

All of Paul's sufferings and hardships were for the cause of the Christian gospel to which he was called to become an apostle and a preacher to the Gentiles. Paul was not ashamed of his mission to the Gentile world, nor was he ashamed of his preaching to the non-Jews. He assures Timotheus that he is loyal to that which he has preached, so that Timotheus may think of him as the preacher of the gospel and an example of the true doctrine.

Many of the Christian converts had strayed from the truth, and some of them had deserted Paul; still others were denying the resurrection of the body and the life hereafter. But we must not forget that these young churches were situated right in the heart of paganism, and were far away from Judea and Syria, where Christians were remaining steadfast to the teaching of their Lord Jesus Christ.

3. SNARE OF THE DEVIL

> . . . And that they may recover themselves out of the snare
> of the devil, who are taken captive by him at his will.
>
> II Tim. 2:26

Some of the Christian converts had reverted to paganism, and Paul admonishes them to think things over in order to save themselves from the trap which Satan had set for them.

The rewards which pagan religion offered to the people were so alluring that many Christian converts became backsliders. Then again, many of them were formerly enslaved by immoral pagan practices, which made them more easily caught again in the "snare of the devil."

4. SCRIPTURES INSPIRED

> All scripture is given by inspiration of God, and is profitable
> for doctrine, for reproof, for correction, for instruction
> in righteousness.
>
> II Tim. 3:16

The Aramaic reads, "All scripture written by the inspiration of the Holy Spirit is profitable for doctrine, for reproof, for correction, and for instruction in righteousness."

The apostle here speaks of that portion of the Scriptures which came through divine revelation, such as the books of the law and the prophets. Note: Some of the books of the Bible were rejected by the Jews because they were state records and accounts of wars and revolutions which were written by royal scribes, for instance, the books of the Apocrypha. Jesus never quoted from these books, but he quoted often from the law and the prophets, the Psalms and other portions of the Scriptures which were inspired and were accepted by the Jewish religion.

5. ADMONISHING AND REPROVING

Preach the word; be instant in season, out of season; reprove, rebuke, exhort with all longsuffering and doctrine.

II Tim. 4:2

The Eastern text reads, "Preach the word; and stand by it zealously in season and out of season; rebuke, reprove, through all patience and teaching."

Timotheus is exhorted to preach the word of God zealously, and to exhort and rebuke when he sees that it is necessary. Timotheus is told not to be afraid to condemn those who teach falsehoods. On the other hand, he is to commend those who are faithful and hard-working.

"In season, out of season" means "whenever and wherever men who need admonition and exhortation are encountered."

The Epistle of Paul the Apostle to the Hebrews

1. JESUS AN EXPRESS IMAGE OF GOD

. . . Who being the brightness of his glory, and the
express image of his person, and upholding all things by
the word of his power, when he had by himself purged
our sins, sat down on the right hand of the Majesty on
high.

Heb. 1:3

The Eastern text reads, "For he is the brightness of his
glory and the express image of his being, upholding all things
by the power of his word; and when he had through his
person cleansed our sins, then he sat down on the right hand
of the Majesty on high."

The term "brightness" is used metaphorically, meaning "hidden things brought to light," that is, the enlightenment which
Jesus Christ brought into the world.

Man, by receiving spiritual understanding and the truth, is
enabled to see the glory of God, which is hidden from the
eyes of mortal man.

"The express image of his person" means that if you have
seen Jesus Christ you have seen God Himself. Jesus as a sinless
man was the expression of God. His perfect life, his knowledge
of God, and his love for humanity made him the express image
of God. No one can see God, but we can see Him through
Jesus Christ, who is His image and likeness, the true Adam,
the spiritual man.

"Sat down on the right hand of the Majesty" means that
God has given him power and entrusted everything to him.
In the East, faithful princes, governors, and ministers of state
sit on the right hand of the king and are trusted by him.

2. FIRE

And of the angels he saith, Who maketh his angels spirits, and his ministers a flame of fire.

Heb. 1:7

Fire in ancient languages symbolizes speed, power, and prompt action. After all, "fire" is another term for "energy." In Aramaic we often say, "He is like fire," or, "He is fire," which means that he has unlimited speed and power. Elijah rode to heaven in a chariot of fire.

Angels are God's ministers or messengers, who are figuratively sent on missions. Moreover, the Aramaic word *malakha,* "an angel" or "a minister," also means "God's counsel." God is always ready to answer prophets and those who seek His divine and infinite counsel.

3. MEN BROUGHT TO GLORY

For it became him, for whom are all things, and by whom are all things, in bringing many sons unto glory, to make the captain of their salvation perfect through sufferings.

Heb. 2:10

The Eastern (Aramaic) text reads, "And it was meet and proper for him, in whose hand is everything and for whom are all things, to bring many sons to glory, so that from the very beginning of their salvation, they are made perfect through suffering."

The Aramaic term *benaya,* "sons," also means "children." Paul here states that Jesus, through his trials and suffering, brought many men and women into glory. That is, he saved them and brought them out of darkness into the light of God, so that they might be able to enter into the heavenly kingdom and be called His children. In other words, Jesus restored man to his former glory and thus made him an heir to God's kingdom.

4. DECLARING JESUS' NAME

. . . Saying, I will declare thy name unto my brethren, in the midst of the church will I sing praise unto thee.
Heb. 2:12

"I will declare thy name" means, "I will preach the teaching which is known by your name, and tell everyone about your wonderful works."

"In the midst of the church" means "in the midst of the congregation." When Easterners are moved by religious ecstasy they stand and shout. Some clap their hands and dance. David danced before the Ark when it was brought to Jerusalem, because he could not suppress his emotion and joy.

5. JESUS ENTRUSTED WITH POWER

But Christ as a son over his own house; whose house are
we, if we hold fast the confidence and the rejoicing of
the hope firm unto the end.

Heb. 3:6

The reference here is to the Christian Church for which
Jesus died on the cross. Being the son of God, everything had
been entrusted to him by God.

In the East, only faithful sons are given authority over their
fathers' households. Jesus, because of his obedience to God and
his trustworthiness, was granted all power in heaven and on
earth. All of those who follow him will be rewarded and will
rejoice because Jesus is the head of the Church; the cornerstone which the builder rejected became the foundation of a
new kingdom. Jesus has the power to bestow rewards upon
his faithful servants.

6. JESUS WAS OBEDIENT

Though he were a Son, yet learned he obedience by the
things which he suffered;
And being made perfect, he became the author of eternal
salvation unto all them that obey him.

Heb. 5:8–9

The Aramaic term *tab*, "good," here means a good or
wonderful son who has been obedient to the father. Jesus
proved his sonship through his suffering on the cross and his
resurrection from the grave. Jesus was completely obedient to

283

God in every respect, even willing to die for the sake of God's true revelation. So he became perfect, and was the first fruits of the eternal life. That is, Jesus, through his obedience even to death, proved that life is eternal and indestructible, because God is eternal and indestructible. And man, being in His image and likeness, is also indestructible. This is why Jesus was not afraid to die, for he knew that he would rise again.

Jesus became a high priest after the order of Melchizedek —that is, a king and priest whose ordination is from God, and not from man. (See Heb. 5:10.)

The term "order of Melchizedek" is used simply because no one knew who ordained Melchizedek. But we do know that Melchizedek was the high priest of the most high God, the God of Abraham.

7. ONE FOUNDATION

Therefore leaving the principles of the doctrine of Christ, let us go on unto perfection; not laying again the foundation of repentence from dead works, and of faith toward God.
Of the doctrine of baptisms, and of laying on of hands, and of resurrection of the dead, and of eternal judgment.
Heb. 6:1–2

The Eastern text reads *mamodita*, "baptism."

Paul here warns of a new foundation different from that which was laid by Jesus Christ, while Jesus' foundation was sufficient. According to Jesus' teaching, sinners could repent at any time, and God, being their loving Father, would always be ready to receive them with open arms.

The Hebrew Christians were still relying on the old doctrine of the flesh, and were trying to advance diverse and contrary teachings to complicate man's repentance and return to Christ. In other words, they were making repentance difficult and at times impossible.

Paul states that Jesus' one foundation was sufficient for repentance. Dead works and useless ordinances, which had failed to save the people, were not needed.

Some Christian teachers maintained that people could sin at any time they were so inclined, and be restored through a second baptism. (See Heb. 6:4, Eastern text.)

These Hebrew Christians were grounded in Mosaic law and its rigid ordinances. It was hard for them to believe that sins could be so easily forgiven, just by saying to a man, "Go and sin no more." They wanted something more difficult and complicated. Simple religion is hard to understand and appreciate, and yet the truth is as simple as two plus two equals four.

8. ONLY ONE TRUE BAPTISM

For it is impossible for those who were once enlightened, and have tasted of the heavenly gift, and were made partakers of the Holy Ghost,
And have tasted the good word of God, and the powers of the world to come,
If they shall fall away, to renew them again unto repentance; seeing they crucify to themselves the Son of God afresh, and put him to an open shame.

Heb. 6:4–6

The Eastern text reads, "But this is impossible for those who have once been baptized and have tasted the gift from heaven and have received the Holy Spirit." Paul in this instance is admonishing the Christians and warning them against false teachers of religion.

There were some false teachers who told the people that they might sin if they wished, provided they were baptized again, repented and received forgiveness. Paul attacks this false doctrine because those who had once been baptized and had tasted the spiritual gift of the Holy Spirit could hardly sin again and expect to receive forgiveness through a second or third baptism.

To sin again, to be converted again, would amount to crucifying Christ a second or third time. Jesus died on the cross only once, and we became partakers in his baptism by only one baptism to the remittance of sin. Members of some cults, in the time of Paul, were baptized every time they sinned. (See Heb. 6:1–2, Acts 19:4.)

9. GOSPEL WILL TRIUMPH

And they shall not teach every man his neighbour, and every man his brother, saying, Know the Lord: for all shall know me from the least to the greatest.

Heb. 8:11

The Eastern text reads, "And no man shall teach his neighbor, neither his brother, saying, Know the Lord; for all shall know me, from the youngest to the oldest." That is to say, in due time the Christian gospel will embrace many lands and peoples; that everyone will know God and His laws. Then there will be no need for teachers and missionaries.

When the light of God shines, darkness and ignorance will flee. As long as we do not know the law of God we need prophets and teachers of religion and pathfinders who will direct and guide us in His way. But when we become well versed in the law, in God's religion, there will be no need for teachers and preachers, because the light of God will shine day and night, and no one will stumble. Moreover, the truth will reign, and the evil forces will be replaced by the good. (See Isa. 54:13.)

10. TIME IS NOT RELEVANT

For yet a little while, and he that shall come will come, and will not tarry.

Heb. 10:37

Paul here is referring to the second coming of Jesus Christ. The Eastern text reads, "For the time is all too short, and he who is to come will come and will not delay." That is to say, the time from now until the coming of Christ is short; time is not relevant in the realms of the spirit. A thousand years are like a minute in the eyes of God.

Paul and the Hebrew Christian converts of his day expected an early return of Jesus Christ notwithstanding the fact that Christ had never left his followers. He had told them, "Lo, I am with you until the end of the world; Whenever two or three are together I am with them." Christ, the spirit, is eternal and universal. He is above time and space. There is no place where the spirit is not, for all space is filled with the spirit of God; He is omnipotent and omnipresent—all-embracing.

The term *come* in Eastern languages is sometimes used to mean "succeed"—to fulfill the mission. Note: Jesus died as a malefactor, a defeated prophet and preacher of a new religion. In the eyes of the enemy he was gone forever, but Jesus never left the world. He is always with those who are sincerely preaching his gospel and hastening the coming of the kingdom of God.

11. PROMISE MADE EFFECTIVE THROUGH CHRIST

And these all, having obtained a good report through faith, received not the promise:
God having provided some better thing for us, that they without us should not be made perfect.

Heb. 11:39–40

The Eastern (Aramaic) text reads, "Thus these all, having obtained a testimonial through the faith, did not receive the promise. Because God from the beginning provided for our help, lest without us they should not be made perfect."

Paul here refers to the patriarchs, Moses, the judges and the prophets, who by faith performed wonders and overcame insurmountable difficulties. But despite their faith and hard work, not one of them received the promise. In other words, all of them expected the coming of the Great One, the Messiah, but not one of them saw him. Nevertheless, all these who worked and prepared the way for the coming of the promised Messiah were perfected by his religion. Their dreams of a great savior and a universal state without boundaries will be fulfilled.

The Christian gospel is marching on, preparing the way for the reign of God and His righteousness, and all those who had worked for it before the coming of Christ will be partakers in the eternal joys which Jesus' gospel ushered into the world.

12. MOSES CHOSE TO SUFFER

By faith Moses, when he was come to years, refused to
be called the son of Pharaoh's daughter;
Choosing rather to suffer affliction with the people of God,
than to enjoy the pleasures of sin for a season;
Esteeming the reproach of Christ greater riches than the
treasures in Egypt: for he had respect unto the recompence
of the reward.

Heb. 11:24–26

The term "Christ" in this instance means the truth of the
Messianic promises for which the Hebrew race was called by
God and for which it has suffered so many persecutions. Moses
chose to dwell with the suffering people of his race, and participate in the divine plans of salvation rather than enjoy the
sensual life of the palace and the honors and glory which the
Pharaohs offered him in Egypt.

Moreover, Moses suffered many reproaches, persecutions, and
deprivations in the Mindina and Sinai deserts for the sake of
the truth which was embedded in the Hebrew race, which
in those early days carried the torch of God in their hands
and His standards upon their arms.

Christians also were to suffer for the sake of the gospel, and
to carry the lamp of God despite persecutions and death.

13. PUTTING ASIDE
NEGATIVE THOUGHT

Wherefore seeing we also are compassed about with so
great a cloud of witnesses, let us lay aside every weight,
and the sin which doth so easily beset us, and let us run
with patience the race that is set before us.

Heb. 12:1

The term *sin*, in this instance, means "the negative thought
which at times harassed the believers." All things which weaken
people's faith and cause them to go astray were to be put
aside in order to run the race and receive the crown of victory.
In other words, victory was the ultimate objective of the followers of Jesus Christ, who were laboring to make the kingdoms
of this earth the kingdom of Jesus Christ.

It takes patience and perseverance to win a battle. The
Christians were seemingly impatient because of the slow progress of the gospel, and at times they were tempted by the
material things which were offered by the pagan religions.

Jesus Christ's teaching is the objective of all workers for the
gospel. Paul admonishes the Hebrew Christians to be patient
and to endure suffering for the sake of their faith, as Jesus
himself had done. (See Heb. 12:2.)

14. SOULS MADE PERFECT
THROUGH CHRIST

To the general assembly and church of the firstborn, which
are written in heaven, and to God the Judge of all, and
to the spirits of just men made perfect.

Heb. 12:23

Paul in this instance compares the advantages of the
Christian converts and their congregations with the Israelites
at Mount Sinai when the earth shook and the mountain quaked
so that no one could draw near it.

The word "spirit" in this instance means "the souls of pious
men who had witnessed for the coming of the Messiah." Their
souls were made perfect through the fulfillment of their expectations and prophecies.

15. SPRINKLING OF BLOOD

. . . And to Jesus the mediator of the new covenant,
and to the blood of sprinkling, that speaketh better things
than that of Abel.

Heb. 12:24

The word "speaketh," in this instance, means "cries out."
Abel's blood cried out for vengeance against his brother Cain,
but Jesus' blood was sprinkled for the forgiveness of our sins.

In the Old Testament ritual the blood of animals was sprinkled on the altar. (See Gen. 4:10, I Pet. 1:2.)

The blood of Jesus Christ which was shed because of our

sins did away with all human and animal blood sacrifices. This is because Jesus through his death on the cross triumphed over death, the grave and the evil forces, and brought man close to his Creator. Therefore, there is no more need for sacrifice, for Jesus reconciled men to God by making them aware that they were His children. He also demonstrated that God is the only power in the universe.

The General Epistle of James

1. THE ENGRAFTED WORD

Wherefore lay apart all filthiness and superfluity of naughtiness, and receive with meekness the engrafted word, which is able to save your souls.

James 1:21

The term "engrafted" in this instance refers to the blending of Christian teachings with Judaism. Grafting is sometimes needed in order for a tree to bear good fruit.

The apostles' work was chiefly among the people of the Jewish religion. Their Lord, Jesus Christ, had admonished them to go first to the Jews, and later to the others.

For a long time, many of these Christians continued to be loyal to the Jewish faith with its ordinances and rituals. They were so deeply rooted that they could not part from them. They fasted and prayed in the temple, even while they accepted Jesus Christ as the promised Messiah, the savior of the world. In other words, the Christian truth was grafted into Judaism.

The Jews would not do away with the teachings of Judaism completely, and they could not depart from the ancient customs and manners which were a part of the culture of the time. But the grafting of the Christian gospel was slowly but surely permeating the Jewish religion. Christianity was acting as a leaven which permeates the meal, or as a seed which grows slowly but finally becomes a plant.

2. THE DEVILS ALSO BELIEVE

Thou believest that there is one God; thou doest well: the devils also believe, and tremble.

James 2:19

The apostle James places more emphasis on charity and good works than on mere belief in God or Jesus Christ. (See James 2:14–18.) This is because faith without works is dead. That is to say, no one can prove that he believes in God if he leads an evil life. Jesus made this very clear when he said, "By their fruits ye shall know them."

Pharisees, Sadducees, and scribes believed in God and His law, but they refused to do the good works which the law had commanded. Even today millions of Christians believe in God and in Jesus Christ, but refuse to do the good works which they are admonished to do.

A tree is known by its fruits and not by its leaves. Even devils (the insane) fear God, and even communists and unbelievers admit that there is a supreme power which rules over the universe. When one does the works of Christ he is a follower of Christ. Jesus said, "If you love me, keep my commandments." He also said, "It is not the one who says, My Lord, my Lord, but the one who hears my words and does them." Christian religion is an activity and not a mere belief in something mysterious.

293

3. SHUN FALSE TEACHINGS

My brethren, be not many masters, knowng that we shall
receive the greater condemnation.
For in many things we offend all. If any man offend not
in word, the same is a perfect man, and able also to
bridle the whole body.

James 3:1–2

The reference here is to diverse teachers of religion who
taught contradictory doctrines, and thus tried to weaken the
faith of the believers in Jesus Christ.

There were many such teachers of false philosophies during
the time of the apostles. Christians were admonished to beware of these false teachings, to shun these teachers, and to
remain steadfast to the true doctrines which had been imparted
to them by the apostles. Jesus is the only teacher and the
cornerstone of the Christian religion. (See Matt. 23:8.)

4. EVIL CAN BE DEFEATED

Submit yourselves therefore to God. Resist the devil, and
he will flee from you.

James 4:7

When Christians surrender to God, evil forces flee. When
truth comes, falsehood disappears; as, for instance, when you
find the true way of working out a mathematical formula the
erroneous way vanishes like a vapor before the sun.

The term "Satan" is derived from the Aramaic word *sata*,
"to slip," "to slide," "to miss the mark" or "to mislead." *Satana*

is the noun of the verb *sata*. Anything which deviates from the truth is evil. When the truth is known, evil departs. This is why Jesus said, "And you will know the truth, and that very truth will make you free." (John 8:32, Eastern text) When you know the truth, the truth will set you free from the bondage of evil forces and evil inclinations, and from all strife.

The First Epistle General of Peter

1. FREED THROUGH CHRIST

Blessed be the God and Father of our Lord Jesus Christ, which according to his abundant mercy hath begotten us again unto a lively hope by the resurrection of Jesus Christ from the dead.

I Pet. 1:3

The Eastern (Aramaic) text reads, "Blessed by God, the Father of our Lord Jesus Christ, who by his abundant mercy has again renewed us spiritually to a lively hope by the resurrection of Jesus Christ from the dead."

The term "begotten" is confusing, for God does not beget nor is He begotten. Such terms are at times used figuratively, here meaning "a new life," or "born again."

The converts who had left all false concepts of religion were like newly born children without any thought of evil. A child knows nothing but good until he is exposed to evil.

Moreover, these Christians were free from laws, rituals and ordinances of the flesh which had held them in bondage. Now they were living a new and happy life through the resurrection of Jesus Christ, which gave them hope of life hereafter.

2. MYSTERY HIDDEN FROM ANGELS

Unto whom it was revealed, that not unto themselves, but unto us they did minister the things, which are now reported unto you by them that have preached the gospel unto you with the Holy Ghost sent down from heaven; which things the angels desire to look into.

I Pet. 1:12

Peter here states that even the angels in heaven desire to look upon the glorious things revealed by the gospel of Jesus Christ through the faithful men who had preached it.

The mystery of God's salvation through the gospel of Jesus Christ was hidden even from His angels who are His ministers, but were made manifest through Jesus Christ who was the son of God. The angels were only the messengers or the servants of God, who carried out His orders.

The messenger of a king does not know the secrets in the hearts of the king, but the king later reveals them to his son, who is to become his heir and sit upon his throne. God had revealed all the secrets of His kingdom and granted all power to Jesus Christ, who through his obedience had become His heir.

3. THE TERM "HOLY"

Because it is written, Be ye holy; for I am holy.

I Pet. 1:16

The term "holy" means "set aside," "dedicated to a cause" or "vowed to God." No man can be holy as God is holy, but men have the power to become holy. The apostle does not promise being holy to the same degree that God is holy.

4. BORN AGAIN

Being born again, not of corruptible seed, but of incorruptible, by the word of God, which liveth and abideth for ever.

I Pet. 1:23

"Born again" means "regenerated," or "like little children," who are free from evil thoughts and harmful actions. Men must be like little children in order to receive the new Christian teaching, which was contrary to the teachings of religions in which they were nurtured. A child believes and accepts everything which his parents impart to him. Christians are to get rid of all former teachings and practices which would hamper the truth of the Gospel. (See commentary on John 3:3, *Gospel Light*.)

5. JESUS' DESTINY

But with the precious blood of Christ, as of a lamb without blemish and without spot:
Who verily was foreordained before the foundation of the world, but was manifest in these last times for you.

I Pet. 1:19–20

Peter had heard Jesus speak of his rejection and death on the cross, on the mount of transfiguration. He had told Peter, James, and John that the Messiah must suffer death on the cross in order to enter into his glory, and the prophecies concerning him must be fulfilled. Moreover, on their way to Jerusalem, he had told them that they would leave him alone, and flee, but that his Father would not leave him. "For behold, the hour is coming, and it has now come, when you will be dispersed, every man to his own country, and you will leave me alone; and yet I am never alone because the Father is with me." (John 16:32, Eastern text)

Also, when Peter assured Jesus of his loyalty, Jesus had told him that even he would denounce and deny him. Moreover, Peter had heard him saying, ". . . O, my Father, deliver me from this hour; but for this cause I came to this very hour." (John 12:27, Eastern text)

Jesus' death was preordained, and was predicted by the great prophet Isaiah. God, from the very beginning of time, knew that the Messiah would be rejected and that the cross was his destiny. That is to say, only through his death on the cross could Jesus reveal God's love for His children and triumph over the forces of evil. (See Matt. 27:46, Mark 15:34.)

6. JESUS' PREACHING IN SHEOL

For Christ also hath once suffered for sins, the just for the unjust, that he might bring us to God, being put to death in the flesh, but quickened by the Spirit:
By which also he went and preached unto the spirits in prison;
Which sometime were disobedient, when once the long-suffering of God waited in the days of Noah, while the ark was a-preparng, wherein few, that is, eight souls were saved by water.

I Pet. 3:18–20

Jesus' death on the cross was foreseen by the Hebrew prophets. They knew that anyone who would admonish the people to leave Baal worship, and the material interests of this life, would be rejected and crucified as a revolutionary, a disturber of the world order.

Through Jesus' death on the cross, God revealed His love for His children in that He let a righteous man die for the sake of sinners. Moreover, through Jesus' death many people understood God's love, and His fatherhood, and learned to forgive one another.

Jesus, while he was in Sheol, preached to the departed souls, so that they might also share in his resurrection and his gospel, which would free men not only from evil forces, but also from death and the sinister Sheol.

7. THE DEAD BECOME PARTAKERS

For for this cause was the gospel preached also to them
that are dead, that they might be judged according to
men in the flesh, but live according to God in the spirit.
I Pet. 4:6

Jesus Christ was in Sheol three days, where he preached to the souls of the departed ones, that they might also become partakers of his gospel, and that they might be judged after the resurrection. (I Pet. 3:19)

No judge can condemn a man who has transgressed a law of which he knows nothing. Wherever there is no law, there is no judgment and condemnation. Without law, sin is dormant.

These people had died before the revelation of the gospel of Jesus Christ. This also shows that the dead are still partakers in the mysteries of God even though they have departed from this temporal life, and in His saving grace which is offered to the living.

8. LOVE IS SUPREME

> And above all things have fervent charity among your-
> selves: for charity shall cover the multitude of sins.
>
> I Pet. 4:8

The Eastern text reads, "And above all things have fervent love towards one another, because love covers a multitude
of sins."

Apparently the term "charity" was introduced later. Love is
the supreme virtue in the Christian religion. Love is the cement,
the cohesive force, that unites people of all races and colors.
This is because God is love. (See James 5:20.)

The term "cover" is used to mean "obliterate." Love causes
people to forget any offenses committed against them. The
Eastern text reads, "Shame covers the wicked."

9. CHRISTIANS WILL BE JUDGED

> For the time is come that judgment must begin at the
> house of God: and if it first begin at us, what shall the
> end be of them that obey not the gospel of God?
> And if the righteous scarcely be saved, where shall the
> ungodly and the sinner appear?
>
> I Pet. 4:17–18

The apostle asks, If the members of the Christian Church
are to be judged first, what will happen to those who have
not received the gospel? The judgment will begin with the
believers, simply because they will be held responsible for any

un-Christian conduct. The unbelievers will come later, because
they have not yet received the light of God. The condemnation
of Christians who have fallen from the grace of God is greater,
because they knew that they were doing evil, and had transgressed against the law of God.

Moreover, Peter here hints that if the Christians, who live
under the light of the gospel, were to be called to judgment,
what is to happen to those who had refused to accept the
gospel?

10. AS A ROARING LION

Be sober, be vigilant; because your adversary the devil,
as a roaring lion, walketh about, seeking whom he may
devour.

I Pet. 5:8

"Roaring lion" means "a lion who is vicious and ready to
strike." Satan is like a roaring lion, always ready to deceive,
to injure, and to cause men and women to go astray from the
word of God.

Again, Christians are admonished to be sober, alert and
vigilant, because the world is full of temptations, and evil
forces are always ready to snare and destroy those who are
not vigilant.

Christians must not be satisfied just to say, "I am a member
of the Church of Christ," and do nothing about it; they must
work harder and harder to overcome the world, just as their
Lord overcame it.

The Second Epistle General of Peter

1. CHRISTIANS MUST EXCEL

For so an entrance shall be ministered unto you abundantly into the everlasting kingdom of our Lord and Saviour Jesus Christ.

II Pet. 1:11

The Eastern text reads, "For by so doing, an entrance shall be given freely to you into the everlasting kingdom of our Lord and Savior Jesus Christ."

Christians are admonished to excel in good works, such as godliness, brotherly love and kindness, and to love one another.

Those who did these good deeds would enter into the promised kingdom, and those who failed to do them would not. (See II Tim. 4:8.)

Jesus, in his parable of the ten virgins, stated that only the five wise virgins whose lamps were burning could enter into the wedding feast, which symbolized heaven. The others were left in utter darkness outside because of their negligence.

Men's good works are their lights; they must let their lights shine continually, for life is full of difficulties which cause men to stumble and fall.

2. EYEWITNESS TO THE TRUTH

For we have not followed cunningly devised fables, when
we made known unto you the power and coming of our
Lord Jesus Christ, but were eyewitnesses of his majesty.
II Pet. 1:16

Peter states that the gospel they had preached is a true
gospel, not just something cunningly put across in order to
deceive. The apostles were eyewitnesses to the truth they
preached. They had heard Jesus, and had witnessed his glorious
resurrection and ascension. Moreover, they had seen the things
that he had predicted fulfilled. They were also the witnesses
of his sonship and his calling by God. (II Pet. 1:17, Matt. 17:5)

The disciples were sincere preachers of the simple and true
gospel which led people into the kingdom of God. They gave
freely. Therefore, there was no reason to tell fables and deceive
the people.

3. BACKSLIDERS

Whereas angels, which are greater in power and might,
bring not railing accusation against them before the Lord.
II Peter 2:11

Peter here speaks of angels, or spirits. In Aramaic, the
term "angels" also means "good men," "messengers," and "innocent men," but in this instance means "the messengers, or
the ministers, of God."

The angels, being God's thoughts, and free from physical

bodies, space, and time, have greater power than men. They do not dare to blaspheme and thus bring condemnation upon themselves. But the evil converts who had once been Christian blasphemed against a doctrine when they misunderstood it.

Peter calls such evil men natural brute beasts, because they could not discern between truth and error, between light and darkness. (See II Pet. 2:12–14.)

These men whom the apostle condemns had been converted, but later had reverted to paganism and Baal worship. (See II Pet. 2:20–22.)

4. EATING THEIR VOMIT

For if after they have escaped the pollutions of the world through the knowledge of the Lord and Saviour Jesus Christ, they are again entangled therein, and overcome, the latter end is worse with them than the beginning. For it had been better for them not to have known the way of righteousness, than, after they have known it, to turn from the holy commandment delivered unto them. But it is happened unto them according to the true proverb, The dog is turned to his own vomit again; and the sow that was washed to her wallowing in the mire.
II Pet. 2:20–22

All of these people to whom the apostle points were former converts and had tasted the true life as Christians, but now they were backsliders. Peter believes that it would have been better for them not to have become Christian at all, if they were to revert to paganism. He likens them to a dog who returns to eat what he has vomited. (Prov. 26:11)

Many of the early Christians who joyously accepted the

304

gospel of Christ returned to paganism and to their former way of life. Some of Jesus' disciples left him while he was on his way to Jerusalem to die on the cross. These Christians were like the seed that springs up fast and dies quickly.

5. SCOFFERS AT THE GOSPEL

Knowing this first, that there shall come in the last days scoffers, walking after their own lusts.

II Pet. 3:3

Jesus said that when the Son of man came he would find no faithful on earth.

Peter, in this instance is speaking of men who would be disappointed in the Christian teaching because they would see no rapid changes and no worldly rewards. The strong would still continue to oppress the weak and devour them. The powerful nations would still harass the small nations, and war and evil forces would continue on a larger scale than before. This condition would cause many to renounce Christianity.

On the other hand, some who would be expecting Jesus' second coming would become impatient and even disappointed and turn against all the promises the apostles had made. They would not realize that the growth of the Christian gospel would be slow, like the growth of a seed. Jesus warned his disciples against the expectation of sudden changes in the world, and he told them that those who would follow him must be ready to take up their crosses and die for the cause of the gospel. (See II Pet. 3:4.)

6. SLOW CHANGES

And saying, Where is the promise of his coming? for since the fathers fell asleep, all things continue as they were from the beginning of the creation.

II Pet. 3:4

The reference here is to the second coming of Jesus Christ. When Jesus ascended into heaven on the Mount of Olives, two angels spoke to his disciples: "And while they looked steadfastly toward heaven as he went up, behold two men stood by them in white robes; and they said to them, Men of Galilee, why do you stand gazing up into heaven? This same Jesus who has ascended from you into heaven shall so come in like manner as you have seen him ascend into heaven." (Acts 1:10–11)

But centuries have elapsed and Jesus has not yet returned. Peter predicted that the time would come when scoffers and unbelievers would say, "Where is his second coming?" And the evil would moreover continue as of yore, which would make people even more doubtful about the Christian religion.

Even today, millions of people wonder about his second coming, and some even question his first coming. This is because the followers of Jesus have failed to implement the things for which he gave his life. This is why today we have wars, and rumors of wars, and fears of wars.

The Christian gospel will at last triumph over the material world, and usher in the kingdom of heaven, but in order to hasten this, the Christian disciples must renew the spirit which once pervaded the hearts of the apostles and their immediate followers.

7. INTENSE HEAT

But the day of the Lord will come as a thief in the
night; in the which the heavens shall pass away with a
great noise, and the elements shall melt with fervent heat,
the earth also and the works that are therein shall be
burned up.
Seeing then that all these things shall be dissolved, what
manner of persons ought ye to be in all holy conversation
and godliness,
Looking for and hasting unto the coming of the day of
God, wherein the heavens being on fire shall be dissolved,
and the elements shall melt with fervent heat?

II Pet. 3:10–12

Jesus had touched on the last day. He had stated that
when the Day of the Lord comes, stars and other heavenly
bodies will fall off. (Matt. 24:29)

Peter goes even further than the Master in describing the
melting of the elements with intense heat. It is interesting to
note that even two thousand years ago people knew that the
world was constructed of elements. Only recently have scientists
discovered that intense heat can cause the molecules to separate
from one another, and that the nucleus of an atom is split
with intense heat. Heat causes the particles to lose their forms
and to melt.

Indeed, Peter was an illiterate man, far from being a physicist, but the Lord God revealed to him that intense fire could
melt the elements and cause the destruction of all forms.

Nearly three thousand years ago the prophet Elijah was told
that water is a conductor of lightning, or fire of God. (See
Old Testament Light, I Kings 18:38.) Scientists discovered this
only a few centuries ago. Elisha used salt to purify a spring
whose water had been polluted. Salt is made of two elements,
sodium and chloride, and is still used even today to purify
water.

All wisdom and knowledge come from God, who is the author of the universe. Our planet earth may collide with some other planet and catch fire, and thus become like a brilliant star or like our sun. Jesus did not state when this would happen; neither did Peter touch on the time when this would take place. Such things are secrets which are known only to God, the creator of the universe.

The First Epistle General of John

1. THE ANOINTING

But the anointing which ye have received of him abideth in you, and ye need not that any man teach you: but as the same anointing teacheth you of all things, and is truth, and is no lie, and even as it hath taught you, ye shall abide in him.

I John 2:27

The apostle John admonishes the Christians to be aware of false teachers of religion who were causing the people to go astray from the gospel of Jesus Christ. Many of these teachers offered the people material and sensual rewards. There were other teachers who were teaching Neoplatonism, similar to communism. (Plato tried to modify what Socrates had taught.) Paul had confronted the same situation in Greece and Asia Minor. Many new teachers who came from Judea and other lands tried to weaken the teaching of the apostles and to discredit them.

John assures the Christians that their anointing, that is, their calling, or ordination, was sufficient to lead them to the truth of the gospel of Jesus Christ. They needed no other teachers with strange doctrines and no new philosophies which were contrary to the gospel of Jesus Christ which the apostles had delivered to them.

"Anointing" is another word for "ordination," "appointment," or "calling." Prophets, kings, and priests were anointed with oil in the olden days, for oil is tangible light. Light is symbolic of God and of understanding. "And God said, Let there be light . . ." "Let there be light" means "let there be understanding."

In the Holy Scriptures, God is called the Light of the World. Jesus said, "I am the light of the world." (John 8:12, Eastern text)

In the East, dark temples are lighted with olive oil or butter. The ordained men were lighted with the light of God, which was to direct them and all their activities and administrations of the church, and to remind them of their dedication and their sacred duties. This light was sufficient for the Christian converts to be guided thereby, because it was imparted to them by the apostles. The apostles had received it from Jesus Christ, who is the light of the world.

2. THE SONS OF GOD

Beloved, now are we the sons of God, and it doth not yet appear what we shall be: but we know that, when he shall appear, we shall be like him; for we shall see him as he is.

I John 3:2

During this period the Jewish concept of God was totally different from that of the early days, when God was called Father and His children were called the sons of God. During the time of the apostles the word "God" was so holy that it could not even be uttered by human lips. Moreover, God was only approachable through intermediaries and sacrifices.

Jesus, by his teaching and his death on the cross, had revealed to humanity that God is a loving Father and people are His children. This was a new concept during the time of the apostles. This sonship was obtained through the grace of Jesus Christ.

The Christians were sons of God and heirs of the kingdom, but being in human bodies they were unable to comprehend what kind of body they would have when they entered into the heavenly kingdom. They knew that their present physical forms could not enter into the kingdom of God, for Jesus had said, flesh and blood cannot inherit the kingdom of God.

The apostle assures the people that during the resurrection all things which were difficult to grasp will be revealed when we greet his coming. Jesus arose in a spiritual body and his followers will rise in like manner. It is then we will see him with our spiritual eyes.

3. BORN OF GOD

Whosoever is born of God doth not commit sin; for his seed remaineth in him: and he cannot sin, because he is born of God.

I John 3:9

"Born of God" is an Eastern idiom which means "God-like." God is eternal spirit. He never begets nor is begotten. The term "born of God" is used in order to reveal that those who are Godlike cannot sin. Jesus used this term when he spoke to Nicodemus: ". . . if a man is not born again, he cannot enter into the kingdom of God." (John 3:3, Eastern text) To be "born again" means "to start over," "to become like a child," receptive, like the first Adam before the transgression.

The apostle speaks of those who are pure in heart and who are Godlike, or those who have given up this world and surrendered to God. Indeed such men never sin again, because they have tasted the true life. They will never exchange it for anything else.

These words should not be taken at face value, for not all who claim to be Christian are Christians, and not all who call themselves saints are saints. The apostle refers to those who have completely surrendered to God and have become heirs of His heavenly kingdom. Indeed many have attained this high mark in true Christian discipleship.

Jesus said, ". . . there are some men who stand here who will not taste death . . ." (Matt. 16:28) The reference here is to men and women who had sacrificed everything for the sake of the kingdom. They were the sinless pious. Indeed, the sinful man cannot inherit the kingdom of God. Jesus revealed this through the parable of the tares and the wheat, because the tares, or evil, will at the end be burned.

4. "SPIRIT" MEANS "PERSON"

Beloved, believe not every spirit, but try the spirits whether they are of God: because many false prophets are gone out into the world.

I John 4:1

The term "spirit" in this instance means "person." In Aramaic, we often say, "How many spirits are here?" or, "How many souls?" At times in colloquial speech, "spirit" and "soul" are used interchangeably. The apostle, in this instance, does not mean that there are many spirits. There is only one Holy Spirit, and God is the Eternal Spirit. Then again, the term "spirit" also means "inclination," "wind," "temper," "pride," "rheumatism," and many other things. One has to know the context to know how the word is used.

311

The false prophets, when they presumably prophesied, pretended that they had contacted the Holy Spirit, the spirit of God, but they spoke falsehoods and lies in the name of God. Jesus warned that many false prophets would come in his name. (Matt. 24:5)

The apostle John had heard Jesus warn them against false prophets, who were to come and try to prophesy in his name, just as in olden days false prophets had prophesied in the name of God and thus deceived kings, princes, and the people by their false legends.

5. CHRIST AMONG YOU

Ye are of God, little children, and have overcome them: because greater is he that is in you, than he that is in the world.

I John 4:4

The apostle in this instance warns again against false teachers of religion and false christs, whom Jesus himself had predicted would come from time to time. Now these false teachers were already among the Christians, teaching false philosophies and destructive doctrines. The apostle assures the Christian converts that Jesus Christ, who was among them, was greater than all these false teachers and deceivers, who were preying on the converts. This is because no greater truth has ever been revealed to the world than that which was revealed by Jesus Christ and sealed by his death.

Note: all the teachings of these false teachers were washed away in a few generations, and their imprints in the sand were obliterated by the wind.

6. BAPTISM OF SPIRIT, WATER, AND BLOOD

This is he that came by water and blood, even Jesus
Christ; not by water only, but by water and blood. And
it is the Spirit that beareth witness, because the Spirit
is truth.
For there are three that bear record in heaven, the Father,
the Word, and the Holy Ghost: and these three are one.
And there are three that bear witness in earth, the Spirit,
and the water, and the blood: and these three agree in
one.

I John 5:6–8

The apostle here refers to the two forms of baptism, the
baptism by water and the baptism by blood. Jesus was baptized
by John in the River Jordan, and on the cross he was figuratively
baptized with his own blood.

Pagans baptized sinners with blood. It is said that they killed
an ox and let the blood flow over the sinner's body to wash
away the sin. This is why the early Christians said. "We have
been cleansed with the blood of Jesus Christ." Prior to their
conversion to the gospel of Jesus they were supposedly cleansed
by the blood of animal sacrifices. Even in the Jewish religious
system, blood was used to absolve the sinner. On the day of
atonement, the high priest would enter the holy of holies and
sprinkle the animal blood upon the mercy seat, and then upon
the children of Israel, to absolve their sins. Even today in
biblical lands, when offerings of dedication are performed, the
blood of the slaughtered animal is placed on the forehead of
the person for whom the animal was sacrificed. The author
himself went through this ritual when he was a boy.

Christians have an additional baptism besides water and
blood, that is, the baptism of the Holy Spirit which was given
to them by the grace of God through the gospel of Jesus Christ.
This baptism of the Holy Spirit is the true baptism; the other
forms are mere shadows, or reminders, of the true baptism.

The General Epistle of Jude

1. REPENTERS RECEIVE MERCY

And others save with fear, pulling them out of the fire; hating even the garment spotted by the flesh.

Jude 1:23

The Eastern (Aramaic) text reads, "And when they repent, have mercy on them with compassion; despise even a garment which is spotted with the things of the flesh."

Jude emphasizes the mercy of God, that is, that God will have mercy and forgive everyone, but the only assurance of God's mercy is true repentance. After repentance and forgiveness the people will look back on the spotted, old garments they had worn when they were living an un-Christian life. When people truly repent, they hate their past and the evil works they did when they walked in darkness.

The Revelation of St. John the Divine

1. READERS ARE BLESSED

Blessed is he that readeth, and they that hear the words of this prophecy, and keep those things which are written herein: for the time is at hand.

Rev. 1:3

Eastern writers and copyists always say a short prayer in which they bless the readers of the books they write or copy. This is a general custom. They also admonish the people to keep the prophecy, or not to add anything to or omit anything from, what they have written. This is done in order to safeguard the true teachings from falsification.

Christians at this time were expecting the early return of our Lord; therefore they were eager to see that the followers of Jesus Christ read the prophecy of John, which means the whole Book of Revelation.

The apostle John had predicted that many evil things would befall the Church, and foretold extreme trials which the believers were to face in the future. That is to say, the Christians were soon to be persecuted by kings and princes of this material world. Moreover, false prophets and teachers would deceive the faithful and cause them to go astray from the way of Jesus Christ. Heresies had already started in some of the churches of Asia Minor and Greece, and many Christians had reverted to paganism.

The author wants Christians to be on guard against the frightful events which were to come.

2. FAITHFUL WITNESS

And from Jesus Christ, who is the faithful witness, and the first begotten of the dead, and the prince of the kings of the earth. Unto him that loved us, and washed us from our sins in his own blood.

Rev. 1:5

"Faithful witness" is an Aramaic saying which means "one who willingly gives his life for the sake of the truth." Jesus died on the cross not because he had done any evil, but because he had been a faithful witness to the truth which God his Father had revealed to the Hebrew prophets, which truth was hidden from the eyes of the people of his day.

315

"First begotten of the dead" means "the first concept of a new religion that believes in the resurrection and in the life hereafter." In other words, Jesus was the first fruits of this new teaching. Jesus through his resurrection won victory over death, the grave, and evil. Therefore he has become the prince of the kings of the earth. The term "prince" in this instance means "the chief" or "the head." The Aramaic word *resha* means "the head man." The Latin is "principal." God had given Jesus power, glory and honor, and made him ruler over the kingdom and principalities of this earth. (John 8:14)

3. KINGS AND PRIESTS

And hath made us kings and priests unto God and his Father; to him be glory and dominion for ever and ever. Amen.

Rev. 1:6

Jesus, through his resurrection and his triumph over the kingdoms of this earth, death, and the forces of evil, has freed us from the dominion of the political kingdoms and the material world, and made us heir, or princes of the kingdom of God, the spiritual kingdom.

In this new and spiritual kingdom there is no place for priests and intermediaries, or for intercession and sacrifices. The true Christians are priests themselves through Jesus Christ. They can approach God as a child approaches his father, without ceremony or fear. In Christ the greater one is servant of the lesser.

4. HE COMETH WITH CLOUDS

Behold, he cometh with clouds; and every eye shall see
him, and they also which pierced him: and all kindreds
of the earth shall wail because of him. Even so, Amen.

Rev. 1:7

The term "coming with clouds," or "upon the clouds" is
an Aramaic idiom which means "coming in glory and honor."
In the East when a man is successful, people say he is riding
on the clouds, for in those days clouds were the highest thing
people could see, higher even than the highest mountains.

A physical Christ coming in a mortal body and riding on a
cloud could only be seen in the area close to the cloud.
"Cloud" is quite often used metaphorically, and is never taken
literally. God is often portrayed as riding on the clouds, or
making clouds His chariot, but no cloud can hold God.

Jesus' coming will be spiritual. He will come in a spiritual
body, free from all physical limitations, from time and space.
Paul says that we die in a corruptible body but rise in a
spiritual body. Every eye will see him; even those who had
crucified him will see him and will lament for their mistakes
on the Resurrection Day.

When Jesus' kingdom becomes a reality and the evil forces
created by man himself are destroyed, people will think and
see spiritually. Then Christ will appear to every eye, just as
he appeared to his disciples and followers who believed in
him. This will come to pass when men change their hearts
and become new creations worthy to be the citizens of the
everlasting kingdom over which Christ will reign, the kingdom of justice and right.

5. FIRST LOVE

Nevertheless I have somewhat against thee, because thou
hast left thy first love.

Rev. 2:4

The Christians at Ephesus were converted to Christianity
by the apostle John and his co-workers. The Christian religion
was their first love because it freed them from the bondage
of evil, and gave them hope of eternal life. In other words,
the Christian gospel to the Ephesians was the pearl of great
price.

The Ephesians had left the teachings of Christ and turned
back to the destructive pagan teachings and immoral practices.
The church is upbraided for its failure to stand steadfast in
the true doctrine which had been imparted to them by the
apostle. John, while at Ephesus, saw the impact of paganism
upon the small Christian centers in the heart of the pagan
world.

6. THE TREE OF LIFE

He that hath an ear, let him hear what the Spirit saith
unto the churches; To him that overcometh will I give to
eat of the tree of life, which is in the midst of the paradise
of God.

Rev. 2:7

The Revelator states that whoever triumphs over this physical life and the alluring sensual rewards of pagan religions
will eat of the tree of life, which means he will live forever.
That is to say, just as transgression of the law by Adam brought

death, obedience to the law through Jesus Christ will bring life.

"In the midst of the paradise of God" means "in the midst of the garden of God, Eden," or "in the safest and most delightful part of the garden." In the East, the best trees which bear precious fruits are planted in the center of the garden. This is because thieves do not venture into the center of the garden; they usually steal from the edges. The owner's booth is usually in the center to watch over the vineyard.

Heaven is a spiritual place. There will be no trees or gardens in it. The terms "tree" and "paradise" are used metaphorically. (Read comments on "The Tree of Life," Gen. 2:9, in *Old Testament Light*.)

In the Old Testament, nations are often called vineyards and trees, because they multiply and increase like trees and plants. Moreover, in deserts and arid places, where trees and vegetation are lacking, people visualize heaven as a place full of trees and vegetation and water.

7. SYNAGOGUE OF SATAN

I know thy works, and tribulation, and poverty, (but thou art rich) and I know the blasphemy of them which say they are Jews, and are not, but are the synagogue of Satan. Fear none of those things which thou shalt suffer: behold, the devil shall cast some of you into prison, that ye may be tried; and ye shall have tribulation ten days: be thou faithful unto death, and I will give thee a crown of life.

Rev. 2:9–10

John commends the head of the church, or the minister, who has suffered many tribulations and persecutions from the enemies in the church.

Most of the Smyrna converts were Jews, former members

of the synagogue, who were looked upon by the Jews as rene-
gades who had left the religion of their forefathers to join a new
religion of a man who had been condemned by Jewish authorities in Jerusalem.

Some of the Jews in Smyrna did everything they could to
hamper the work of the gospel among their people, which
was a natural thing. Nevertheless, some of the loyal Christian
leaders who were former Jews were blamed and persecuted
for weakening Judaism. These men at the end will receive
crowns of glory. No doubt the Jews who were opposed to
the Christian doctrine knew all about Paul, his zeal for Judaism
and his conversion to Christ.

John here refers to the Jewish synagogue, which he calls
the "synagogue of Satan," that is to say, a Jewish congregation
that has rejected the Word of God and the Messianic prophecies
and followed the misleading teachings of the scribes and Pharisees, the doctrines of the elders.

The "devil" in this instance means "the opposition," the evil
people who would cause many Christians to be arrested.

"Ten days" refers to the duration of the sentence.

8. SATAN'S SEAT

I know thy works, and where thou dwellest, even where
Satan's seat is: and thou holdest fast my name, and hast
not denied my faith, even in those days wherein Antipas
was my faithful martyr, who was slain among you, where
Satan dwelleth.

Rev. 2:13

"Satan's seat" is used metaphorically, meaning "Ephesus."
This city was the home of the worship of the goddess Diana,
where images of this goddess were made and sold, and where

the artisans resisted the teaching of the gospel of Jesus Christ. Paul and Barnabas were stoned and expelled from this city. (Acts. 14:5)

The author of Revelation nevertheless commends the minister who is in charge of the church at Ephesus. This is because, despite the persecutions and martyrdoms, he had held steadfast and remained loyal to the gospel.

There will always be opposition against the truth and its adherents will always be persecuted; but there is always a remnant of those who remain loyal and are willing to die for it.

9. SWORD OF THE MOUTH

Repent; or else I will come unto thee quickly, and will fight against them with the sword of my mouth.

Rev. 2:16

The term "repent," in this instance, is used as a warning against the Christians who had returned to paganism. The term in Aramaic does not mean just to be sorry for the evil you have done, but to stop doing what you have been doing, and to make restitution for it or face the consequences.

The Revelator is threatening these people by saying that he will come and fight against them with the "sword of my mouth," which means "the truth," which will expose and destroy the error.

The term "sword" is used figuratively. In the East we often say, "his words were like a sword; they pierced my heart."

10. JEZEBEL

Notwithstanding I have a few things against thee, because thou sufferest that woman Jezebel, which calleth herself a prophetess, to teach and to seduce my servants to commit fornication, and to eat things sacrificed unto idols.

Rev. 2:20

The term "Jezebel" is used figuratively, meaning "a bad woman." Jezebel was the wife of Ahab, the King of Israel. She introduced the immoral Baal worship in Israel and brought hundreds of false prophets to the royal court to supplant the prophets of God. Jezebel was denounced strongly by Elijah and Elisha, the two great Hebrew prophets, and hence had become the symbol of whoredom and deceit. (I Kings 16:31-32)

The Revelator does not call this woman by name, but he likens her to Jezebel because, like Jezebel, she had introduced Baal worship and immorality and corrupted the people of the Christian congregations at Pergamos. The church at Pergamos, as in other places bordering the pagan world, was constantly harassed by false teachers of religion, some of whom identified themselves with Christianity in order to weaken the Christian congregation.

11. SICKBED

Behold, I will cast her into a bed, and them that commit adultery with her into great tribulation, except they repent of their deeds.

And I will kill her children with death; and all the churches shall know that I am he which searcheth the reins and hearts: and I will give unto every one of you according to your works.

Rev. 2:22–23

The Eastern text reads, "Behold I will cast her into a sickbed, and those who commit adultery with her into great tribulation, unless they repent of their deeds."

"Sickbed" is an Aramaic idiom which means "an incurable disease."

The Revelator here warns the people to repent from their evil doings or suffer tribulations. This is because evil deeds sooner or later produce evil fruits, and good deeds produce good fruits. On the other hand, evil, not having a divine originator, returns to the one who originates it. In other words, one reaps what he has sown, and gathers what he has gathered. The people were to punish themselves with their own evil deeds.

The term "children" in this instance means "the members of the congregation." Members of the church are called the sons and daughters of the church in the East. When the Israelites joined the worship of Baal and committed immoral acts in Moabite temples, 24,000 people died of disease. (Num. 25:9)

12. THE ROD OF IRON

And he that overcometh, and keepeth my works unto the
end, to him will I give power over nations:
And he shall rule them with a rod of iron; as the vessels
of a potter shall they be broken to shivers: even as I
received of my Father.
And I will give him the morning star.

Rev. 2:26–28

Those who repented and remained loyal to the teachings
of the gospel would be granted authority over nations by God.
To shepherd them means to discipline them; a shepherd leads
and disciplines the lambs with a small and tender twig, but
in this instance the evildoers will be disciplined with an iron
rod, which was often used by wicked rulers to punish citizens
who had broken their laws and had committed crimes against
the state. John in this instance is speaking in a language which
the people could understand. Most of his statements are figurative speech. (Ps. 2:8–9, Rev. 19:15)

"Morning star" symbolizes "the light," "the dawning of truth."

13. LOYAL MEMBERS

Thou hast a few names even in Sardis which have not
defiled their garments; and they shall walk with me in
white: for they are worthy.

Rev. 3:4

The Eastern text reads, "But you have a few members . . .
who have not defiled their names. . . ."

John here upbraids the congregation at Sardis. They had not done well, and he warns them to do better.

Nevertheless, there were some members of the congregation who had remained loyal to the true doctrine and had overcome the temptations to which the majority of the congregation had fallen. Thus he commends them very highly and assures them of the heavenly reward, that they would walk with Jesus, dressed in white. White is symbolic of purity, innocence, and victory. This is why priests dress in white when ministering before the altar. Black is symbolic of evil, darkness and mourning. (Rev. 7:9)

14. PILLAR IN THE TEMPLE

Him that overcometh will I make a pillar in the temple of my God, and he shall go no more out: and I will write upon him the name of my God, and the name of the city of my God, which is new Jerusalem, which cometh down out of heaven from my God: and I will write upon him my new name.

Rev. 3:12

The phrase "pillar in the temple" is used figuratively to mean an outstanding member of the congregation. In Aramaic we often say, "He is the pillar in my group," meaning "the leading supporter." This is because just as a temple is upheld by strong pillars, so a church or a congregation rests upon the loyalty and devotion of its members.

Names of deities were often inscribed on the pillars of the temple. "Jerusalem" is used symbolically, meaning "the heavenly city," or "the perfect worship." Jesus was known by several names such as "the Lamb," "the Prince of Peace," "King of Kings," etc. (Rev. 14:1)

15. TO SIT WITH JESUS

To him that overcometh will I grant to sit with me in
my throne, even as I also overcame, and am set down
with my Father in his throne.

Rev. 3:21

The reference here is to Jesus Christ who overcame all
worldly temptations and then won the crown of glory.

"In" should read "upon." A throne is like a chair, and kings
sit upon it and not in it. Kings usually have several thrones,
some large and some small, according to the greatness of the
king. But all the thrones are on the same level. No two kings sit
on the same throne.

The term "throne" in this instance means "glory and authority." In the Scriptures we read that Jesus sat on the right
hand of God. That is to say, God entrusted him with honor
and authority. In the East when a ruler loves or has confidence
in one of his ministers, he always asks him to be seated in a
chair on his right. Even today, cardinals and other high church
dignitaries sit around the Pope, but always in smaller chairs.

Only the loyal princes and governors of the realm sit on
the right hand of the ruler. Christians who had overcome
the temptations and stood steadfast in the truth of Jesus
Christ sit in high places with Jesus. (Matt. 19:28)

16. THE SLAIN LAMB

And I beheld, and, lo, in the midst of the throne and of the four beasts, and in the midst of the elders, stood a Lamb as it had been slain, having seven horns and seven eyes, which are the seven Spirits of God sent forth into all the earth.

Rev. 5:6

The slain lamb is symbolic of Jesus Christ, who was crucified. Lambs were slain as offerings for the sins of the people. Moreover, the lamb is the meekest animal; it does not resist the wild animals who devour it, or the men who slaughter it. Jesus went to the cross like a lamb; he offered no resistance. (Isa. 53:7, John 1:29)

The elders are those of the Old Testament and the apostles. The beasts before the throne denote glory and the majesty of God. In the East, a king is considered a god. In the olden days, kings kept lions and tigers in front of their palaces as a means of protection. This is still done by the Emperor of Ethiopia and the King of Jordan. (Note: the beasts are not mentioned in the Eastern text.)

The number "seven" is a sacred number. People in the early days knew about only seven planets, which are represented by the seven stems in the Jewish candlestick. Two more planets have since been discovered, Uranus and Pluto.

All of these symbols refer to the seven churches to which the letters are addressed. Each congregation is seen with a different eye. As we can see from the book, all of them are judged differently. Some had failed, some had done well and are highly commended, and others are rebuked. (Zech. 3:9)

17. HIDING IN CAVES

And the kings of the earth, and the great men, and the
rich men, and the chief captains, and the mighty men,
and every bondman, and every free man, hid themselves
in the dens and in the rocks of the mountains.

Rev. 6:15

The reference in this instance is to the end of the world,
when the wicked and the righteous will be separated and the
wicked will hide themselves because of the wrath (which means
the displeasure) of the Lamb, or Jesus Christ.

Jesus told the Jews that the day was coming when they
would hide themselves in caves because of the fearful day of
the Lord. This prophecy was fulfilled when Titus, in the year
A.D. 70, besieged Jerusalem, destroyed the temple, and mas-
sacred thousands of Jews. Many of the inhabitants of the
historic city fled into the mountains, where they hid themselves
in caves. (Matt. 24:16)

18. WASHED THEIR ROBES

And I said unto him, Sir, thou knowest. And he said to me,
These are they which came out of great tribulation, and
have washed their robes, and made them white in the
blood of the Lamb.
Therefore are they before the throne of God, and serve
him day and night in his temple: and he that sitteth
on the throne shall dwell among them.

Rev. 7:14–15

"Washed their robes and made them white in the blood"
symbolizes martyrdom. In the East, when a man is seriously
wounded and his garments smeared with blood, it is said
figuratively that he is washed in his own blood. In English, we
say "bathed" in blood. White signifies innocence. Martyrs died
for the sake of truth. Since their white garments were washed
with their own blood for the sake of the gospel, the garments
remained white. When a man is accused falsely and put to
death, he becomes a martyr, free of guilt and reproach.

All those who had suffered for truth will serve in the presence
of God and rejoice at the sight of the Lamb, Christ, the Truth.

19. GOLDEN CENSERS

And another angel came and stood at the altar, having a golden censer; and there was given unto him much incense, that he should offer it with the prayers of all saints upon the golden altar which was before the throne.

And the smoke of the incense, which came with the prayers of the saints, ascended up before God out of the angel's hand.

And the angel took the censer, and filled it with fire of the altar, and cast it into the earth: and there were voices, and thunderings, and lightnings, and an earthquake.

Rev. 8:3–5

Censers are used even today in many churches during the services, to offer incense to God. Moreover, Mohammedanism, Hinduism and many other religions still use incense.

In the olden days, people thought the smoke of the incense would mingle with their prayers and carry them up before the throne. of God, Who was supposed to be seated on the clouds. Gold symbolizes purity. Most of the censers were made of bronze, but the censer wherewith the priests ministered in the holy of holies was made of gold.

The fire was thrown upon the earth to burn it. The learned people of that time, like scientists today, believed that someday the earth would catch fire and burn. On the other hand, fire was the most destructive force known at this time, and therefore was greatly feared. Peter in his second epistle tells us that when the end comes, the elements will melt with the fierce fire which will cause them to separate and then be burned. (II Pet. 3:12)

20. HAIL AND FIRE

> The first angel sounded, and there followed hail and fire
> mingled with blood, and they were cast upon the earth:
> and the third part of trees was burnt up, and all green
> grass was burnt up.
>
> Rev. 8:7

The Eastern text reads, "mingled with water instead of mingled with blood." This is because the intense fire would cause the hail to melt and turn into water. Hail and fire are symbolic of great disaster. Vineyards, fruit trees and crops are generally destroyed by hail; forests and cities, by fire. Moreover, lightning, which often sets forests afire, is called "the fire of God." This is because fire, while burning, arises to the skies, but lightning comes down from the skies, which in Aramaic and Hebrew also means heaven.

Hebrew prophets also foresaw similar catastrophes falling upon the world, caused by great natural forces. (Ezek. 38:22)

21. THIRD PART OF LIFE DESTROYED

> And the second angel sounded, and as it were a great
> mountain burning with fire was cast into the sea: and
> the third part of the sea became blood;
> And the third part of the creatures which were in the
> sea, and had life, died; and the third part of the ships
> were destroyed.
>
> Rev. 8:8–9

The catastrophes whereof the Revelator speaks which are to fall upon man are to fall upon nature, too. In other words,

John implies that the calamities will be so great that even nature will share in them.

Fire symbolizes a great disaster. The word "mountain" means "a large fire," not large enough to destroy the whole sea, but only one-third thereof.

22. STAR FALLING

And the third angel sounded, and there fell a great star from heaven, burning as it were a lamp, and it fell upon the third part of the rivers, and upon the fountains of waters;

And the name of the star is called Wormwood: and the third part of the waters became wormwood; and many men died of the waters, because they were made bitter.

Rev. 8:10–11

A star usually signifies a potentate, an emperor, a king, a great person, or a realm. Seemingly, the astronomers in ancient days knew that a falling star would cause intense heat, explode and catch fire. The Chaldean astronomers who studied the stars and planets in order to devise our calendar knew that the stars were far away from the earth, and they must have known something about the law of gravity.

John here again emphasized the impending disaster. Water is symbolic of life, and its transmutation into wormwood, bitterness, signifies the bitter end of life.

Note that all these things are seen by the Revelator in a vision during the night. In order to understand the vision, one must be familiar with Eastern symbology, and know something about the figurative speech which is so common in the Aramaic language.

23. NATURE SHARES HUMAN TRAGEDY

> And the fourth angel sounded, and the third part of the
> sun was smitten, and the third part of the moon, and the
> third part of the stars; so as the third part of them was
> darkened, and the day shone not for a third part of it,
> and the night likewise.
>
> Rev. 8:12

Sun and moon "darkened" means "the universe mourns over the human tragedy." In the East, when poets compose songs at the death of a king, they often say, "The sun refused to shine and the moon to give her light."

In the history of Alexander the Great, we read that when he died the sun refused to come out, and the stars did not give their light. This is also true about the death of Jesus. We read that when he was on the cross, the sun became darkened.

This is not all. In the Old Testament we often read that the sun darkened or did not move, and the stars fought on the Jewish side against the Amorites. The people in the olden days understood that the writers intended that their poetic writings and figurative speech should not be taken literally. The darkening of the sun brings forth this truth: that the whole universe shares in the joys and tragedies of man, who was created in the image and likeness of God. (Isa. 13:10)

24. BOTTOMLESS PIT

And the fifth angel sounded, and I saw a star fall from heaven unto the earth: and to him was given the key of the bottomless pit.

And he opened the bottomless pit; and there arose a smoke out of the pit, as the smoke of a great furnace; and the sun and the air were darkened by reason of the smoke of the pit.

And there came out of the smoke locusts upon the earth: and unto them was given power, as the scorpions of the earth have power.

And it was commanded them that they should not hurt the grass of the earth, neither any green thing, neither any tree; but only those men which have not the seal of God in their foreheads.

Rev. 9:1–4

A star is symbolic of kings, princes, ministers, and other prominent personalities.

"The bottomless pit" is Sheol, which is supposed to be the large pit where the souls of the departed ones rest. The star, here representing a great person, had the key to the pit to open it and bring out locusts and scorpions to destroy man. The Revelator is describing another catastrophe which befalls evildoers.

25. DESIRING TO DIE

And in those days shall men seek death, and shall not find it; and shall desire to die, and death shall flee from them.

Rev. 9:6

"Seek death" means that the suffering will be so intense that people would be happy to depart from this life. "And shall not find it" means that the suffering will be continuous; that is to say, the mental suffering, the agony, and the suffering will be so great that death will seem like paradise. Easterners use this type of symbolism in their daily speech. One often hears, "I wanted to die but the death fled from me, in order to keep me suffering."

Job, who during his trials was suffering agony, sought death, but death fled from him. (Job 3:21)

Death, no matter how sinister, is a blessing to those who have done wickedness, and are punished for it. On such occasions, death becomes sweeter than life and more difficult to attain.

26. ARMY OF LOCUSTS

And the shapes of the locusts were like unto horses prepared unto battle; and on their heads were as it were
crowns like gold, and their faces were as the faces of
men.
And they had hair as the hair of women, and their
teeth were as the teeth of lions.
And they had breastplates, as it were breastplates of iron;
and the sound of their wings was as the sound of chariots
of many horses running to battle.
And they had tails like unto scorpions, and there were
stings in their tails: and their power was to hurt men
five months.

Rev. 9:7–10

Most of the symbolism in the Book of Revelation is
taken from the books of the prophets. This is because this type
of symbolism or figurative speech was familiar to the people.
Then again, such spiritual and profound ideas could hardly
be expressed without metaphors and figurative speech. For
example, the portion which pertains to the locusts is found
in Nahum 3:17: "Your Nazarites are as the locusts, and your war-
riors as the swarms of locusts which settle on the hedges on
a cold day, but when the sun arises they fly off, and it is not
known where they are."

The Easterners believe that locusts, like bees, have a king
which leads them from one place to another. During the time
when ravaging locusts appear, one can see the ground and
the bushes covered with them. They are motionless as though
dead, but suddenly they all fly at once, and no one knows
their destination except their king.

The figure of the locust resembles that of an armed soldier
who wears breastplate and hat for protection. "Faces of men"
signifies intellect; the locusts would act like a well-trained
army. "Teeth of lions" symbolizes devouring; "tails like unto

scorpions" means the destructive venom which they carry. "Hair as the hair of women" indicates dignity and order. The locusts' resemblance to horses in battle symbolizes speed. The locusts are symbolical of the fortified war planes of today.

27. ABADDON

And they had a king over them, which is the angel of the bottomless pit, whose name in the Hebrew tongue is Abaddon, but in the Greek tongue hath his name Apollyon.

Rev. 9:11

"King" symbolizes authority, and "angel" is the guardian of the pit. The Hebrew word *Abaddon* means "the one who is constantly active or destructive." The root of the word is *abad*, "to perish," "to come to nought." The Devil is usually described as taking no vacation. The Aramaic meaning for this word is the same as the Hebrew. (John 12:31, Eph. 2:2)

28. THE RIVER EUPHRATES

Saying to the sixth angel which had the trumpet, Loose the four angels which are bound in the great river Euphrates.

Rev. 9:14

The River Euphrates was the boundary between Palestine, Syria, and Assyria, or Mesopotamia, and also between the Roman and Persian empires. This is the richest and most civilized land in the Near East, and is called "the cradle of civilization" and also "the fertile crescent."

In the twelfth and thirteenth centuries A.D. this land was invaded by the Chinese warlords Genghis Khan and Tamerlane. They destroyed all the palm trees in Mesopotamia, captured the cities and put its inhabitants to the sword.

It is prophesied in Revelation 16 that the kings of the East will cross the River Euphrates in their invasion of the world or during the Battle of Armageddon, which will take place in the vast plains of Israloon near the ancient city of Magido. In the olden days this place, because of its vastness, served as a battleground between the King of Babylon, Nebuchadnezzar, and Neco, King of Egypt. The latter was slain in the battle.

In the Eastern language, when describing the size of an army, we often say the river dried before them; that is to say, the army was so large that they drank all the water of the river. Note: A writer who had been born and reared in Palestine, accustomed to drinking water from a well, could easily imagine that a river like the Euphrates would be insufficient for a large army. He had often seen wells, cisterns, and other small water sources completely exhausted when large armies invaded the land. (Rev. 16:12)

29. THIRD OF MEN KILLED

And the number of the army of the horsemen were two hundred thousand thousand: and I heard the number of them.

And thus I saw the horses in the vision, and them that sat on them, having breastplates of fire, and of jacinth, and brimstone: and the heads of the horses were as the heads of lions; and out of their mouths issued fire and smoke and brimstone.

By these three was the third part of men killed, by the fire, and by the smoke, and by the brimstone, which issued out of their mouths.

For their power is in their mouth, and in their tails: for their tails were like unto serpents, and had heads, and with them they do hurt.

And the rest of the men which were not killed by these plagues yet repented not of the works of their hands, that they should not worship devils, and idols of gold, and silver, and brass, and stone, and of wood: which neither can see, nor hear, nor walk.

Rev. 9:16–20

The large size of the army indicates that this invasion would be carried out by China, which has the largest population of any country in the world, and by other Asiatic powers. The number of cavalry is two million. Note: The Revelator uses a large number figuratively, meaning a huge army. (See Ps. 68:17, Dan. 7:10.) Such an army would occupy all Asia.

The breastplates of fire are symbolic of the strength of the shining armor, and the destruction which the large army was to cause. The term "lion" symbolizes courage and destruction. The army would march ahead. Fire and smoke symbolize disaster. When large cities are burned, many inhabitants perish by fire.

When the Mongolian armies invaded the Near East in the twelfth and thirteenth centuries A.D., they burned the cities, cut down the palm trees, and put the people to the sword.

30. CLOTHED IN A CLOUD

And I saw another mighty angel come down from heaven,
clothed with a cloud: and a rainbow was upon his head,
and his face was as it were the sun, and his feet as pillars
of fire:
And he had in his hand a little book open: and he set
his right foot upon the sea, and his left foot on the earth.
And cried with a loud voice, as when a lion roareth:
and when he had cried, seven thunders uttered their voices.

Rev. 10:1–3

"Clothed in a cloud" is an Aramaic idiom which means
"gloriously arrayed." The rainbow is symbolic of beauty and
majesty. (Rev. 1:13–14)

The sun is symbolic of truth, and is often figuratively used
for God. The angel, or the messenger, would judge the people.
(See Matt. 17:2.)

The book, or the scroll, open, symbolized the time for the
final judgment. In the East, judges open the books when they
judge the people. This is because judges are not trained in the
law. They are guided by the sacred book. For example, Mosaic
law touched on most of the problems in jurisprudence in Moses'
time. All the judges had to do was to find the appropriate
passage relative to the case which was now before them. This
is still done today, in some of the Moslem countries where the
Koran is the only law.

Then again there are the other books, the books of good and
evil deeds, wherein every human act is recorded.

"Lion" in this instance symbolizes the seriousness of the impending calamity and its destructive force. "And he set his
right foot upon the sea, and his left foot on the earth" means
that the angel had complete dominion.

31. SWEARING BY GOD

And sware by him that liveth for ever and ever, who created heaven, and the things that therein are, and the earth, and the things that therein are, and the sea, and the things which are therein, that there should be time no longer:
But in the days of the voice of the seventh angel, when he shall begin to sound, the mystery of God should be finished, as he hath declared to his servants the prophets.

Rev. 10:6–7

In the East, all solemn promises begin by a sacred oath. Therefore, such promises cannot be broken, but must be carried out.

The angel swore by God, the Creator of the heavens and the earth, that he would carry out his mission and cause such destruction that even the heavenly bodies would suffer during the catastrophe. There would be no more time, because even the heavenly bodies would disappear.

The mystery of God means the sealed revelations which were to be fulfilled in due time. All things which the prophets and apostles had predicted were to be fulfilled.

32. THE WITNESSES

And I will give power unto my two witnesses, and they
shall prophesy a thousand two hundred and threescore
days, clothed in sackcloth.

Rev. 11:3

The witnesses are the souls of the men who were slain
because of the preaching of the gospel of Jesus Christ. (Rev.
6:9–10, 19:10)

The term "two" denotes the prophets and the apostles. The
Mosaic law requires two witnesses to testify against, or for,
anyone. Both the prophets and the apostles were witnesses for
God's truth, which was rejected by wicked men.

The witnesses are clothed in sackcloth because they
mourned for their brethren who had rejected the gospel, and
now were ready to perish.

As to the number of days, see Revelation 12:6. Days in this
instance might be symbolic of the number of days wherein the
Church of Jesus Christ suffered persecutions under the Roman
emperors.

33. TWO OLIVE TREES

These are the two olive trees, and the two candlesticks standing before the God of the earth.

And if any man will hurt them, fire proceedeth out of their mouth, and devoureth their enemies: and if any man will hurt them, he must in this manner be killed.

These have power to shut heaven, that it rain not in the days of their prophecy: and have power over waters to turn them to blood, and to smite the earth with all plagues, as often as they will.

Rev. 11:4–6

The two olive trees are symbolic of the remnant in the Old and New Testaments, that is, the pious men who had never been defiled by pagan teachings, heresies and evil practices. Moreover, the olive tree is symbolic of truth, light and life. The olive tree lives longer than any other tree, and its oil is used to light the temples. It was a branch of an olive tree which a dove brought after the flood, which heralded the good news that the disastrous flood was over. Then again, an olive branch is symbolic of peace, protection and understanding.

These pious men were not to be hurt by the impending disasters. God was to protect them because they had been loyal to Him and to the gospel of Christ. (Rev. 19:8) Anyone hurting them would be consumed by fire, or truth. This is because as fire destroys fuel, truth destroys error. Ultimately, God's truth will be revealed, and will prevail, and will triumph over the evil forces, and the kingdoms of this world will become the kingdom of God.

34. JERUSALEM CALLED SODOM

And their dead bodies shall lie in the street of the great
city, which spiritually is called Sodom and Egypt, where
also our Lord was crucified.

And they of the people and kindreds and tongues and
nations shall see their dead bodies three days and an
half, and shall not suffer their dead bodies to be put
in graves.

Rev. 11:8–9

The reference here is to Jerusalem, which is metaphorically
called Sodom because of its evils, and to Egypt, two places
which in the olden days were hated by the Jews because of
corruption and oppression. Jerusalem had murdered God's prophets and His messengers, and there Jesus was crucified. Moreover, in the Scriptures, Sodom is symbolic of immorality and
homosexuality, while on the other hand, Egypt represents oppression.

The Christian believers were to suffer persecution and to be
killed, and their corpses left on the streets unburied, but they
were to rise again.

The beast, or the evil forces, was given power. In other
words, these disasters were brought about by the people themselves, because of their own evil works, heresies, and corrupt
practices. Even the righteous were to suffer during these calamities.

35. WITNESSES SLAIN FOR TESTIMONY

And after three days and an half the Spirit of life from
God entered into them, and they stood upon their feet;
and great fear fell upon them which saw them.
And they heard a great voice from heaven saying unto
them, Come up hither. And they ascended up to heaven
in a cloud; and their enemies beheld them.

Rev. 11:11–12

The reference here is to the resurrection of the dead and
the ultimate triumph of truth over error. The witnesses who
were slain for the testimony of Jesus Christ would rise again. In
the days of the prophet Ezekiel, both Israel and Judah were
crushed by their enemies; but the prophet saw in a vision the
bones of the dead receiving flesh and rising up again, which
indicated that Israel was to rise again. (Ezek. 37:5–13) Christianity was to suffer many persecutions and harassments, but
the truth of the gospel could not be destroyed, nor could God's
light be put out.

These true witnesses were wearing crowns of victory, and
they were rewarded for their suffering.

36. THE KINGDOM OF OUR LORD

And the seventh angel sounded; and there were great
voices in heaven, saying, The kingdoms of this world are
become the kingdoms of our Lord, and of his Christ; and
he shall reign for ever and ever.

Rev. 11:15

There were two concepts of the kingdom: the first, the
kingdom of heaven, which means a universal state which em-
braces all races and colors, and which was envisioned by the
Hebrew prophets; and the second, the kingdom of God.

The difference between these two concepts of the kingdom
was this: The kingdom of heaven would be a universal kingdom
embracing both the Jews and the Gentiles, and there would
be both good and bad in it. Jesus illustrated this by the parable
of the wheat and the tares, and that of the net which contained
both good and bad fish. In the kingdom of God, all evil would
be eradicated.

Jesus Christ is the king of the universal kingdom, that is,
the Church, but God Himself would rule over His kingdom.
Of course, all this is related in human terms in order to be
understood by man. What the Revelator means here is "the
good" will rule over the universe, and all those who are good
will participate in it. The evil will ultimately be annihilated.
The kingdoms of this world will ultimately become the kingdoms of Jesus Christ and of God, where truth will reign.

37. THE TEMPLE OF GOD

And the temple of God was opened in heaven, and there was seen in his temple the ark of his testament: and there were lightnings, and voices, and thunderings, and an earthquake, and great hail.

Rev. 11:19

The temple which King Solomon had built in the tenth century B.C. was symbolic of the temple in heaven. Every pattern of the magnificent temple in Jerusalem had a spiritual meaning, and therefore it was a true pattern of the kingdom of God. But sooner or later the spiritual and inner meaning of this earthly temple was lost completely.

When the law was given to Moses, Mount Sinai shook. There was thunder and lightning, heralding the introduction of God's law and his way of life to men. (Ex. 19:16)

On the other hand, the pattern of the spiritual and moral tablets which contained the Ten Commandments was in heaven, where no one could steal or destroy it. But the stone tablets were lost.

"The temple of God was opened" means "the secrets of religion were revealed." Pagan temples were dark and closed, and had many curtains, and the rituals were performed in a mysterious way. (Heb. 9:4) This is because the priests were engaged in magic and in the deliverance of oracles and the practice of tricks, and they never wanted the people to know their secrets. When truth shall come, all mysteries of religion will be revealed.

38. GREAT RED DRAGON

And there appeared another wonder in heaven; and behold
a great red dragon, having seven heads and ten horns,
and seven crowns upon his heads.
And his tail drew the third part of the stars of heaven, and
did cast them to the earth: and the dragon stood before
the woman which was ready to be delivered, for to devour
her child as soon as it was born.

Rev. 12:3–4

A great red dragon is symbolic of a great imperial wizard,
or a religious ruler with supreme authority over the people.
Both emperors and high religious authorities wore scarlet garments symbolizing their devotion to their high offices, and
their readiness to die for them. Red symbolizes blood. Moreover, emperors marched ahead of their armies and were always ready to die for their people. A great many of them
were slain in battle.

The "seven heads" means "seven kings under the emperor."
In the Roman system, there were vice caesars. "Seven crowns"
means "the king of kings." "Ten horns" mean "ten small kingdoms," or "princely states." (See Rev. 17:1–17, 13:1.)

39. MICHAEL AND HIS ANGELS

And there was war in heaven: Michael and his angels
fought against the dragon; and the dragon fought and his
angels,
And prevailed not; neither was their place found any more
in heaven.
And the great dragon was cast out, that old serpent,
called the Devil, and Satan, which deceiveth the whole
world: he was cast out into the earth, and his angels were
cast out with him.

Rev. 12:7–9

"Michael" means "God has humbled me." It is the name
of a noted angel, like Gabriel, the man of God.

The war in heaven is symbolic of the struggle between the
truth of Jesus Christ and the error; between good and evil
forces; between the true doctrine and heresy. Messages in a
vision are related in a symbolic manner. The dragon means
gross deception, the Devil, or the opposition to the truth. (See
Dan. 10:13, Rev. 20:2.) The term "dragon" is another name
for the serpent who beguiled Adam and Eve.

The dragon is finally conquered and the error has been
overcome by the truth of the Christian gospel.

Jesus said the Devil is a liar and father of lies. The dragon
and his angels cast down to the earth symbolizes the utter
defeat of the evil forces.

The doctrine of demonology started during the exile. The
Babylonian, or Persian, religion had two gods, the god of evil
and the god of good, which were constantly at war against
one another. This Babylonian concept of religion exerted considerable influence on the Jewish people in exile, just as pagan
religions had also exerted some influence on Christianity.

Prior to the exile, there is very little mention of devils,
demons, or angels in the Hebrew Scriptures. Note: the term

"angel" in Aramaic means "counsel." It was used in this sense. Angels are God's counsel. The term "devil," which means "demented" or "wild," comes from the Persian language.

40. ACCUSERS CAST DOWN

And I heard a loud voice saying in heaven, Now is come salvation, and strength, and the kingdom of our God, and the power of his Christ: for the accuser of our brethren is cast down, which accused them before our God day and night.

And they overcame him by the blood of the Lamb, and by the word of their testimony; and they loved not their lives unto the death.

Therefore rejoice, ye heavens, and ye that dwell in them. Woe to the inhabiters of the earth and of the sea! for the devil is come down unto you, having great wrath, because he knoweth that he hath but a short time.

Rev. 12:10–12

The "accuser" is the exponent of the heretical doctrines. When the church councils met, they met at large cathedrals and churches. The heretical accusers of the pious men who stood firm for the true teachings of Jesus Christ, accused them before the altar, the throne of God. But sooner or later the adversary was overcome by the testimonies of the saints who were willing to die for the truth of the gospel of their Lord.

There were already many heresies at the time of the apostle John, and many heretical teachers were supported by the so-called Christian leaders and corrupt government officials whose intent was to use religion for political ends and worldly gain.

Finally, and in due time, the truth was to triumph, and the

opposition was to be overcome, and the kingdom of God was soon to be heralded.

The "inhabiters of the sea" means "the inhabiters of the islands." The evil forces were soon to spend their fury and come to an end.

41. DRAGON DEFEATED

And the serpent cast out of his mouth water as a flood after the woman, that he might cause her to be carried away of the flood.
And the earth helped the woman, and the earth opened her mouth, and swallowed up the flood which the dragon cast out of his mouth.
And the dragon was wroth with the woman, and went to make war with the remnant of her seed, which keep the commandments of God, and have the testimony of Jesus Christ.

Rev. 12:15–17

The serpent symbolizes evil and opposition to the truth. The woman is the Virgin Mary. The evil forces wanted to destroy the Christ, the truth, or drown it in pagan practices. Note: King Herod had many infants in Bethlehem slain, and Joseph, Mary, and the infant fled to Egypt.

The earth helped by opening her mouth and swallowing the flood which the dragon (Satan) spat out. In other words, nature was on the side of the truth; it helped the woman, the truth, to escape. "So shall they revere the name of the Lord from the west, and his glory from the rising of the sun. For the oppressor shall come in like a flood, and the Spirit of the Lord shall humble him." (Isa. 59:19)

The opposition to the truth continued, and still continues

today. Those who are obedient to the word of God are often persecuted, and the evil forces are still in power.

The woman might be Eve, with whose descendants the evil forces had made, and are making, war.

The Revelator sees the past, the present, and the future. There is no time in a vision.

42. BEAST RISING OUT OF THE SEA

And I stood upon the sand of the sea, and saw a beast rise up out of the sea, having seven heads and ten horns, and upon his horns ten crowns, and upon his heads the name of blasphemy.

And the beast which I saw was like unto a leopard, and his feet were as the feet of a bear, and his mouth as the mouth of a lion: and the dragon gave him his power, and his seat, and great authority.

Rev. 13:1–2

The beast is an oppressor, a ruler who is opposed to the truth of the gospel. The beast rising out of the sea symbolizes the Roman naval power, which dominated all the lands around the Mediterranean Sea. Rome was to oppose this new religion, which condemned war and oppression and which declared all people equal.

The dragon is symbolic of a deception, a false teaching and the teacher thereof. An emperor or a false religious leader would deny the true teaching, and blaspheme against it.

Some of the Roman and Byzantine emperors did suppress the truth and persecute the saints, that is, the faithful. There were ten persecutions under Rome, starting with Nero and ending with Galerius. The Christians were put to death and thrown to the lions.

43. PATIENCE OF THE FAITHFUL

He that leadeth into captivity shall go into captivity:
he that killeth with the sword must be killed with the
sword. Here is the patience and the faith of the saints.

Rev. 13:10

At last the gospel of Jesus Christ was to triumph over
the Roman Empire and the evil forces. (See Rev. 13:8.) And
the oppressors who carried Christians and Jews away captive
were soon to be captive themselves, and those who had slain
the innocent by the sword were to perish by the sword.

The term "saints" means "the dedicated ones," "the faithful,"
those who are willing to die for the sake of the truth.

The faithful are admonished to be patient until justice catches
up with the oppressors. (See Isa. 14:2.)

Patience is an answer to many difficult human problems.
This is because today we see a thing in part, but tomorrow
or the next day we may see it as a whole. All human problems
could be solved, provided that people take enough time to
consider them from every angle. A person without patience is
like a ship without a rudder or compass, constantly drifting in
the turbulent sea of life.

44. BEAST WITH TWO HORNS

And I beheld another beast coming up out of the earth; and he had two horns like a lamb, and he spake as a dragon.

And he exerciseth all the power of the first beast before him, and causeth the earth and them which dwell therein to worship the first beast, whose deadly wound was healed.

And he doeth great wonders, so that he maketh fire come down from heaven on the earth in the sight of men.

And deceiveth them that dwell on the earth by the means of those miracles which he had power to do in the sight of the beast; saying to them that dwell on the earth, that they should make an image to the beast, which had the wound by a sword, and did live.

And he had power to give life unto the image of the beast, that the image of the beast should both speak, and cause that as many as would not worship the image of the beast should be killed.

And he causeth all, both small and great, rich and poor, free and bond, to receive a mark in their right hand, or in their foreheads:

Rev. 13:11–16

The beast is symbolic of oppression and an exponent of heresies. "Two horns" means he had two powers. "Two horns like a lamb" refers to religious power; "he spoke as a dragon" symbolizes political power. Byzantine emperors were both political and religious, and some of them did all they could to weaken or even to destroy Christianity.

Fire coming from heaven symbolizes unlimited authority and excessive power to do wonders in order to deceive the faithful. Some of the emperors compelled the people to worship images. And many images were supposed to perform miracles.

In other words, the Revelator in his vision saw the restoration of paganism. Those who were willing to accept his edict and worship his image were marked for favor over others. The others could not buy or sell because they were not marked. In the East, sheep are marked for the slaughter.

The "beast" in this case is Nero, Caesar, who started the first persecution against the Christians. His name is given in figures in Aramaic as 666. (See comment on the Number of the Beasts, *New Testament Commentary*, Rev. 13:18.) In the East, when people are warned about a government official, they use the number of his name in order to avoid being persecuted. Moreover, in Aramaic, every name can be expressed in numbers. This is because every letter has a numerical value.

45. ONE HUNDRED AND FORTY-FOUR THOUSAND

And I looked, and, lo, a Lamb stood on the mount Sion, and with him an hundred forty and four thousand, having his Father's name written in their foreheads.

Rev. 14:1

The reference here is to the remnant, or the number of the Israelites who returned from Babylon after the captivity: 12,000 from each tribe, that is, 144,000.

This remnant was the people who were marked to be spared to return from Babylon and establish the second Jewish Commonwealth during the time of Ezra and Nehemiah. The term "marked" means "identified," as sheep are marked on their ears in the East. The lamb is symbolic of Jesus Christ. (Rev. 14:3; see comment on Rev. 7:4, *New Testament Commentary*.)

46. DIED BELIEVING IN THE LORD

And I heard a voice from heaven saying unto me, Write,
Blessed are the dead which die in the Lord from henceforth: Yea, saith the Spirit, that they may rest from their
labours; and their works do follow them.
And I looked, and behold a white cloud, and upon the
cloud one sat like unto the Son of man, havng on his head
a golden crown, and in his hand a sharp sickle.

Rev. 14:13–14

The author of the Book of Revelation is here admonished
to write the message which came unto him in a vision, namely,
"Blessed are the dead who die in the Lord," that is to say,
men and women who died professing the Christian gospel, so
that they may rest from earthly labors.

The term "cloud" is an Aramaic idiom which means "glory
and majesty"; white is symbolic of purity and truth, which is
free from any kind of falsehood. (Dan. 7:13, Rev. 7:13)

The "golden crown" is symbolic of glory and long dominion;
the sickle is symbolic of the end, as, when the harvest is ready,
the wheat is cut. At the end, the people will be gathered as
a reaper gathers sheaves of wheat, and then good and evil will
be separated. (Matt. 13:39)

47. THE VIALS

And the first went, and poured out his vial upon the earth;
and there fell a noisome and grievous sore upon the men
which had the mark of the beast, and upon them which
worshipped his image.
And the second angel poured out his vial upon the sea;
and it became as the blood of a dead man; and every
living soul died in the sea.
And the third angel poured out his vial upon the rivers
and fountains of waters; and they became blood.

Rev. 16:2–4

The term "vials" symbolizes plagues or catastrophes
whereby the wicked were to be punished. These vials were
disasters similar to those which befell the Egyptians during
the time of the exodus. (Ex. 9:9)

All those who had the mark of the beast, that is to say,
those who were immune to persecution and suffering in this
life because they worshiped the beast, were inflicted by sores
(blains). In other words, justice was to catch up with them.

When the Nile turns red, the fish generally die. The Aramaic
and Hebrew word *dam,* "blood," also means "red." The term
Adam means "red earth." (See Ex. 7:17, Rev. 8:8–9.)

48. BLASPHEMED THE NAME OF GOD

And the fourth angel poured out his vial upon the sun; and power was given unto him to scorch men with fire. And men were scorched with great heat, and blasphemed the name of God, which hath power over these plagues: and they repented not to give him glory.

And the fifth angel poured out his vial upon the seat of the beast; and his kingdom was full of darkness; and they gnawed their tongues for pain,

And blasphemed the God of heaven because of their pains and their sores, and repented not of their deeds.

Rev. 16:8–11

This vial, or plague, was caused by the intense heat of the sun. The suffering from the scorching heat was so intense that the wicked blasphemed against the name of God during their torment. This is because He did not stop the plagues, nor did He take their lives away to relieve their suffering. (See Isa. 8:21.)

The fifth angel brought the plague upon the seat of the imperial government; and those who were faithful also suffered from the catastrophe. (See Rev. 16:10.) Nevertheless, these men did not repent of their evil doings.

Some of the above calamities had already befallen the people, and the others were to come in due time.

49. UNCLEAN FROGS

And I saw three unclean spirits like frogs come out of
the mouth of the dragon, and out of the mouth of the
beast, and out of the mouth of the false prophet.
For they are the spirits of devils, working miracles, which
go forth unto the kings of the earth and of the whole
world, to gather them to the battle of that great day
of God Almighty.

Rev. 16:13–14

The term "unclean spirits" in this instance means "evil
inclination," or "insane people." In Aramaic, the term "spirit"
is often used to refer to a person. Thus "evil spirits" means
"evil people." It is also used when describing insane men.

Frogs were and still are considered unclean. In the East,
neither Jews, Moslems, nor Christians eat frogs or any unclean
creature prohibited by Mosaic law. The dragon symbolized the
highest pagan religious authority. Pagan priests aroused the
government officials against other religions. The beast is the
imperial power, or an emperor who resorts to persecution and
tyranny. The false prophet is the false teaching, that is the
evil counsel, which the dragon, or deceptive teacher, gave to
the beast, or the emperor.

These were the spirits of men who had the evil inclination
to deceive the people. Both the political and religious leaders
were to convince the people of the world to go to the great
battle of the great day of God Almighty—the Battle of Armageddon.

50. COVERING THE SHAME

Behold, I come as a thief. Blessed is he that watcheth, and keepeth his garments, lest he walk naked, and they see his shame.

Rev. 16:15

One who "keepeth his garments" means "one who is alert and ready for the second coming of Christ," who will come as a thief during the night. In other words, one who is careful, sparing his garments and preserving them clean to wear to meet the Lord. Easterners always have a special garment which they wear during weddings and festivals. Some men, being careless about keeping them, find themselves ashamed at weddings and festivals. Such garments are often called the wedding garments. Christians must be constantly alert, their lamps burning, and their garments clean, for no one knows the day and hour of his coming.

Moreover, in the East, when people sleep on the roofs of their houses, their clothes are kept in the house so they will not be stolen. When sudden disaster comes, they have no time to go down to don their clothes, so they escape naked. The term "naked" in this sense means "ashamed." (Matt. 25:13, Mark 13:33, Luke 21:36)

51. THE BEAST THAT WAS IS NOT

The beast that thou sawest was, and is not; and shall
ascend out of the bottomless pit, and go into perdition:
and they that dwell on the earth shall wonder, whose
names were not written in the book of life from the
foundation of the world, when they behold the beast
that was, and is not, and yet is.
And here is the mind which hath wisdom. The seven
heads are seven mountains, on which the woman sitteth.
And there are seven kings: five are fallen, and one is,
and the other is not yet come; and when he cometh,
he must continue a short space.
And the beast that was, and is not, even he is the eighth,
and is of the seven, and goeth into perdition.

Rev. 17:8–11

The beast was the imperial power, Rome, which persecuted the Church, but Constantine, in the fourth century A.D.
changed the capital of the empire to Constantinople. Hence,
the city of Rome lost its imperial power. The whole pagan
world, or the people, as they are called here, whose name
was not written in the book of life, wondered because Rome
suddenly lost its power, and priests and believers in pagan
religions went underground, for Constantine I, through an imperial decree, abolished paganism. But Rome regained her
power again in the sixth century A.D. when the Byzantine
Empire was plagued with church controversies and weakened
by long wars against the Persian Empire.

Rome and Constantinople are built on hills. Some of the
emperors of both capital cities persecuted the Christians, introduced heresies and suppressed the truth. Moreover, both
Roman and Byzantine emperors exerted tremendous influence
over the Christian Church. The Byzantine Empire lost its power
completely in the fifteenth century A.D., when the Church took
Constantinople, but as we have said, Rome regained her power

and became even greater. Despite many persecutions and changes in government, the lamp of God was kept burning, and the Christian truth was preserved.

52. TRUTH TRIUMPHS OVER IMPERIAL POWERS

And a mighty angel took up a stone like a great millstone, and cast it into the sea, saying, Thus with violence shall that great city Babylon be thrown down, and shall be found no more at all.

Rev. 18:21

Babylon was used by the Hebrew prophets as a symbol of oppression, drunkenness, violence, corruption and injustice. In other words, the word "Babylon" came to be used when describing an evil city. Previously, Sodom and Amorah (wrongly called Gomorrah) were used as symbols of corruption, sensuality and materialism.

"Babylon" in this instance means either Constantinople or Rome. This is because Babylon was no longer in power. But imperial Rome and the Byzantine Empire often persecuted the Christians and put many people to death because of their belief in Jesus Christ.

Note: These two capitals of the ancient world were established on hills. There are no hills in Babylon. In the East, when a prostitute receives notoriety, all other prostitutes are called by her name. Even today, many immoral women are called "Jezebel."

Be that as it may, both imperial cities tried to suppress the Christian truth, and used Christianity for political and economic gains. This interference by the state resulted in schism and division in the Church.

53. RESURRECTION AND JUDGMENT

And the sea gave up the dead which were in it; and death
and hell delivered up the dead which were in them: and
they were judged every man according to their works.
And death and hell were cast into the lake of fire. This
is the second death.

Rev. 20:13–14

These sayings are used metaphorically to mean that death
and Sheol had come to an end. It also means that the fearful
day, the Day of Judgment, was at hand. Fire consumes everything; moreover, metals are purified by fire. In the new realm
of life, death and Sheol would no longer be remembered.

Both death and Sheol were greatly feared by the Jewish
people, and are feared by Christians as well. Sheol was supposed to be a place beyond the dominion of God. Jesus through
his death and resurrection, gave death and Sheol a new synthesis, and life a new meaning. Today, through Jesus' teaching,
we know there is no place in the universe where God does
not reign. This is because God is spirit, and spirit is everywhere.
Thus Sheol and death have no power over those who believe
in Jesus Christ and adhere to his teaching.

54. A NEW HEAVEN, A NEW EARTH

And I saw a new heaven and a new earth: for the first
heaven and the first earth were passed away; and there
was no more sea.

Rev. 21:1

The phrase "a new heaven and a new earth" is used
figuratively, meaning "a new order, free from all evil, suffering,
and injustice"; that is, the kingdom of God wherein all people
will be like brothers and sisters, and where perfection will
reign, and evil be destroyed.

The first heaven and the first earth were symbolic of the
mortal man, but the new heaven and the new earth symbolize
the spiritual and perfect man, who was created in God's own
image and likeness.

The Revelator here quotes from Isaiah 65:17 and II Peter
3:13. Christ's teaching heralded a new heaven and a new
earth; the old heaven and the old earth, as the prophet Isaiah
foresaw, had passed away.

55. ALEPH AND TAU

And he said unto me, It is done. I am Alpha and Omega,
the beginning and the end. I will give unto him that is
athirst of the fountain of the water of life freely.
He that overcometh shall inherit all things; and I will be
his God, and he shall be my son.

Rev. 21:6–7

The Aramaic reads, "I am Aleph and Tau," the first and
the last letters in the Aramaic alphabet; that is to say, "I am

the first and the last," or "the beginning and the end." The
Greeks translated this literally to Alpha and Omega, the first
and last letters in the Greek alphabet, which was borrowed
from the Aramaic.

The fountain of the water of life means the true teaching,
which brings about salvation from evil forces and relief from
injustices. In some parts of Palestine, water is so scarce that
it has to be purchased at a price. At times the people go to
sleep thirsty. Until a few decades ago, water was sold by
water carriers, vendors, in the streets of large cities where
water was scarce.

Water is often used to symbolize truth. Jesus said to the
woman in Samaria, "I will give you the living water, and you
will never be thirsty again." (John 4:14) Ezekiel speaks of the
water issuing from the foundation of the temple, which means
the truth of the Jewish religion would survive even though
the temple, or material religion, would be destroyed. The people were thirsty for the truth of God. (See John 7:37,
Matt. 5:6.)

56. JESUS' TEACHING THE LIGHT OF THE WORLD

And I saw no temple therein: for the Lord God Almighty
and the Lamb are the temple of it.
And the city had no need of the sun, neither of the moon,
to shine in it: for the glory of God did lighten it, and
the Lamb is the light thereof.

Rev. 21:22–23

When falsehood is replaced by truth, and true religion is
revealed and accepted, there will be no more need for the
temples made by human hands. The truth itself will be the

lamp of light, and the law of God will guide the people in the right way. All the things of the material world will cease.

"Sun" is symbolic of the light of God, the Truth. In the liturgies of the Church of the East, "sun" is often used metaphorically to mean Deity, another name for God. In due time, the light of God will supersede the light of the sun which is needed only for our physical eyes, through which we see earthly things. "The Lamb" means Jesus Christ, who went to slaughter like a lamb. The light thereof will also shine. (See Isa. 24:23.)

57. THEY SHALL SEE HIS FACE

And they shall see his face; and his name *shall be* in their foreheads.
And there shall be no night there; and they need no candle, neither light of the sun; for the Lord God giveth them light: and they shall reign for ever and ever.
And he said unto me, These sayings are faithful and true: and the Lord God of the holy prophets sent his angel to shew unto his servants the things which must shortly be done.

Rev. 22:4–6

In the East, kings and princes generally refuse to see their enemies and those whom they hate. Only the favored ones whom they love and trust and their faithful officials and servants can see their faces and stand in their presence. "Blessed are the pure in heart, for they shall see God." (Matt. 5:8)

When the spiritual light comes, the light of the planets will cease, for the light of the planets is temporal and good only for this life, but the light of God is the spiritual light through which we can see His face, His heavenly kingdom and His reign of justice. God is the Eternal Spirit; therefore, He can only be seen in spirit. The Psalmist says, "For with thee is the fountain of life; in thy light shall we see light." (Ps. 36:9)

Note: all of these sayings came through a revelation from God, but are written in symbolic language, and should not be taken literally.

58. THE TREE OF LIFE

Blessed are they that do his commandments, that they may have right to the tree of life, and may enter in through the gates into the city.

Rev. 22:14

"The tree of life" symbolizes the perfect humanity; that is, the immortal man who was created in the image and likeness of God, free from evil and death.

Those who obeyed God's commandments and received the true gospel of Jesus Christ would enter into the heavenly kingdom, that is, the reign of righteousness, which is symbolized as a new, perfect, and harmonious Jerusalem. Note: The word "Jerusalem" means "a place of peace." Peace, harmony, and understanding are the ultimate goal of all true religions.

59. THE MORNING STAR

I Jesus have sent mine angel to testify unto you these
things in the churches. I am the root and the offspring
of David, and the bright and morning star.
And the Spirit and the bride say, Come. And let him
that heareth say, Come. And let him that is athirst come.
And whosoever will, let him take the water of life freely.

Rev. 22:16–17

"The root and the offspring of David" means "the Messiah
Christ who would sit on the throne of the spiritual kingdom."
The kingdom of David preceded the Messianic kingdom, and
was symbolic of the Messianic reign. David tried hard to be
faithful to God's word. His reign was emulated by all Jewish
kings.

"The bright and morning star" symbolizes a new day, bright
and free from oppression and the forces of evil. (Isa. 11:1)

The spirit, the truth and the bride symbolize the true Church.
The Church is called "the bride of Christ."

SUBJECT INDEX

Abaddon, see Rev. (27), *page 337*

According to the Flesh, see Acts (4), *page 154*

Accusers Cast Down, see Rev. (40), *page 350*

Admonishing and Reproving, see II Tim. (5), *page 279*

Aleph and Tau, see Rev. (55), *page 364*

Angel at the Tomb, see Mark (27), *page 86*

Angel Communed with Paul, see Acts (22), *page 170*

Angel Opened the Door, see Acts (7), *page 156*

Angels Ministered, see Matt. (3), *page 3*

Anointing, see I John (1), *page 308*

Anti-Christ, see II Thess. (5), *page 269*

Armor of God, see Eph. (10), *page 254*

Army of Locusts, see Rev. (26), *page 336*

As a Roaring Lion, see I Pet. (10), *page 301*

Awake and Pray, see Matt. (54), *page 49*

Backsliders, see II Pet. (3), *page 303*

Baptism for the Dead, see I Cor. (23), *page 215*

Baptism of Fire, see Matt. (1), *page 1*

Baptism of Spirit, Water, and Blood, see I John (6), *page 313*

Beast Rising Out of the Sea, see Rev. (42), *page 352*

Beast That Was Is Not, see Rev. (51), *page 361*

Beast with Two Horns, see Rev. (44), *page 354*

Binding the Strong Man, see Matt. (17), *page 15*

Blasphemed the Name of God, see Rev. (48), *page 358*

Born Again, see I Pet. (4), *page 297*

Born of God, see I John (3), *page 310*

Born to Die on the Cross, see John (35), *page 144*

Bottomless Pit, see Rev. (24), *page 334*

Breaking of Bread, see Acts (18), *page 166*

Bribes Were Common, see Acts (20), *page 168*

By Him, see Acts (17), *page 165*

Calling Peter "Satan," see Matt. (26), *page 23*

Caught in the Clouds, see I Thess. (2), *page 264*

Caught up into Paradise, see II Cor. (22), *page 236*

Chastity, see Rom. (21), *page 192*

The numbers in parentheses refer to the items listed in the contents.

Children's Angels, see Matt. (30), *page 27*

Christ among You, see I John (5), *page 312*

Christ Is Our Hope, see Luke (2), *page 91*

Christ Is the Head, see Col. (4), *page 261*

Christ Stands by You, see II Thess. (1), *page 265*

Christ the Main Objective, see Col. (3), *page 260*

Christian Challenge, see I Tim. (8), *page 275*

Christians at Corinth, see II Cor. (4), *page 221*

Christians, see Rom. (25), *page 194*

Christians Must Excel, see II Pet. (1), *page 302*

Christians Must Remain Faithful, see II Tim (1), *page 276*

Christians Suffer, see II Cor. (1), *page 218*

Christians Will Be Judged, see I Pet. (9), *page 300*

Christ's Suffering Foretold, see Luke (27), *page 113*

Church in Rome, see Rom. (1), *page 173*

Clothed in a Cloud, see Rev. (30), *page 340*

Comforter, see John (30), *page 140*

Coming in a Cloud, see Luke (24), *page 110*

Confess, see Matt. (12), *page 11*

Confessing, see Rom. (24), *page 194*

Confessing Jesus Christ, see Phil. (2), *page 256*

Corinthians Admonished, see II Cor. (25), *page 238*

Covering of the Head, see I Cor. (15), *page 208*

Covering the Shame, see Rev. (50), *page 360*

Crush Satan, see Rom. (26), *page 195*

Cup of Death, see Matt. (33), *page 31*

Cut Off Your Hands, see Matt. (7), *page 6*

Dangers of Being a Christian, see Luke (14), *page 101*

Dead Become Partakers, see I Pet. (7), *page 299*

Dead to Meet Christ, see I Thess. (1), *page 263*

Dead Will Hear Jesus, see John (11), *page 124*

Death of a Sinner, see II Cor. (13), *page 228*

Deceptive Men, see Matt. (41), *page 39*

Declaring Jesus' Name, see Heb. (4), *page 282*

Delusion, see II Thess. (6), *page 269*

Demons Cast Out, see Matt. (16), *page 14*

Descendants Through Christ, see Gal. (9), *page 245*

Desert Place, see Matt. (22), *page 20*

Desiring to Die, see Rev. (25), *page 335*

Devil Is a Liar, see John (19), *page 130*

Devils Also Believe, see James (2), *page 293*

Diana of Ephesus, see II Cor. (2), *page 219*

Did God Pay a Ransom?, see John (5), *page 117*

Died Believing in the Lord, see Rev. (46), *page 356*

Disciple's Love, see John (23), *page 134*

Divine Gifts, see Eph. (8), *page 252*

Divorce of Eunuch, see Matt. (31), *page 28*

Dragon Defeated, see Rev. (41), *page 351*

Eagles, see Luke (17), *page 104*

Earthly Home, see II Cor. (9), *page 226*

Eating Their Vomit, see II Pet. (4), *page 304*

Enemies of the Soul, see Luke (7), *page 95*

370

Engrafted Word, see James (1), *page 292*

Enlightenment, see John (20), *page 131*

Entrusted with Power, see Matt. (57), *page 52*

Esau Put Aside, see Rom. (17), *page 187*

Evil, see Matt. (9), *page 8*

Evil Can Be Defeated, see James (4), *page 294*

Evil Forces at Work, see II Thess. (4), *page 268*

Eyewitness to the Truth, see II Pet. (2), *page 303*

Faith in His Name, see Acts (5), *page 155*

Faith Increased, see Luke (16), *page 103*

Faith Might Be Lost, see Luke (18), *page 105*

Faithful Witness, see Rev. (2), *page 315*

Falsehood, see I Cor. (14), *page 207*

Figs Were Picked, see Mark (13), *page 70*

Filthiness of Spirit, see II Cor. (16), *page 231*

Fire, see Heb. (2), *page 281*

First Adam, see I Cor. (24), *page 216*

First Fruits of the Spirit, see Rom. (15), *page 184*

First Love, see Rev. (5), *page 318*

First Will Be Last, see Luke (12), *page 99*

Freed from the Law, see Rom. (11), *page 181*

Freed Through Christ, see I Pet. (1), *page 295*

Friday Not Preparation Day, see John (38), *page 147*

Fruit of the Vine, see Mark (18), *page 74*

Gentiles, see Rom. (20), *page 191*

Gentiles Declared Righteous, see Gal. (6), *page 243*

Gift of God, see Rom. (8), *page 179*

Giving Alms in Secret, see Matt. (8), *page 7*

God Cannot Be Seen, see John (1), *page 114*

God Does Not Harden Hearts, see Rom. (18), *page 188*

God Is Aware of Everything, see Matt. (11), *page 10*

God of the Living, see Matt. (39), *page 37*

God of This World, see II Cor. (7), *page 224*

God Raised Jesus, see Acts (3), *page 153*

God's Divine Care, see Luke (8), *page 96*

God's Kingdom, see I Cor. (22), *page 214*

God's Name Is Holy, see Matt. (40), *page 38*

Gods Wisdom Hidden, see Eph. (7), *page 251*

Golden Censers, see Rev. (19), *page 330*

Golden Rule, see Matt. (10), *page 9*

Golgotha a Cemetery, see Luke (26), *page 112*

Good Things Out of Good Treasure, see Matt. (18), *page 16*

Gospel Will Triumph, see Eph. (1) and Heb. (9), *page 247; page 286*

Great Calamity, see Mark (17), *page 73*

Great Red Dragon, see Rev. (38), *page 348*

Great Signs Wanted, see Mark (9), *page 65*

Greater Prophet, see Acts (10), *page 159*

Hagar and Sarah, see Gal. (10), *page 246*

Hail and Fire, see Rev. (20), *page 331*

Handling Serpents, see Mark (29), *page 88*

He Cometh with Clouds, see Rev. (4), *page 317*

He Will Be Called, see Luke (1), *page 90*

Heaven Opened, see John (3), *page 116*

Heirs, see Rom. (16), *page 186*

Hellenistic Jews, see Acts (8), *page 157*

Helmet of Salvation, see Eph. (11), *page 254*

Hiding in Caves, see Rev. (17), *page 328*

High Mountain, see Matt. (2), *page 2*

Holy Angels, see Matt. (28), *page 25*

Hour of Crucifixion, see Mark (24) and John (37), *page 79; page 146*

Human Deities, see II Thess. (3), *page 267*

Human Teachers, see I Cor. (5), *page 199*

Husband and Wife, see I Cor. (11), *page 205*

Hypocritical Teachers, see Rom. (3), *page 175*

In a Sponge, see Mark (26), *page 85*

In a Vision, see II Cor. (21), *page 235*

In the Name of the Lord, see Matt. (43), *page 40*

Iniquity Shall Abound, see Matt. (45), *page 42*

Insane Confess Jesus, see Mark (4), *page 61*

Insane, Lunatics, see Luke (3), *page 92*

Insincere Teachers, see Phil. (1), *page 255*

Intense Heat, see II Pet. (7), *page 307*

Interpreters, see I Cor. (21), *page 213*

Invited, see I Cor. (1), *page 196*

Jerusalem Called Sodom, see Rev. (34), *page 344*

Jesus Admonished the Leper, see Mark (2), *page 59*

Jesus an Express Image of God, see Heb. (1), *page 280*

Jesus Aware of Cross, see John (27), *page 137*

Jesus Confident, see Matt. (56), *page 51*

Jesus Crucified by Romans, see Luke (19), *page 105*

Jesus Denounced by Relatives, see Mark (5), *page 61*

Jesus Destined to Die, see John (25), *page 135*

Jesus Died to Save All, see II Cor. (12), *page 228*

Jesus Entrusted with Power, see Heb. (5), *page 283*

Jesus Knows His Own, see John (22), *page 133*

Jesus Mindful of His Death, see Luke (10), *page 98*

Jesus of Nazareth, see Acts (12), *page 161*

Jesus Promises a Place, see John (34), *page 143*

Jesus Questions the Sick Man, see John (8), *page 122*

Jesus Refused to Meddle, see Luke (9), *page 97*

Jesus Shared His Teaching, see Mark (11), *page 67*

Jesus Sought No Publicity, see Mark (8), *page 54*

Jesus Spoke for God, see John (28), *page 138*

Jesus the Resurrection, see John (24), *page 135*

Jesus Was Obedient, see Heb. (6), *page 283*

Jesus' Death Foretold, see Mark (25), *page 80*

Jesus' Destiny, see I Pet. (5), *page 297*

Jesus' Great Power, see John (21), *page 132*

Jesus' Method, see John (29), *page 139*

Jesus' Name, see Eph. (2), *page 248*

Jesus' Peace, see John (31), *page 141*

Jesus' Preaching in Sheol, see I Pet. (6), *page 298*

Jesus' Relatives, see Mark (6), *page 62*

Jesus' Second Coming, see Acts (1), *page 151*

Jesus' Sudden Coming, see Matthew (51), *page 47*

Jesus' Sudden Return, see I Cor. (25), *page 217*

Jesus' Teaching the Light of the World, see Rev. (56), *page 365*

Jewish People Back Jesus, see Luke (22), *page 108*

Jewish Race, see Matt. (50), *page 46*

Jewish Sects, see Mark (14), *page 71*

Jezebel, see Rev. (10), *page 322*

John Lived a Longer Life, see John (42), *page 150*

Judge of the Living and the Dead, see Acts (14), *page 163*

Judging Angels, see I Cor. (9), *page 203*

Judging One's Neighbors, see Rom. (2), *page 174*

Judgment Before Christ, see II Cor. (11), *page 227*

Key of Knowledge, see Luke (5), *page 94*

Kingdom of Our Lord, see Rev. (36), *page 346*

Kings and Priests, see Rev. (3), *page 316*

Land of Naphtali and Zebulun, see Matt. (4), *page 4*

Law Cannot Save, see Gal. (5), *page 242*

Law of Nature, see Rom. (12), *page 182*

Life Eternal, see John (33), *page 142*

Life of Jesus Manifested, see II Cor. (8), *page 225*

Light of the World, see Matt. (6), *page 5*

Like Angels, see Mark (15), *page 72*

Living and the Dead, see Rom. (23), *page 193*

Love Is Supreme, see I Pet. (8), *page 300*

Love of Money, see Mark (12), *page 68*

Loyal Members, see Rev. (13), *page 324*

Loyalty to Christ, see Col. (5), *page 262*

Man of Sin, see II Thess. (2), *page 266*

Man with Two Sons, see Matt. (36), *page 34*

Mary of Magdala, see Matt. (61), *page 55*

Meeting in Galilee, see Mark (19), *page 75*

Men Brought to Glory, see Heb. (3), *page 281*

Men of Nineveh, see Matt. (19), *page 17*

Messenger, see Matt. (14), *page 12*

Michael and His Angels, see Rev. (39), *page 349*

Mind of God, see I Cor. (4), *page 199*

Minister to Be above Reproach, see I Tim. (4), *page 273*

Minister's Conduct, see I Tim. (3), *page 272*

Miracles of Paul, see II Cor. (24), *page 237*

Moderation, see I Cor. (10), *page 204*

Morning Star, see Rev. (59), *page 368*

Moses Chose to Suffer, see Heb. (12), *page 289*

Mount of Ascension, see Matt. (62), *page 56*

Mustard Seed, see Matt. (21), *page 19*

My Cup You Shall Drink, see Matt. (34), *page 32*

Mystery, see Col. (2), *page 260*

Mystery Hidden from Angels, see I Pet. (2), *page 296*

Naked, see II Cor. (10), *page 226*

Nature Shares Human Tragedy, see Rev. (23), *page 333*

373

Nazarenes, see Acts (19), *page 167*

Near in Spirit, see I Cor. (7), *page 201*

New Heaven, a New Earth, see Rev. (54), *page 364*

New Man, see Rom. (14), *page 184*

No Advantage in Circumcision, see Rom. (4), *page 176*

No Marriage in Heaven, see Matt. (38), *page 36*

No Wine in Heaven, see Matt. (52), *page 47*

Not One Stone upon Another, see Matt. (44), *page 41*

Obedience to Jesus Christ, see II Cor. (17), *page 231*

Old Order and the New, see Luke (15), *page 102*

One Foundation, see Heb. (7), *page 284*

One Hundred and Forty-four Thousand, see Rev. (45), *page 355*

One Sows, Another Reaps, see Luke (20), *page 106*

Only One True Baptism, see Heb. (8), *page 285*

Only Son, see John (6), *page 120*

Open Face, see II Cor. (6), *page 223*

Open Sepulchers, See Rom. (6), *page 177*

Others Will Tie Your Girdle, see John (41), *page 149*

Pagan Jews, see I Cor. (16), *page 209*

Partaker of His Suffering, see Phil. (3), *page 257*

Past Example, see I Cor. (12), *page 205*

Patience of the Faithful, see Rev. (43), *page 353*

Paul a House Prisoner in Rome, see Acts (24), *page 171*

Paul at Appii Forum, see Acts (23), *page 171*

Paul Exhorts the Passengers, see Acts (21), *page 169*

Paul's Name Changed, see Acts (16), *page 164*

Paul's Rank, see II Cor. (20), *page 234*

Paul's Sincerity, see II Cor. (3), *page 220*

Paul's Trials and Suffering, see I Tim. (1), *page 270*

Perfection, see I Cor. (18), *page 210*

Perish by the Sword, see Matt. (55), *page 50*

Peter's Loyalty, see John (40), *page 148*

Pharisees, see Matt. (24), *page 21*

Pilate Had No Power, see John (36), *page 145*

Pilate Marveled at Jesus, see Mark (22), *page 78*

Pillar in the Temple, see Rev. (14), *page 325*

Pious Not Judged, see John (10), *page 124*

Political and Religious Power, see John (32), *page 142*

Preacher among the Gentiles, see Eph. (6), *page 250*

Prince of the Air, see Eph. (3), *page 248*

Prince of This World, see John (26), *page 136*

Promise Made Effective Through Christ, see Heb. (11), *page 288*

Promise Made to Abraham, see Gal. (7), *page 244*

Prophet from Nazareth, see John (2), *page 115*

Prophets Revered, see Matt. (13), *page 11*

Pure in Heart, see Matt. (5), *page 4*

Putting Aside Negative Thought, see Heb. (13), *page 290*

Queen of Sheba, see Matt. (20), *page 18*

Rabbi, see Mark (20), *page 76*

Readers Are Blessed, see Rev. (1), *page 314*

374

Receiving a Child, see Mark (10), *page 66*

Reconciliations, see Rom. (7), *page 178*

Rejected Stone, see Matt. (37), *page 35*

Repentance, see Acts (6), *page 156*

Repenters Receive Mercy, see Jude (1), *page 314*

Resting in Heaven, see Eph. (4), *page 249*

Resurrection and Judgment, see Rev. (53), *page 363*

Revelation, see Gal. (3), *page 241*

Right Time, see II Cor. (14), *page 229*

Righteous Believe, see Rom. (19), *page 190*

Righteousness of God, see Rom. (5), *page 176*

River Euphrates, see Rev. (28), *page 337*

Rod of Iron, see Rev. (12), *page 324*

Sadducees, see Matt. (25), *page 22*

Samaritan Woman, see John (7), *page 121*

Satan's Angel, see II Cor. (23), *page 237*

Satan's Seat, see Rev. (8), *page 320*

Saved by Grace, see Eph. (5), *page 249*

Scarlet Robe, see Matt. (59), *page 53*

Scoffers at the Gospel, see II Pet. (5), *page 305*

Scriptures Inspired, see II Tim. (4), *page 278*

Sealed, see John (12), *page 125*

Secret Councils, see Luke (6), *page 95*

Servants Are Not Heirs, see John (18), *page 129*

Shepherd Smitten, see Matt. (53), *page 48*

Shun False Teachings, see James (3), *page 294*

Sickbed, see Rev. (11), *page 323*

Sign in Heaven, see Matt. (49), *page 45*

Sign of the Kingdom, see Luke (25), *page 111*

Simon the Carpenter, see Acts (15), *page 163*

Simple Gospel, see I Cor. (2), *page 197*

Simple Teaching, see II Cor. (18), *page 232*

Sin Has No Power, see Rom. (9), *page 180*

Sins Forgiven, see John (39), *page 147*

Slain Lamb, see Rev. (16), *page 327*

Slow Changes, see II Pet. (6), *page 306*

Snare of the Devil, see II Tim. (3), *page 278*

Some Will Not Enter, see Luke (11), *page 98*

Son of David, see Matt. (35), *page 33*

Sons of God, see I John (2), *page 309*

Sorrow Causes Death, see II Cor. (15), *page 230*

Souls Made Perfect Through Christ, see Heb. (14), *page 291*

Speak with New Tongues, see Mark (28), *page 87*

Speaking Plainly, see Rom. (10), *page 181*

"Spirit" Means "Person," see I John (4), *page 311*

Spirit Is Life, see Rom. (13), *page 183*

Spiritual Food, see Luke (13), *page 100*

Sprinkling of Blood, see Heb. (15), *page 291*

Star Falling, see Rev. (22), *page 332*

Stephen Was a Jew, see Acts (9), *page 158*

Strict Sabbath Observance, see John (9), *page 123*

Struggle Against Evil, see Eph. (9), *page 253*

Sudden Coming of Jesus, see Matt. (46), *page 42*

Suffering for the Gospel, see II Tim. (2), *page 277*

Suffering from Evil, see I Cor. (8), *page 202*

Swearing by God, see Rev. (31), *page 341*

Sweet Savior, see II Cor. (5), *page 222*

Sword of the Mouth, see Rev. (9), *page 321*

Synagogue of Satan, see Rev. (7), *page 319*

Tabernacle of Malcom, see Acts (11), *page 160*

Take Your Cross, see Matt. (27), *page 24*

Taxes, see Matt. (29), *page 26*

Temple of God, see Rev. (37), *page 347*

Temple Overthrown, see Mark (16), *page 72*

Term "Holy," see I Pet. (3), *page 296*

They Shall See His Face, see Rev. (57), *page 366*

Third of Men Killed, see Rev. (29), *page 339*

Third Part of Life Destroyed, see Rev. (21), *page 331*

Thirsty for Truth, see John (16), *page 128*

Thirty Pieces of Silver, see Matt. (58), *page 53*

Time Is Not Relevant, see Heb. (10), *page 287*

Time of the Gentiles, see Luke (23), *page 109*

Time to Awake, see Rom. (22), *page 192*

Time Too Short, see John (15), *page 127*

Titus and Aramaean, see Gal. (4), *page 242*

To Guard the Teaching, see Matt. (63), *page 57*

To Him Who Has Shall Be Given, see Luke (21), *page 107*

To Sit with Jesus, see Rev. (15), *page 326*

Touching His Garment, see Mark (7), *page 63*

Transgression, see Gal. (8), *page 245*

Transgression of Moral Law, see I Tim. (2), *page 271*

Tree of Life, see Rev. (6, 58), *pages 318, 367*

Trials in This Life, see I Cor. (13), *page 206*

True Christian Doctrine, see I Tim. (7), *page 275*

True Gospel, see Gal. (2), *page 240*

True Judgment, see John (17), *page 129*

True Religion Is Simple, see John (13), *page 126*

Truth Triumphs Over Imperial Powers, see Rev. (52), *page 362*

Turned to Another Gospel, see Gal. (1), *page 239*

Two Olive Trees, see Rev. (33), *page 343*

Unclean Frogs, see Rev. (49), *page 359*

Unclean Spirit, see Mark (1), *page 58*

Universe Mourns, see Acts (2), *page 152*

Universe Shares in Calamity, see Matt. (48), *page 44*

Unknown Tongues, see I Cor. (19), *page 211*

Unlearned, see I Cor. (3), *page 198*

Untrue Doctrines Uprooted, see Matt. (23), *page 21*

Vials, see Rev. (47), *page 357*

Vineyard—God's Religion, see Matt. (32), *page 29*

Vultures and Carcasses, see Matt. (47), *page 43*

Warning Against False Teachers, see II Cor. (19), *page 233*

Washed Their Robes, see Rev. (18), *page 329*

Way of the Wind, see John (4), *page 117*

We Know Things in Part, see I Cor. (17), *page 210*

Widows' Behavior, see I Tim. (6), *page 274*

Wine and Gall, see Matt. (60), *page 54*

Wine Mixed with Myrrh, see Mark (23), *page 79*

With You in Spirit, see Col. (1), *page 259*

Wisdom and Works, see Matt. (15), *page 13*

Witnesses, see Rev. (32), *page 342*

Witnesses Slain for Testimony, see Rev. (35), *page 345*

Women Keep Silent, see I Cor. (20), *page 212*

Words Without Action, see I Cor. (6), *page 200*

Worshiping Peter, see Acts (13), *page 162*

Written in Heaven, see Luke (4), *page 93*

Yokefellows, see Phil. (4), *page 258*

Young Man, see Mark (21), *page 77*

Young Widows, see I Tim. (5), *page 273*

Your Sins Are Forgiven, See Mark (3), *page 60*

Zechariah, Son of Barachiah, see Matt. (42), *page 39*